So Much
& More

SO MUCH & MORE

An Invitation to Christian Spirituality

Debra Rienstra

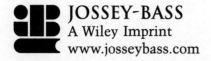

JOSSEY-BASS
A Wiley Imprint
www.josseybass.com

Published by Jossey-Bass
A Wiley Imprint
989 Market Street, San Francisco, CA 94103-1741   www.josseybass.com

No part of this publication may be reproduced, stored in a retrieval system, or
transmitted in any form or by any means, electronic, mechanical, photocopying,
recording, scanning, or otherwise, except as permitted under Section 107 or 108 of
the 1976 United States Copyright Act, without either the prior written permission
of the Publisher, or authorization through payment of the appropriate per-copy
fee to the Copyright Clearance Center, Inc., 222 Rosewood Drive, Danvers, MA
01923, 978-750-8400, fax 978-646-8600, or on the web at www.copyright.com.
Requests to the Publisher for permission should be addressed to the Permissions
Department, John Wiley & Sons, Inc., 111 River Street, Hoboken, NJ 07030,
201-748-6011, fax 201-748-6008, e-mail: permcoordinator@wiley.com.

Jossey-Bass books and products are available through most bookstores. To contact
Jossey-Bass directly call our Customer Care Department within the U.S. at 800-
956-7739, outside the U.S. at 317-572-3986, or fax 317-572-4002.

Jossey-Bass also publishes its books in a variety of electronic formats. Some content
that appears in print may not be available in electronic books.

Unless otherwise noted, Scripture is taken from the HOLY BIBLE, NEW
INTERNATIONAL VERSION®. NIV®. Copyright © 1973, 1978, 1984 by
International Bible Society. Used by permission of Zondervan. All rights reserved.

Library of Congress Cataloging-in-Publication Data
Rienstra, Debra.
So much more: an invitation to Christian spirituality / Debra Rienstra.
p. cm.
Includes bibliographical references (p.) and index.
ISBN 0–7879–6887–0 (alk. paper)
1. Spirituality. I. Title.
BV4501.3.R535 2005
248.4—dc22
2004024483

Printed in the United States of America
FIRST EDITION
HB Printing   10 9 8 7 6 5 4 3 2 1

CONTENTS

To all my mothers and fathers in the faith

PREFACE

Who will welcome me? Every time I've moved—off to college or graduate school or to my husband's first job or overseas for a few months—part of me has wondered how I will get my bearings in the new place. Of course, there are street maps and phone books, but they provide too much information. I don't need to know every street to make it through the first few weeks, only which streets will get me to a good grocery store or a place to buy children's socks or a reliable car repair shop. I need insider knowledge to help me find the essentials. Even more than that, I need insider friendship. I need someone who will be available as a helpful friend, at least for a while. Someone who will understand that it's hard, encourage me, and help me sort out the important basics from the thousands of confusing details.

This book is a gesture of welcoming friendship for people who are new or newly returned to the Christian faith—those who are searching, lurking, longing, or learning. Even more than moving across the country, committing or recommitting oneself to a Christian life can feel disorienting. Christian beliefs are presented in many different ways, so it can be difficult to find the heart of the faith and to imagine how it might affect your life. Christian practices vary a great deal too, and it's hard to know where to begin, especially without a lot of prior knowledge, experience, or mastery of insider vocabulary. For those who find themselves in this new place, with eagerness or hesitation or a little of both, I have sought to set the confusing details aside as much as possible and instead give a good account of the main things.

What are the main things? I have struggled with that knotty question throughout the process of writing this book. C. S. Lewis, when he wrote his enduringly successful book *Mere Christianity* in the middle of the last century, sought to focus on "the belief that has been common to nearly all Christians at all times."[1] This book inherits the challenge of trying to find the center of all the variations of Christian belief and explain that center in plain terms. However, Christianity is more than a set of beliefs; Lewis knew this very well too, as his many other writings amply demonstrate. Christian belief and practice go together; and if all goes well, they reshape the passions, the imagination, and every part of ourselves—reshape them through a growing relationship with God.

So although I certainly affirm the importance of rational arguments for Christian beliefs, I am not attempting that task here. For one thing I'm not qualified. For another, satisfying one's reason is only one of many concerns people have in coming to faith; and it may not be the concern of highest priority in this twenty-first-century world. Instead, in our increasingly fragmented world, people want a way to heal their hurts and to find integrity and authenticity. They want all the parts of their lives, blessed and terrible and everything in between, to make sense together in light of some big answers to the big questions of our existence. In a world in which the future seems to rush at us, we also long to feel grounded in a tradition—to take seriously the hard-won wisdom of those who have lived before us and sought God in their own places and times. Although the great truths of Christianity do not change, in different periods of history, we seek them from slightly different places of need; we use different terms to explain those truths; and we live in response to them in ways particular to our own time and place. Taking all this into account, I have tried to create a picture of how Christian belief, practice, passion, and imagination might create that coming together we all long for and how that might look when lived out in an ordinary life today. In calling this book *So Much More: An Invitation to Christian Spirituality,* that's what I mean by spirituality: a way of letting God bind together all parts of ourselves, all parts of our lives into a vibrant, enduring wholeness.

When Sheryl Fullerton, my editor at Jossey-Bass, first invited me to write this book, I assured her that I was not a pastor or theologian, only an ordinary Christian who for some reason has been given the compulsion to write. Sheryl, savvy person that she is, overcame my hesitation in two main ways. She presented this project as an intriguing challenge, knowing, I suppose, that I would have a hard time resisting such a challenge. She also reminded me that sometimes the most welcome guidance for readers comes not from an expert but from a fellow traveler. I had to admit that this is true. I remember that as a middle schooler, when I had been playing the viola for only a few years, I was far more inspired to practice when I heard a high schooler play a viola concerto than when I listened to professional recordings. The pros played with such speed and facility that I could not imagine ever reaching their level. What the high schooler was doing, on the other hand, seemed wonderful but not quite so far off. So we need, as well as the expertise of the real professionals, the special encouragement that can come only from companions closer to where we are on the journey.

In that spirit I have tried to keep the book on ordinary ground as much as possible. Rather than hunting for the most amazing stories about the most famous people, I took examples and stories whenever possible from my own life and from the lives of people I know. I find the extraordinary stories inspiring too, and I certainly try to listen to professional recordings, as it were, by reading what the wisest and most famous Christians from ages past and present have to say. But we live most of our lives among ordinary things and people and events, and it's on that day-to-day level that we have to weave our own stories into the great Christian story.

As a welcoming friend, as a companion on the journey, I'm offering a particular and very personal perspective. In this way I'm in the position of the orientation-group leaders at the college where I teach. These orientation leaders welcome new students, not as officials of the college but only as fellow students a year or two along in their own college experience. Each orientation leader presents every aspect of the college from a point of view deeply colored by his or her background, opinions, experience, and style. This kind of biased introduction has limitations, of course. Alternatively, the college could hand new students an electronic audio guide and send them trotting about campus listening to general, officially sanctioned lectures about each building and activity. But it's much more welcoming and useful and definitely more fun to go around with a real person. Besides, new students are smart enough to recognize that sooner or later, when they get their bearings, they will develop a fuller picture of the whole place and begin to claim their own experiences and perspectives.

In the same way, I hope readers will understand that as much as I have tried to account for the center of the Christian faith, I see that center from the perspective of a Protestant, Midwestern, middle-class, American woman who was raised in the church. If you have been around long enough to catch the ethos of some other enclave of Christianity, you may find that I say things a little differently from what you've heard or that I emphasize some things and not others. Feel free to respond to some passages with "Well, that *would* be how a Protestant would put it, wouldn't it?"—or whatever else might come to mind in acknowledging my perspective. If you do find some things I say making you uncomfortable, I hope you will simply take that as a starting point for discussion with other Christians whom you trust and with whom you can talk face-to-face.

I've organized the book beginning with foundational Christian beliefs in the first five chapters, including some attention to Christian history and much attention to the Bible. Topics in these chapters loop back on each other like the stitches in a knitted sweater; if something seems oddly missing in one chapter, do be patient. The missing element will probably turn up in another chapter. In the second section of the book, I describe how the foundational beliefs play out in the central Christian practices of prayer, Bible reading, worship, community, and service. The book ends where it begins, with a recognition of the wonder and mystery that characterize a faith-filled response to our loving and great God.

Allow me to mention a few practical matters, lest they become distracting as you read along. First, I have generally used a masculine pronoun for God only because other alternatives are either awkward or, to some, offensive. I strongly believe that imagining God as exclusively masculine is not only untrue to the nature of God but also deeply damaging to us. Although I hope I have pointed to a full range of God's attributes in the book, I did not think this the appropriate place to work out a point about pronoun usage.

When referring to the two parts of the Christian Bible, I have usually used the terms *Old Testament* and *New Testament*. Some people object to the term *Old Testament* and prefer *Hebrew Bible* as more respectful to Jews and to the Hebrew origins of the text. I certainly mean no disrespect by using the traditional Christian terms. I have loved and studied the older portion of the Bible all my life and, like many Christians, remain deeply grateful for and respectful of the Jewish heritage. I simply felt that those less familiar with the texts would more readily understand the parallel terms.

As to different translations of the Bible, I almost always quote the New International Version (NIV), primarily because it's a widely used contemporary translation whose language I find both poetic and clear. Where biblical citations appear in this book, the reader can assume I am using the NIV. Occasionally I quote from other translations, and very occasionally I paraphrase a passage for one reason or another. In crucial places I have supported my comments with study of the original-language texts.

In the chapters that follow, I'm doing what many have done before me: telling a great and ancient story over again in a fresh way. I invite you to explore how you might live your own life into this story. As you do, my hope and earnest prayer is that this book will make you feel welcome, encouraged, intrigued, and challenged to discover the *so much more* that is waiting for us all.

So Much & More

IMAGINING
THE
CHRISTIAN WAY

CHAPTER ONE

SOMETHING MORE

Transcendence

YOU HAVE SET YOUR GLORY ABOVE THE HEAVENS.
—Psalm 8:1

There must be something more. More than the material universe with its frenetic subatomic particles and unfathomably vast, cold space. More than the pines whispering to the stolid mountains. More than the morning commute, the coffee in paper cups, the lady at the newsstand, the half-lies we tell to get by. More than the evening news routine of crime and war, embroidered with empty banter and car advertisements. More than our fragments of longing, our tattered and fleeting gladness.

In simple dailiness something more whispers to us. We hear it in the jaunty fretting of the chickadee at the feeder, see it in the creases around an old woman's eyes or in the sunlight warming the curves of a vase—wherever ordinary things become luminous. And in the joy that bursts out the edges of life, something more cries out, as the newborn the moment after birth, or the apple blossoms fallen like confetti in modest celebration of spring, or the symphonies and sonatas and all the genius of art. And in our desolations, something more roars. At the graveside of the child, the scene of the accident, the arenas of war. In all our tableaus of anguish, when our hearts crack or our civilizations, in the blackness between the jagged edges, we perceive this something more. For many of us, the suspicion that there is something more is the beginning of faith.

Such a delicate beginning. Do we perceive it? We are not always sure. We live in the wake of a distrustful age. In the West at least, we have learned to regard with skepticism any sense of that which is beyond, any sort of reality we cannot see and touch and measure. Such skepticism is nothing new; every age has its own form of it. But with the magnificent rise of science, industry, and technology in the last several centuries, skepticism found its legs and strutted about with great arrogance. Skepticism is still fashionable, if somewhat chastened, and it finds expression these days in the form of a kind of melancholy aesthetic commitment. Because I teach literature for a living, I'm most familiar with the beautiful, hopeless novels, the poems full of absence, the essays with glitter on the surface and sadness at the core. In literature, song, film, and many other domains, this fashionable angle on the world pays homage to the enduring human spirit, acknowledges the mysteries of existence—but remains ironic. In other words, it wishes there were something more but, in an attempt to be heroic and relentlessly honest, ruefully concludes that there is not. Much of our art and public discourse throws a kiss of admiration to transcendence as a concept or psychological phenomenon, but it is a kiss of betrayal: "You are lovely," we say to transcendence, "but you are not really there." A devastating rejection.

Skepticism may earn nods of agreement at parties, but perhaps, like me, you have suspected that it is a needless heroism. Ultimately skepticism capitulates to the cold universe as the end of the question and resolves merely to suffer it in style. It may seem brave to lean your body against the subzero winds of the cosmos in chic little chiffon scarves, but why? Must cold be the truth, and the means to warmth merely an illusion? Perhaps the hat, the boots, the very long coat hanging in the vestibule are also real and exactly your size. Those who endure Minnesota winters know enough to muss their hair with a big, warm hat, no matter how silly or unfashionable it seems. To believe there is indeed something more is to admit that the wise thing in this existence is to put on the available gear.

ASKING WHY

Collective wisdom is not always true, but it's certainly worth pondering. And some notion of a transcendent reality appears everywhere in every age. The very recent phenomenon sometimes called scientific naturalism or scientism is among the few exceptions. Put together Eastern thought and Western thought, northern and southern thought, jungle, desert, whatever variety of thought; and what emerges from the sweep of it all is the recognition that human beings have a physical, a psychological, and a spiritual nature. We participate in a material world, in the world of our individual perceptions and mind, and in the something more. There is plenty of argument about what the nature of that transcendent reality might be. But for now let's define transcendence as some dimension of existence that is not contained within the material world or within the human mind, collective or individual. This dimension of what it is may be intertwined with the other two, but it is not the same thing. In short, *something* exists beyond space dust and brains.

When you give your assent to intimations of a dimension of existence exceeding both the material and the human mind, you place yourself in agreement with all the great wisdom traditions of history.[1] You choose not to shrug resignedly at the whispers, the cries, and the roars but instead to admit that some of your experiences cannot be truly explored or explained unless you say yes to the something more.

Perhaps you are a woman who has studied all the pregnancy books thoroughly, followed every detail of conception, fetal development, and labor equipped with well-researched information. But when through pain and ecstasy you push that strange, slippery creature out of your body and you look into his eyes, you meet a new being altogether, a presence, a consciousness. And you know this is a mystery that all your information can only lap against like little waves.

Or maybe you are a graduate student, completely committed to science, who has spent years of your life peering at instruments in labs and scribbling equations into notebooks. You used to be rather arrogant about scientific method and about empiricism; but now that you have worked with some of the best people in your field, you are beginning to realize that the cutting edge of science is where knowledge is not most powerful but most humble. Why is there something rather than nothing? How did the universe achieve the exact density necessary for existence as we know it? Why are things this way and not some other way? You love science and the pursuit of knowledge as much as ever. But you now believe that the very questions science by definition cannot answer are the most, well, beautiful.

Or perhaps you were once a young girl who loved to visit the zoo. You loved the giraffe with his handsome spots and his rhythmically swaying tower of a neck; the elephant poking around with her preposterous nose; the lion shaking his mane and licking his enormous paws; the otter making her quick, lithe undulations through the water. You read the placards with their cheerful comments on the evolutionary usefulness of this and that physical adaptation. But you wondered. Is the penguin's waddle merely useful? His black-and-white tuxedo? And the stunning amber color of the owl's eyes? Why are all the animals so funny and gorgeous? And you knew that somehow, in this world, it's not all about getting through the next day or the next eon. At the center of nature's utility you found, most naturally, delight.

Perhaps you have lived less than twenty years, but already certain peculiar things have fallen into place for you in ways no one could have engineered. A stranger said something to you unknowingly that steered you away from danger or toward something you love. A little incident here, a feeling there. Could there be some design to all this, some purpose?

Or perhaps you are a man still living in the shadow of your father's death, still picturing his body in the coffin, emaciated from the cancer and looking fake anyway with the makeup and the sewn-shut lips. It was not him at all. You feel a profound separation from your father now but also a heavy, dusky love. Although you have never thought much about it all before, having been busy making your own place in the world, now you have questions. Why should you insist that this ordinary man's life has some value beyond the slender perimeters of his first breath and his last? Why should you long for an existence after death, if there is no such thing? What good would such a longing serve?

Human personality, the incredibly intricate structures of the universe, the delights of other living creatures, odd sequences of events, the profound connections between people that urge us to protest death and insist that such an obvious and common thing simply cannot be right: let us grant that these are realities that require explanation beyond a usefulness for survival or the bizarre sparklings of our neurons. Maybe it's other things for you—a Mahler symphony that seems to press your heart into your throat; the ocean's ancient, ceaseless roar; the frescoes on the ceiling of St. Peter's; the way your two-year-old lays her head on your shoulder. Maybe it's the simple observation—this is what seals it for me—that human beings can feel wonder and love and ask why.

SPIRITUAL BUT NOT RELIGIOUS

If we are willing to agree that a transcendent reality exists and that human beings can, one way or another, perceive it, then we find ourselves in the position of trying to name this reality. Is there an impersonal life force? A God? Many gods? If you go so far as to concede the existence of a personal deity, you are still faced with many alternatives. Some have the force of major religious traditions behind them: Allah of Islam, the God of the Jews, the Trinitarian God of Christians, the variety of Hindu deities. Other possibilities, with less force of the masses behind them, are nonetheless available. There is probably a Web site, for example, for worshipers of the Egyptian sun-god Ra. We are keenly aware in our age of a colorful marketplace of explanations, a kind of worldview bazaar. Somehow we have to cope with this confusion.

One mode of coping these days is to call oneself spiritual but not religious. I've heard this formula so often that I was actually pleased when my friend Jeff, a self-defined "indifferent, agnostic Jew," wrote me a letter in which he admitted, "I've grown comfortable with the idea that I'm just not a very spiritual person." *How refreshing,* I thought, *to hear from someone who's not insisting how spiritual he is!*

"Spiritual but not religious" often means that a person acknowledges a transcendent dimension to existence but prefers to keep its nature undefined, nebulous, and usually impersonal. A very understandable impulse. The options for defining transcendent realities are maddeningly diverse. More ominously, no one can deny that firm convictions can be dangerous. We have looked over our shoulders at the landscape of the previous century, at the charred trenches, smashed buildings, shattered bodies, at the gaping, smoking holes in the foundations of modernist optimism about human nature and progress. We are suffering from collective traumatic stress disorder. We know only too well that the lust for power, when combined with convictions about race, forms of government—and yes, religion— creates the most lethal alchemy on earth. Never mind that the Stalins, Hitlers, and Husseins of the last century followed Nietzsche as their prophet more than anyone else. They draped themselves with some other ideology to cover their arrogant nihilism, so that we are now quite suspicious of drapes.

So to be spiritual but not religious seems the humane, peace-loving thing to do. It doesn't quite follow that the antidote for bad convictions is to have very few or very fuzzy or very contradictory ones. But the desires behind nonreligious spirituality are among the noblest humanity has to offer: peaceful coexistence, personal bliss, human well-being (and often animal and tree well-being too). On a more individual level, indefinite beliefs about the transcendent avoid the troubles of a God with personality. The minute you move from a life force to a personal God, you are dealing with an other who could potentially make demands on you that you would rather not conform to, like giving up sex or giving away money or explaining to people that you routinely talk to invisible beings. Better to meditate rather than pray, mix beliefs as they seem pleasant and helpful to your own happiness, keep your options open, and stick with what works. It's a gesture of humility to say, "I mean, it's true for *me*." It may also be an admission of defeat.

Somewhere along the line, we all make two choices. The first is to decide whether some perceptions of a transcendent God are closer to the truth than others or not. Perhaps, you might propose, all notions of the transcendent are equally far from an astoundingly incomprehensible truth. In that case you could indeed say that all religions lead to God or are equally mistaken about God. The other viable possibility is this: no matter how astoundingly incomprehensible the truth, some notions represent a more accurate perception than others. I live by this latter option, because it seems to me that the minute you grant any notion of truth at all, it follows as a matter of human dignity that we ought to pursue this truth as ardently as we can. Perhaps we will stumble; perhaps we are limited in our perceptions; but we ought to try. After all, we live by various notions of truth whether we attend to them or not; better therefore to attend. If this makes sense, then the questions that follow are the most difficult yet: Which beliefs come the closest to the truth? How do we weigh different beliefs against one another?

LADDERS AND LEAPS

When C. S. Lewis wrote *Mere Christianity* in the middle of the last century, he made his argument for the Christian faith as the best account of the truth by beginning with universal moral law and reasoning his way from there, with ingenious congeniality, to Christian doctrine. The only drawback of this strategy today is that reason has since suffered some bruising blows. We have lost confidence in reason as the all-in-one tool of truth. Excessive optimism that reason, science, technology, and capitalism could at last solve humanity's age-old problems was exploded by the great wars and other moral disasters of the twentieth century. Reason, we have had to concede, is neither the social savior nor the ultimate arbiter that the West has believed it to be. And only rarely has reason been the path to religious faith.

Reason must be satisfied, nevertheless, in order for faith to endure. As the medieval European allegorists might put it, Reason is a beautiful and imperious figure. She wears a crown. One of the last century's greatest philosophers, Alvin Plantinga, who has taught for many years at the University of Notre Dame, has spent much of his career thinking and writing about knowledge and belief. In his recent works, he demonstrates with utmost philosophical rigor that belief in God is rationally warranted: that it is as "properly basic" to believe in God as it is to believe that other minds exist, that we can remember events, or that our senses can provide reliable information under the right circumstances. He has provided such a convincing case for the rationality of theism in general and Christianity in particular that even his secular colleagues have had to relinquish the "knockout punch of the sheerly logical objection" to belief.[2]

Still, although rationality can be compatible with belief in a God, rational structures do not typically get a person from no faith to faith, like a ladder. One gets to this kind of belief through other means. As the philosopher Søren Kierkegaard pointed out, one reaches faith by a leap. For some it is a little hop, and for some it is a gigantic death-defying half-flight. For some a leap is not the right metaphor at all, and faith feels more like a repeated turning or stepping or even just a leaning. But something other than reason nudges a person in that faith direction. One great advantage, then, in our coming to terms with transcendent reality these days is that reason is less of an obsession. We are more ready to give equal or even superior weight to particular experience over complex latticeworks of reason.

Lewis himself did not come to the Christian faith through reason, although he came as close as anyone by the rational road. I think he understood that rational argumentation functions mostly as a brush-clearing exercise, removing branches and stumps to make a space for belief to grow or to free a belief already planted for further growth. Those little nudges in the faith direction come instead by experience. I use the word here to mean an individual's alchemy of perceptions, understanding, and memory. We are always trying to find names for our experiences and build an understanding of them; and to do this we depend on hearing how other people describe their experiences, on their witness to what they have seen and heard. We change our ways of thinking and living when something awakens us to experiences we have had but not understood, when something finally gives a name to our experiences that fits so well it sticks. Other people witness to their own experiences of the transcendent; we have a swirl of these accounts in our heads; and we keep trying to grasp some of these possible explanations and test whether they fit our own experiences of the transcendent. When events and perceptions accumulate and certain names for describing those experiences keep sticking, a shape begins to emerge; and our jumble of understanding slowly transforms into faith.

GETTING A GRIP

For me the most compelling body of witness has always pointed to the Christian faith. The stories of people who have come to believe in Jesus, whether in an extraordinary encounter or an ordinary journey, are the ones that consistently cover *what is* with names that stick.

The Bible is the primary source of such stories. I have avoided quoting the Bible so far because it can be an authoritative text only once you have acknowledged the possibility of God. But even before we consider the particular nature of its authority, it is helpful to think of the Bible as an enormous, messy, glorious body of witness. "Strange things happened to us," say the voices in the Bible. "We did not choose this truth; we did not even know what was happening to us. But God gripped us, and we're telling you about it to help you make sense of what is happening to you." The writer of the Gospel of John concludes his description of the life and work of Jesus with such a declaration (21:24): "This is the disciple who testifies to these things and who wrote them down. And we know that his testimony is true." The Bible as Christians have put it together, from the first book of creation and patriarchs (Genesis) to the last book of apocalyptic vision (Revelation) claims to tell one continuous story in which a great many people encounter the same God. The Old Testament describes a variety of people facing extraordinary experiences with this God: Moses at the burning bush, Hannah praying for a child in the temple, the prophet Isaiah and the seraphim before the throne of God. The figures of the New Testament believe that their experience of Jesus is a new (but not completely unprepared-for) revelation of this same God: Mary and the angel Gabriel, the writers of the gospel accounts, the Jewish legal scholar Paul and the blinding light arresting him on the road to Damascus.

Beyond the pages of the Bible emerge the stories of people since the time of the New Testament whose dramatic experiences of the transcendent fit the explanations of the Christian faith. French mathematician and philosopher Blaise Pascal with his vision of God so ineffable he could only describe it by scribbling on a slip of paper a few words—"fire," "tears of joy," "Jesus Christ."[3] The twelfth-century abbess and composer Hildegard of Bingen and her visions. John Wesley, the founder of Methodism, who after agonizing for years over whether or not he was right with God, one day in Aldersgate, London, felt his "heart strangely warmed."[4] Famous people and ordinary people throughout the centuries and today—the tide of their stories rises in all their drama and dailiness and variety. Their stories cannot easily be dismissed.

I have been speaking of religious belief as if it were a choice one makes quietly and reasonably, like selecting A rather than B on a multiple choice test or croutons rather than cottage cheese at the salad bar. But listening to people's stories suggests that the Christian faith is not first about a set of beliefs carefully chosen but about encounters with a divine person. People explain that something happened to them, whether they wanted it or not, and they were helpless to deny its reality. God, they say, has gripped them.

My friend Paul Willis, a poet and English professor, describes his coming to faith beginning with a Sunday school lesson taught by his mother in the basement of a Baptist church in Oregon. She explained to the first and second graders, using cardboard hearts as visual aids, that we all have black hearts but that Jesus will give us a white heart if we ask. For some reason this explanation took hold in Paul, and later,

in the quiet of his own room, he asked Jesus to perform this operation, "sort of like repainting a bedroom." Within a few weeks, he had
made a public statement of his faith in his church and was baptized.
But a couple of years later, at the age of nine, he found himself restless with hunger and longing for something more. One day after
church, he climbed the stairs to the balcony, praying obsessively, and
upon entering the sanctuary, he recalls, "I walked into a presence that
had been there, I was quite sure, all along. It was quiet, powerful, good,
and deep. It was a presence that included me, and all things around
me. . . . They [these things] were not different, but more themselves,
more what they had been all along, richly sustained, transfigured in
their everyday best."[5] The experience lasted only a few moments. But
Paul attributes to these extraordinary moments the first surrender of
his whole being to the reality and goodness of God. His church
upbringing had captured his imagination, and his intellect had assent-
ed to the faith. But here Paul encountered the person of God for the
first time, encircling him with an irresistible presence.

   Some people testify to dramatic mystical experiences. Others
describe events that seem mundane, almost unimpressive. In the famous
account of his conversion in his fourth-century autobiography,
Confessions, for example, Augustine of Hippo describes his desperate
state of torment, shame, and desire. After all his years of searching for
the truth, he had finally concluded that Christianity was the way. Yet
he could not quite give up his sin, his "one-time mistresses" figurative
and literal. Lust was his particular weakness, and he knew he was helpless unless God gave him the strength to live a new kind of life. One
day, while in a flood of tears, he heard a child chanting, "Take and
read, take and read." He opened the Scriptures randomly and landed
on Romans 13:13—not an especially inspirational verse on its own,
but it seemed to Augustine to speak directly to him: "Not in rioting
and drunkenness, not in chambering and impurities, not in con-
tention and envy, but put ye on the Lord Jesus Christ, and make not
provision for the flesh in its concupiscences." He read that one verse,
and suddenly his whole world shifted. He wrote: "I had no wish to
read further, and no need. For in that instant, with the very ending of
the sentence, it was as though a light of utter confidence shone in all
my heart, and all the darkness of uncertainty vanished away."[6] That
small, improbable event altered the trajectory of Augustine's life. From

there he became a bishop, helped shepherd the Christian church through the internal controversies and external turmoil of the Roman empire's demise, and wrote the many volumes that made him one of Christianity's greatest theologians.

Not all people who have such encounters with God desire them, however. Patron saint of the reluctant is Paul on the road to Damascus, whose story is recorded in the New Testament book of Acts. Paul, whose name was Saul at the time, knew all about God, was trained as a scholar of Jewish law, and thought he had his affairs with God completely sorted out. Going about his business of maintaining the Jewish religious power structures one day by persecuting a little upstart sect of Jesus-followers, Saul was knocked flat on his face and heard Jesus himself calling his name and offering particular instructions: "This is Jesus speaking. Why are you persecuting me? Stop it, because I have work for you to do" (see Acts 9:1–19 and Galatians 1:11–24). Saul reeled from this experience for several years before sorting things out, unlearning many things he thought he knew, and beginning his new life as a Christian missionary named Paul.

A good contemporary example of the unwelcome encounter comes from writer Anne Lamott. In her spiritual memoir, *Traveling Mercies,* she writes that in her lowest hour of misery and fear and loneliness and literal bleeding, she "became aware" of someone with her, and "knew beyond any doubt that it was Jesus." This was no mystical moment of peace and comfort. On the contrary, she writes: "I was appalled." Later, she describes this person pursuing her "as if a little cat was following me."[7] This went on for about a week, with Lamott resisting in every way she knew how, until finally she swore her surrender, in both senses of the word *swore.*

My friend Sean is an example of someone for whom a dramatic experience, while not in the least mystical, eventually became a turning point. One morning in 1997 when Sean had arrived early at the office in lower Manhattan where he buys and sells coffee beans, a man came into the office and held him up at gunpoint. He duct-taped Sean's hands behind his back, duct-taped his mouth, and forced him to lie facedown on the floor. The incident lasted maybe twenty minutes, during which time Sean thought very practical, mundane thoughts such as *I'm glad I have a lot of cash on me so this guy will be satisfied and go away.* Meanwhile, the bigger picture took hold of him, and amid his terror he thought: *I only want to see my wife and daughter again* and *What does my life mean, anyway?* and *I need to get myself right with God.* Before that morning Sean had a few scraps of Catholicism left over from his youth, a nominally religious upbringing that impinged on his life only in the form of occasional good-natured ribbing with his Presbyterian wife. But he began to understand his early morning terror as someone, maybe a transcendent someone, giving him a rather vigorous shake. This small shift in thought became the starting point of a spiritual journey that led him to new convictions about God and a new identity as part of a Christian community.

Swept into Meaning

Some who believe can mark a dramatic moment when vague perceptions of the transcendent or beliefs that seemed plausible but somehow cold gave way to what had to be described as an encounter with an other, a divine person, Jesus, God. Others of us experience moments that seem unremarkable on the surface but still carry with them an unmistakable sense of God. "I just felt this presence," a person might say. Or "I had this overwhelming feeling that Someone was there with me, at my sister's bedside as she died, and I felt such peace." For many people belief is the sum they make of a lot of little experiences: strong suspicion about small coincidences, the experience of beauty, the love of friends and family, and other loose pieces. Some experiences of God are deeply desired and prepared for with years of study, consideration, and formation. Others come as a complete shock, and their full significance can only be understood much later.

As odd and varied as they are, accounts of such experiences tend to raise scornful responses among those who have never had them. Some might assert that experiences of God are just indigestion or hormones or the power of the human imagination and that we *call* them an encounter with God only because that's what we have been taught to call them. Culture or upbringing or both give the person in question some God-language, and that in turn manufactures the experience. To support this argument, one might point to certain styles of Christian storytelling in which everyone's encounter with God sounds exactly like the next person's. In certain kinds of churches, one might hear many speeches that sound much like this: "And then I was con-victed of my sin, and I took Jesus into my heart, and now I have a peace that passes understanding." A skeptic might wonder whether these people are encountering God or just repeating a conventional formula.

Alternatively one might say that the transcendent is so ineffable as to support many descriptions, all of which are equally valid and equally inadequate. People of other faiths have experiences of God too, and they use their own language to describe them. The Muslim girl who perceives the presence of a deity in the universe, for example, is going to describe this with words she knows. Not Ra or Kali but Allah. She's going to give this other a name that her religion provides. The little Baptist boy is, of course, going to understand his experience of God based on his Sunday school lessons. So what's to say that Paul Willis is more accurate in his perception of God than the Muslim girl?

There is a long, sometimes noble, and sometimes ugly tradition of debate concerning which religious faith best describes truth. People have considered which belief system produces the best results—the "by their fruits ye shall know them" argument. Or which one has gathered the most adherents—the vote of the masses argu-ment. Or which has produced the most poignant art—the aesthetic argument. Or which one obtains the most logically coherent belief system or requires the least number of crazy, nonempirical beliefs—the rational dignity argument. These debates are not by any means worthless, and they often help people settle their questions. Yet all of these methods break down at some point and fail to yield an absolute-ly irresistible conclusion.

Doubtless we can understand our experiences of the transcen-dent only with the tools of language we have been given, and we are prone to misperceptions. But it does not follow that the transcendent is only a construction of language or that all descriptions are equally (in)adequate. Any notion of a divine being requires at least this prem-ise in the mix: if God does not show himself somehow, we cannot know him. God must come to us. Acknowledging this puts in quite a different light the two main explanations these days for the way people find meaning and purpose. Some say human beings *discover* meaning; but this implies that our perceptions, on their own, are suf-ficient to that task. Some say we merely *construct* meaning; but this implies that nothing exists outside our minds or, if it does, that we cannot possibly perceive such existence. One view attributes too much to our perceptive powers, the other too little. Neither squares with the experience of religious adherents of every religion from ancient varieties of paganism to all modern major religions. Perhaps the best way to describe it is to say that God reveals. It's not that we discover or construct meaning but that we are swept up in meaning as it blows by us—or through us. We need only be willing. And we become lighter and more susceptible when we have heard the witness of others.

Both the variety and the continuity of transcendent experiences are attributable to a living person who acts independently of our desires and understanding but who also works within our desires and understanding. Heaven and earth reach toward each other, you might say. We are helpless in our clouded perceptions of the transcendent: God is very great and must accommodate to our limited understanding in order to reveal to us. We can desire this, which is certainly an advantage, or not desire it. We can understand it well or mistake it. We can describe it poetically or with conventional formulas. (That there would be conventional formulas is not surprising: it reflects commonalities in the way God acts as much as our difficulty in finding words to describe those actions.) But in response to all this confusion, I can only find a way to live when I concede that one way of describing God-experience approaches the full and true nature of God more closely than another way.

BLINDING LIGHTS AND DARK MIRRORS

We must be gentle with one another's experiences of God and our accounts of these experiences. We can never fully defend them. All of us who believe have our own reasons for coming to the faith we own and for staying there. I will tell you in the chapters that follow some of my own reasons for staying in the Christian faith. However, I admit here and now that language is not entirely up to the task of describing transcendence fully. Words often fumble; and even when language reaches the extent of its powers, it falls short. Barbara Brown Taylor, one of the best contemporary American preachers, likes to describe language as a deck of fifty-two cards. We can play many games with the cards in our efforts to describe God, but in the end we still have only fifty-two cards.[8] Dante, the great medieval Italian poet of mystical vision, routinely complained about the limitations of language:

> But oh how much my words miss my conception,
> which is itself so far from what I saw
> that to call it feeble would be rank deception![9]

Mystics of all religions profess that the transcendent one is beyond our capacity to perceive fully. God is far greater than our doctrines, our imagination, our poetry, our most mystical experiences. As Paul, even after the blinding light of the Damascus road, put it: "We see through a glass darkly" (1 Corinthians 13:12 KJV). As much as I love Christian theology and believe in its hold on truth, I know that even the best theology is still an approximation, limited by our smallness in every sense.

It's all right to be small. We do not all have to be mystics, catching palpable visions of infinity. Most of us just need to answer that question: What are we? We need to find a way to go on that makes sense. One of my favorite hymns expresses this longing that rises in humility from our not-knowing:

> I ask no dream, no prophet ecstasies,
> No sudden rending of the veil of clay,
> No angel visitant, no opening skies;
> But take the dimness of my soul away.[10]

What will give us the light to relieve our dimness? Not only on some rarefied plane of perception but here on the ground? That's where the real test is. We cannot understand it all, but what can we understand that will be enough?

Some people seem to fear that committing to a certain set of beliefs requires giving up too much of the world's diversity and appeal. I have found that once I come into the light of Christian faith, it is not so much that all else is taken from me but that all things are returned to their truest, best nature. With Christ at the center, all things hold together. The world comes alive again, and the delights of nature speak a language of praise. The suffering of all creation is no

longer a mere illusion or a brittle fact or a slide to despair but is occu-
pied with the presence of Jesus and becomes pliable to hope. As for
the poignant beauties of human existence so sadly caressed in the art
of our age, I can love them the more tenderly for the sake of the one
who sustains their existence despite it all. Whatever is true, noble,
right, pure, lovely, and admirable yields up in the light of Christ its
true origin and purpose.

To convince you of all this, I am helpless. That is the work of the
Spirit. I can only point to the threshold of light, with so many before
and beside me, and say: come in.

CHAPTER TWO

ᐵᐺ

THE DIVINE DANCE
God with Us

EVEN THOUGH I WALK THROUGH
THE VALLEY OF THE SHADOW OF DEATH,
I WILL FEAR NO EVIL, FOR YOU ARE WITH ME.
—Psalm 23:4

If in some way we are visited by the presence of God, if through some circumstance or inkling God gets a message through to us, our response might be gratitude and wonder, perhaps confusion or fear, or most likely some complex combination. If God is there, what could this God be like? How do I find out? Is God for me or against me? Should I hide? Or have I finally found shelter from my fears?

All major religions have ways both of rousing our fears and reassuring us, but Christians believe something about God that adherents to other religions do not believe: that God has become one of us—for good. The first chapter of the Gospel of Luke tells a most astonishing story. An angel appears to a young Jewish woman with a message from God. Although the young woman, whose name is Mary, believes in the God of her people, a personal visitation from God's messenger leaves her, at least at first, quite bewildered. But the angel reassures her: "Do not be afraid." The angel tells her that she will give birth to an extraordinary child. In her world, in her life, in her very body, God will make himself known. "The Lord is with you. Do not be afraid" (verses 28, 30).

This astonishing moment sets in motion within human history the most dramatic divine revelation ever known: the birth of a human baby who is, at the same time, God. Christians call this the incarnation, God taking on human flesh.

That the baby Jesus could be both fully divine and fully human, as Christians believe, defies logic. And for those who believe that God's greatness inheres in his distance, in his difference from us, the incarnation is an offense. How can it be, and why should it be? No one can answer *how* it can be. On this point we stand on the precipice of mystery. But *why* it should be is easier to comprehend. A God far distant from us in being and power, if he desires any relationship with us, will have to make himself known to us somehow. The question is how and to what degree. To what extent does God remain above and beyond, and to what extent does God move among us?

We see God in the majesty and complex elegance of nature, yet nature leaves us with many questions about God. We learn more about God from holy books composed through some extraordinary, God-influenced process. Yet even the Scriptures—though precious, instructive, and indispensable—are not enough. Neither the natural world nor volumes of books are sufficient to reveal the fullness of God because neither is like enough to God. If God is a personal being, then the best means to make himself known to us is through personhood, in a form with which we are familiar: the human. Christians believe that God took on human form in order to give us the key to unlock the mystery of himself. To take on our nature like this may seem to reduce God's glory and power, but this is precisely what we most need to know about God: that God's essential nature is love, the kind of love willing to diminish oneself for the sake of another. In the incarnation God in a way reduces his own stature out of love, like a parent kneeling down to comfort a frightened child, pressing the face of compassion to the face streaked with tears and saying: "Do not be afraid. I am with you."

THE INCARNATION STORY

To bend our imaginations around this central Christian belief, we have to spend some time immersed in the New Testament. This collection of writings testifies that God revealed himself to humankind most completely in Jesus of Nazareth, and they record an emerging understanding of how this could be and what it all might mean to us.

The angel who appears to Mary in Luke's gospel (*gospel* simply means "good news") announces that she will give birth to a child named Jesus, then offers an account of who this baby will become: "He will be great and will be called the Son of the Most High. The Lord God will give him the throne of his father David, and he will reign over the house of Jacob forever; his kingdom will never end. . . . The holy one to be born will be called the Son of God" (1:32–33, 35). Through the words of the angel, Luke presents the reader immediately with the full identity of Jesus. Jesus is the long-awaited Messiah, or "anointed one," of the Jewish people, the one from the house of David promised for centuries by the prophets. He would rescue the people of Israel from their suffering, end their exile, and bring the presence of God to the glorious city of Zion—the restored Jerusalem—so that all nations would see it. But Jesus, the angel hints, is even greater than that. He has a closer relationship with God than servant or anointed one; he is the Son of God. The title *son of God* was not a new one in first-century Judaism; it pointed to someone especially holy, with an extraordinary nearness to God. Neither the term *messiah* nor the title *son of God* necessarily implied a divine nature.[1] But in the wake of Jesus' life, death, and resurrection, the term underwent a profound expansion as Jesus' followers began to understand that Jesus, in some unexpected sense, *was* God.

All four of the New Testament books called gospels (Matthew, Mark, Luke, and John) make it abundantly clear, however, that Jesus' identity was not easy for anyone among whom he lived to understand. As Jesus grew up and began to preach, and even more so when he was tortured and killed, those around him struggled to decide whether he was a prophet, a political leader, a determined troublemaker, or someone for whom there was simply no former category of description. To me it's a mark of the authenticity of the gospel accounts that they fully acknowledge the puzzlement even of Jesus' closest followers. They record many examples of Jesus trying to explain his identity. For instance, the Gospel of John records a long conversation the night before Jesus is arrested and killed (14:8–11). His disciples are nervous and frightened, though they don't know exactly what's about to happen. A disciple named Philip asks Jesus to "show us the Father, and that will be enough for us." Jesus replies: "Don't you know me, Philip, even after I have been among you such a long time? Anyone who has seen me has seen the Father. How can you say, 'Show us the Father'? Don't you believe that I am in the Father, and the Father is in me? . . . Believe me when I say that I am in the Father and the Father is in me; or at least believe on the evidence of the miracles themselves." In all four gospels, when Jesus tries to explain or demonstrate his relationship with the God whom his Jewish followers and their ancestors have worshiped for many generations, people often respond with confusion or even offense. The disciples sometimes seem to understand and sometimes seem to bungle terribly.

It might have been easier for Christians to "prove" precise theological formulations about the nature of Jesus if the gospels were more straightforward—if Jesus were simply to say, "Look, here's how it works: I am the second person of a Trinitarian Godhead, eternally begotten, of one being with the Father, etc., etc." and the people in the story were to answer, "Oh, I see. Of course." But in fact, the gospels take a far more savvy approach to presenting who Jesus is. They are both generous to the reader and clear about the central issue. They are generous to the reader in the sense that they present four accounts of the life of Jesus, each in its own way acknowledging the challenge of comprehending this person yet each offering abundant witness and evidence for who he is. The gospels are clear about the central issue in their recognition that each reader must go through the process of discovering Jesus and receiving an invitation to follow his teachings and ways. So the gospel texts allow the main players in the stories to display their own process of discovery, and they invite readers to answer for themselves the question Jesus asks his disciples in the texts: "Who do you say that I am?" (Matthew 16:13–20; Mark 8:27–30; Luke 9:18–22).

The gospels are honest about the confusion of those around Jesus, but they also describe moments when someone finally understands—and these "aha!" moments serve to encourage the reader. In three gospels the bold disciple Peter is the first to offer his confession of who Jesus is. He reaches the conclusion that Jesus is the promised Messiah of the Jews, the Greek term for which is *christos* or "Christ" (Matthew 16:16; Mark 8:29; Luke 9:20). Jesus' friend Martha, even amid her bitter disappointment that Jesus did not arrive at her brother Lazarus's bedside in time to save him from dying, also tells Jesus that she believes he is the Christ (John 11:27). Her confession seems to stir Jesus to perform his most dramatic miracle: calling Lazarus out of the tomb. In the Gospel of Mark, the one most sympathetic to the skeptical reader, no one but Peter has dared to come out and say who Jesus is until, at the very end, just after Jesus dies on a Roman cross, the only other person in the entire gospel to make a confession is not another disciple but a Roman military captain who stands in awe and says: "Surely this man was the Son of God!" (Mark 15:39; Matthew 27:54).

Of course, the greatest stumbling block to all Jesus' followers in understanding his identity was his suffering and death. Even if the disciples managed to believe before he died that he was the promised Messiah of the Jewish people, the gospels admit that after the disciples buried his broken body, they were left devastated with disappointment and fear. The Messiah was supposed to save Israel, not die a horrific death at a young age! Other would-be messiahs had died martyrs' deaths too, and their followers took this as a sign that their leader hadn't quite done the job. The followers scattered or pinned their hopes on someone else.[2] After Jesus' death, however, something very different happened among his followers: their numbers exploded. According to the gospel accounts, the explanation for this comes with the events beginning on the third day after Jesus' death. The women among Jesus' disciples find his tomb empty, see a vision of an angel explaining that Jesus is risen from the dead, and run to tell the other disciples. The Gospel of John (chapter 20) tells the story of Peter and John running to the tomb after hearing the women's report. They see the tomb empty, the burial cloths neatly folded. They believe something miraculous has happened, but they're not entirely sure what. After the events at the tomb, all of the gospels record appearances of Jesus to his disciples—wonderful accounts in which Jesus is different enough that they don't always recognize him at first, yet he is still very much the master they loved.

In regard to Jesus' resurrection, the gospels are again honest about how difficult it is to comprehend these events and accept them as true. First-century Jews were familiar with the idea of resurrection—which does not mean being resuscitated in the same body or simply existing as a spirit after death but actually being reembodied. Some Jews, though not all, believed that the righteous would all be resurrected together eventually as part of a great return from exile once and for all.[3] But even Jesus' closest disciples didn't immediately believe that their teacher would or could actually rise from the dead in this way. No one expected an individual resurrection. The disciple Thomas famously insisted on seeing the risen Jesus with his own eyes; and according to the Gospel of John, Jesus obliged him, appearing to him and inviting him to touch the scars of his crucifixion wounds.

So what could it mean that this teacher and healer, Jesus of Nazareth, was first crucified by the Roman authorities and then resurrected? Apparently the disciples eventually recovered from their shock enough to recall that Jesus had tried all along to explain to them that part of the Messiah's job, according to Jewish prophecies, was to suffer, die, and rise again. In all their expectation and excitement about Jesus being the Messiah, no one had quite wanted to believe that this was what the job entailed. As the gospels portray it, they didn't understand Jesus' words at the time. You know how it is when people try to tell you something ahead of time, and you can hardly hear it: "A baby will change your life!" or "Living abroad expands your perspective!" These are only empty words until you've been through the experience. In the same way, the disciples couldn't quite make sense of Jesus' predictions until they had experienced the cataclysmic events of Jesus' crucifixion, the empty tomb, and his appearances to them. After these things they began to study the Hebrew Scriptures all over again to find how this could be true. There they found a strain of prophecy in the Psalms, the book of Isaiah, and other Hebrew Scriptures indicating that the kingly messiah they expected would also be a suffering messiah. And that at the right moment in history, the suffering of Israel would be focused in the suffering of an individual. Moreover, that individual's suffering would bring about the restoration to God that Israel had longed for, which would in turn open the way for the reconciliation of all peoples and nations to God. The glory of God had returned to Zion, not in a stone-and-gold temple as everyone had supposed but in a person. In fact, the Gospel of Matthew quotes Hebrew Scriptures constantly because its major concern is precisely this: demonstrating how Jesus, in all the contours of his life and teachings, fulfills the promises of the Hebrew Scriptures.

IMMANUEL, GOD WITH US

One of the first passages Matthew quotes is an obscure prophecy from the Old Testament book of Isaiah. The prophetic words during Isaiah's time had to do with King Ahaz of Israel and his dealings with the king of Assyria. But the writer of the gospel understood that prophecies are often fulfilled in more than one way, that they are not simply *predictions* but *patterns* of how God views the world and chooses to make himself known in it. So when Matthew tells the story of Jesus' birth, he quotes this passage from Isaiah (7:14): "The virgin will be with child and will give birth to a son, and will call him Immanuel." The Hebrew name Immanuel means "God with us." Matthew, in quoting this passage, declares to the reader that Jesus' birth fulfills the words of the prophet in a new way. Jesus is the one who most truly bears the name Immanuel; and in Jesus, God is with us in a way more intimate, more humble, and more magnificent than anyone expected.

The rest of the New Testament after the gospels is in essence a record of how early believers began to connect the dots from Jewish history and thought, through the life of Jesus, and into a previously unimagined future. The book of Acts recounts the disciples' actions after the postresurrection appearances, the conversion of the great missionary Paul, and the founding of the first Christian churches. The remaining New Testament books are letters addressed to early believers. (The book of Revelation, however, is a special case belonging to the genre of apocalyptic literature.) The New Testament letters, sometimes called epistles, often contain practical advice for churches on how to get along and how to solve specific ethical problems. But the more practical words are embedded in profound meditations on the meaning of Jesus' miracles, the necessity of his death, and the implications of the resurrection. Most important, the letters reflect an emerging understanding that the promised Messiah was much more than a political and moral leader specifically for the Jews. That expectation was far too small. Jesus came to fulfill Israel's original role as God's chosen people, which was to reconcile God with all nations, with all creation. The particular way in which Jesus did this, his followers came to understand, was through his teaching, his miracles, his suffering, death, and resurrection.[4] In all these things, Jesus displayed authority and power beyond the prophets. In fact, it was the power of God himself. So from the very early days after the resurrection, Christians believed that Jesus was the Messiah, and—here was the bigger surprise—the Messiah was God.

It's possible to reject what the New Testament says about Jesus, especially when popular novels and journalism promote sensational misconceptions. Some skeptics suppose that these texts represent merely the earnest ravings of people who were deeply mistaken. Or perhaps Jesus' followers wrote the texts long after Jesus of Nazareth lived, making up events and putting sayings in Jesus' mouth that reflect what his followers wish had happened, not what actually did occur. I can say here only that no one need hesitate to investigate the New Testament texts and their background. Serious study bears out that the New Testament books are different in their development and conventions from modern texts (naturally) but still represent the testimony of people who sincerely believed that they had experienced extraordinary events and wrote about them—Christians would say, with the help of the Spirit of God—as best they could.

Moreover, if the writers of the New Testament were trying to create a successful religious movement for their own purposes, they could hardly have done a worse job. Jesus' claims about himself are subtle, often metaphorical, deeply symbolic, and require a good knowledge of Hebrew Scriptures and history to come fully clear. The disciples are frequently painted in a less-than-flattering light. And the New Testament writers were not exactly doing themselves a favor or advancing their position in the world by following the teachings of and worshiping a Jewish fellow from a minor backwater who advocated repentance, forgiveness, and nonviolence. Many of those who spread these ideas about Jesus were despised, tortured, and killed for what they preached. Nevertheless, despite persecution, Christianity spread with extraordinary speed through the ancient world. Strange, but it begins to make sense if you can imagine that what these people said about Jesus was true.

A THREEFOLD MYSTERY

In the centuries following the composition of the New Testament, believers in Jesus as the Son of God continued to clarify exactly what that meant. The earliest Christians, Jews whose ancestors had declared for centuries that "the Lord is one,"[5] believed that this Jesus deserved their worship. So what did this reveal about the nature of the God? If the evidently human Jesus is the Son of God and also divine, does that mean he is separate from God? Or the same as God? The relationship between Father and Son gets more complicated when you consider another promise Jesus made. The night before his arrest, Jesus told his disciples he would be going away but that they would not be left alone: "But the Counselor, the Holy Spirit, whom the Father will send in my name, will teach you all things and will remind you of everything I have said to you. Peace I leave with you; my peace I give you. I do not give as the world gives. Do not let your hearts be troubled and do not be afraid" (John 14:26–27).

The book of Acts (chapter 2) describes an event many weeks later in which these same disciples experienced yet another bizarre event, which they understood as the fulfilling of this promise: the arrival of this Spirit as signaled by rushing wind, visions of fire, and the disciples' ability to speak spontaneously in other languages. Christians call this event Pentecost. The book of Acts further explains how the disciples, after this event, believed that the Spirit had given them the power to preach about Jesus, do miracles, and bring people to believe that Jesus made possible a profound change in identity and purpose that they called salvation.

Over the course of the first and second centuries, Christians eventually came to understand that God has shown himself as Father, as Son, and as Spirit. The leaders of the early church decided that, rather than trying to fit God into a simpler, more sensible explanation, there was nothing for it but to contemplate a mystery they did not fully understand. A singularity, however great, was insufficient as traditionally understood to express the fullness of God. To study the question precisely, leaders of the church called councils in the fourth century at Nicaea and Constantinople. They eventually settled on the idea of the Trinity as the best way to explain the nature of God. God is one God in three persons: Father, Son, and Holy Spirit.

The councils were important because there were several opinions at the time on how to put one and one and one together, as it were. In recent decades it has become popular in some circles to imagine that Christian beliefs about the nature of God were established merely through power politics, in which the nasty majority oppressed the noble minority, and the ideas that "won" had no particular merit over those that "lost." Surely, as with any human process, the participants were not free of self-promoting desires and motivations. But studying the early debates on the Trinity reveals that the leaders of the church repeatedly refused to reduce or flatten the mystery of God's nature to make it easier to comprehend. Moreover, they understood that these questions were not merely trivial and academic but had profound implications. Their decisions would have ramifications for the present and for future centuries of believers.

One logical possibility that the councils never seriously considered was a kind of tritheism, the idea that we actually have three gods. The church always insisted that, unlike the capricious and constantly quibbling Greek and Roman gods, the true God *is* a unity, as the Hebrew Scriptures had always declared—God of all creation, steady in purpose and nature, faithful in loving his people. The more important debate involved whether or not the Son was equal to the Father. Couldn't we believe that God created a human Jesus and somehow elevated him to godhood? This was not an unfamiliar idea at the time. The elders concluded, however, that all three persons of the Trinity are co-equal, of the same substance, and have always been so. There's no hierarchy in God, only perfect and eternal harmony. If the elders of the church had wanted to establish power structures in their own favor, they might well have favored the idea that hierarchy originated in the very nature of God. Instead, they articulated a conception of God as a perfect oneness of equal persons.

Another alternative view of God's nature, which existed in several varieties, was Gnosticism. This version of Christianity was espoused in a number of writings that were eventually rejected by the majority of church elders as the New Testament was being established. Gnostics believed that the material world was evil, created by a being called a Demi-Urge. The true God, meanwhile, was revealed by Jesus, but Jesus did not truly become human. His body was an illusion. Moreover, Gnosticism had an elitist strain, claiming that certain people possessed a higher insight and others did not. Early church leaders rejected these ideas and maintained that Christianity was available to everyone, not just a class of enlightened people. They maintained the reality of the incarnation too, because in the fact of Jesus' earthly body, we learn to befriend our physical nature rather than reject it. By rejecting Gnosticism, the elders reclaimed God's love for creation and the human body and God's mercy for people's everyday needs.

THREE IN ONE

All of these theological fine points are fascinating to those of us who enjoy this sort of thing, but it's not necessary to sift through every subtle question in order to accept the wisdom of many centuries concerning the nature of God. Christians, in their study and daily practice of the faith, continue to confirm that the Trinity, though counterintuitive, is the best explanation we've got for understanding the nature of God. I find that counterintuitive quality of the Trinity part of its persuasiveness. Any idea about God's nature that made complete logical sense would have to be too simple. The God who created the universe is beyond any formulation of language: we should expect to have to stretch our understanding and imagination to grasp, even tentatively, the full nature of this God.

On a more practical and less theoretical level, the Trinity gives us a way to organize and speak of our experiences of God. Christians generally understand each person of the Trinity to have particular qualities and roles. Father, Son, and Holy Spirit are the titles, derived from the Bible, that Christians throughout the centuries have given the persons of the Trinity. Another equally biblical but more functionally descriptive way to think about the Trinity is as Creator, Redeemer, and Sustainer. Although all three persons participate in all three of these functions, it sometimes helps us begin to comprehend God's nature and work if we focus on one dimension at a time.

Christians speak of the Father as the Creator of all things, the initiator of relationship with us and all creation, and the source of divine power. In some ways I think the Father is the easiest to comprehend, the first impulse we have when we imagine God. When Christians look in awe on the beauty of the created world, they give praise to the Creator. When a college student feels childlike and helpless in the midst of her parents' divorce, she might pray to God the Father. When a relief worker longs for a God who is just and powerful, the kind who will take terrible injustice and make things right, he might look to the Father.

The Son is the visible face of the Father, the one through whom the Father is most fully made known, the one through whom our relationship to the Father is redeemed or restored. One of the strangest questions early believers in Jesus had to answer was: If Jesus is the Son of God, if Jesus is part of God, then where was he *before* the birth of the human Jesus? And where is he *now* that we don't see Jesus on earth anymore? The author of the Gospel of John strives to solve this problem in his elegant prologue. His answer is that the Son has always existed, always been what we might call the interface between the Father and the world. Echoing the opening words of Genesis, John writes (1:1–3): "In the beginning was the Word, and the Word was with

God and the Word was God. He was with God in the beginning. Through him all things were made." The word translated as "word" in English is the Greek word *logos,* which means not only a small unit of language but the ordering principle behind all language that shapes the world into meaning. John went back to the beginning of Scriptures and began to see the Son everywhere, in the words God spoke to create the world, in the figure of Wisdom eloquently described in the book of Proverbs, everywhere God sought to bridge the gap between himself and his creation. Thus, the historical period during which Jesus walked the earth was a special manifestation of what always existed in the nature of God: "The Word became flesh and lived for a while among us. We have seen his glory, the glory of the one and only Son, who came from the Father, full of grace and truth. . . . No one has ever seen God, but God the only Son, who is at the Father's side, has made him known" (1:14, 18). The Greek word for "lived for a while" can be more literally translated as "tented"—or as we might say, "set up camp." It's a humble description, one that depicts Jesus among us not in a palace but on the ground—an idea borne out rather literally in the gospel accounts of how Jesus lived. The Greek term for "made him known" in this passage is *exegeted,* which means "to lead out or go before" and "to draw out the meaning of," the way one might explicate a literary text. The Son explains the Father. He is the comprehensible pattern of the Father, a pattern exhibited centrally in Jesus' life, death, and resurrection but also rippling outward from those events; he is the leading edge of God in all history and all creation.

This is why Christians focus on the person of Jesus in their prayer and worship: Jesus is the face of God to us. Through the Son we come to the Father, and the Father's power is made available to redeem our struggles and sorrows. When a woman abandoned by her husband desires someone who will come to earth, judge with justice, and reveal the truth, she might look to the Son. When a small child wants to talk to a God who has a face, a God who makes more sense than a distant spiritual being, he can talk to Jesus. When a patient in the hospital feels the friendship of God, the kind and understanding presence, she feels Jesus beside her.

The Spirit is perhaps the most mysterious person of the Trinity. The Spirit creates motion, connection, and change. According to the book of Genesis (1:2 KJV), the Spirit "moved upon the face of the waters" before all creation. According to Jesus, the Spirit delivers the presence of God to us, bringing that presence to our inward being so that we say the Spirit lives within us. Any response we have to the love of God is activated and enabled through the Spirit, the Sustainer of faith. The Spirit reveals truth, enables us to believe, inspires our words, and gives us comfort and peace. The Spirit is also the conduit of God's power. If people do amazing or miraculous things, we say they do so by the action of the Spirit. Christians pray to the Spirit when they seek understanding (especially of Scripture), inspiration, a change of heart, or renewed understanding. Christians understand all their prayer as enabled by the Spirit, who prays along with us, as Paul wrote, "with sighs too deep for words" (Romans 8:26 RSV).

Holding the three persons in balance in our thought and worship of God presents something of a challenge. Perhaps as a result, different parts of the church tend to emphasize one person over the others. Some believers, particularly those who shout and sway and clap as they worship and who seek the kinds of miraculous abilities described in the New Testament, tend to emphasize the Spirit. American evangelicals and others who focus on telling the good news to their neighbors tend to emphasize the Son and his redemptive acts. Individuals might connect better to God through one or another person of the Trinity. And this may change throughout a person's lifetime. As a child, for example, I thought of God mostly as Father. I imagined a fatherly figure of power and love looking down on me. As I grew up and faced the difficulties of adulthood, I felt closest to Jesus, the one who knows our sorrows and walks beside us. In recent years, when my work has required creative energy I feel helpless to summon, I have often found myself praying to the Spirit. Of course, one can always simply say "God" and mean all three persons at once.

Part of the beauty of the Trinity is that it will not allow us to settle into a limited view of God for long. Christian worship and teaching will, if done properly, constantly remind us that our view of God as pure spirit or long-bearded judge or mild teacher—or whatever picture begins to solidify in our mind—is far too simple. God is always more than our imaginations can comprehend and infinitely more than enough to satisfy our most expansive desires.

Matter Matters

Many religions and philosophical systems teach that the physical world is inferior and undesirable, a mere illusion or something to be dispensed with if possible. Even in science fiction, one of the most irreligious of imaginative realms, one old chestnut of a plot device is to arrange for a superior alien species of pure energy to encounter the poor, primitive humans trapped in their prison of physical matter. Sometimes in these stories we watch in amusement as the aliens try on flesh for a while and experience the pleasures of, say, eating or kissing. The poor aliens find out it's not so easy to control oneself in the midst of physical pleasures; and as we watch them fumble, we feel momentarily superior. But then the aliens encounter the other side of fleshly life, pain, and off they go back into their pure energy form. Lucky them.

People want to imagine the flesh as inferior and dispensable for rather good reasons. We are vulnerable to physical pain, decay, and ultimately death. Especially in illness and age, we can feel trapped by our bodies, longing only to be free of these dead weights on our spirits. If we have sufficiently absorbed convictions that the flesh is inherently offensive, that physical matter ought to be regarded as base and inferior to spirit, then we might regard the incarnation—the idea that God took on our human flesh—as silly or offensive. Even Christians sometimes like to avoid talking about Jesus' body (or their own) as much as possible. But the failures of the flesh are exactly the reason we need the incarnation.

One of the most important implications of the incarnation is that physical matter *matters* to God. If the Word became flesh and dwelt among us, then God not only honors but shares our physical nature, even in its vulnerability. In some other religions or mythological systems, a spiritual divinity occasionally becomes incarnated, putting on a garment of flesh to be worn temporarily and then removed. But Christians believe that the Son exists in eternal solidarity (to use an apt term) with our physical nature. God has gathered our physical nature into himself. God bothered to live in a body on this earth; so we can be sure that God loves our bodies, the earth, this whole universe. The great Christmas hymn "O Come, All Ye Faithful," in a verse not usually piped over the loudspeaker in department stores, remarks profoundly on this surprising affirmation of the body:

God of God, Light of Light eternal,
lo, he abhors not the virgin's womb.[6]

Though our bodies sometimes offend or trouble or limit us, Christians believe the body of a young woman named Mary was honored as the dwelling place of God. The figure of Mary, pregnant with the Christ child, an embodied God enfolded in her own body, becomes an emblem of God's reaffirming love for creation.

We ought not to worship nature or the pleasures of the body, because these are not equivalent to God. Instead we are free, even obligated, to love the beauty of the cosmos, to admire the wonders of our bodies, to protect and care for all created things because God created these things, and they are the "work of his fingers" (Psalm 8:3, paraphrase). Even more important, the incarnation is the ultimate sign that God loves this creation enough to fix what is broken about it. Jesus preached about sin and repentance and other spiritual things, but he also healed people's bodies and fed their stomachs and instructed his followers to do likewise. God does not intend to dispose of physical matter and elevate us to a purely spiritual state. God created us as both spiritual and physical beings, and the Bible testifies that God intends to renew and perfect us, and indeed all creation, according to that original blueprint.

The gospels make it clear that when Jesus appeared to his disciples after his resurrection, he was not merely a glowing ball of light. He had a body. Apparently it was an improved body that was not limited by time and space as our present bodies are; but he still had scars from his wounds, still ate food, still spoke and listened. And why not? If God can create the body of a baby in its mother's womb thousands of times a day over thousands of generations, why could not God create an improved version? Christians take Jesus' resurrected body as a herald of what is to come: a physical resurrection. This squares with the Bible's great poetic visions of God's destiny for us and the world. These visions say nothing about floating about as spirits; they feature banquets and mountains, trees and cities and singing. The incarnation and resurrection together affirm that these are not merely metaphors.

Christians from the Orthodox traditions of the East offer us an especially wise understanding of the incarnation. They emphasize that the created world, if we have eyes to see it, is transparent to the glory of God. So often, however, our consciousness is blinded and

the physical world remains opaque to us. We recognize physical pleasures or the laws of nature and see nothing of God through them.
Because God chose to become incarnate, however, every atom is holy.
When we look to Jesus, our vision is renewed and physical realities
become transparent to God. We see how the world is broken in many
ways, but we also see through the world's plenitude and beauty into
the heart of God. Physical and spiritual unite in the illumination of
God's radiance.

In my view anyone who has sighed with delight at a sunset,
wondered at the intricate design of plants and animals, marveled at
the mathematical order of the universe, gasped at the perfectly formed
fingernails of a newborn baby, savored eating an orange or touching
a lover's skin—anyone who has done even one of these things ought
to rejoice in the incarnation. In fact, any poet or artist or craftsperson
who works with the materials of body and sound and matter, attending to them carefully enough to see through them to something divine,
should find the incarnation a most welcome, if mysterious, truth. When
we perceive in the materials of the here and now some transcendence,
something beyond, what more durable explanation is there than that
God has set up camp in this world, infusing it with his presence?

We complain that Christmas has become too materialistic in
our culture, and surely our excessive buying and selling has become a
burden rather than a celebration. But Christmas is a festival of the
incarnation. So to make it purely spiritual—as the Puritans tried to do
in a well-intentioned effort to avoid what they called worldliness—
dismisses the power of the incarnation. It's quite right that we enjoy
good food, beautiful candles and table linens, thoughtful gifts, and one
another's physical presence as we celebrate Jesus' birth. God gave himself in an earthy, material way. So when we offer one another hope
and reconciliation, peace and goodwill, generosity and compassion,
not merely as good wishes but in material ways, we are reflecting the
pattern of God's love.

DESPERATE MEASURES

A week or so after last Christmas, I was packing away our decorations,
and I realized that somehow my family has managed to accumulate
five different crèches—the nativity scenes that Christians have set out

in their homes at Christmastime since the thirteenth century.[7] One of our crèches is about fifty years old and is looking pretty shabby. The figures come from two or three different sets: some are painted realistic colors, and some are gold; they vary in size, so that the shepherds look like giants compared to Mary and Joseph, and the donkey could easily eat several of the sheep. All the figures are cracked or broken or chipped. Because I was feeling a strong impulse to purge our possessions this year, I thought about throwing the whole junky thing away. But I couldn't do it. It occurred to me that this is the most fitting of all our crèches, because a cracked and chipped nativity scene represents rather well why the baby came in the first place.

God did not undertake a magnificent condescension simply to make the world somehow cozier than it already was. God entered the world in order to repair it. The fear God wishes to answer—in Mary, in the shepherds on the hillside who were also visited by angels, and in ourselves—is the result of what has gone wrong with this world. Christians use the word *sin* as a shorthand for all that is wrong in the world and in our own hearts. Sin encapsulates our alienation from God, our clouded vision, the long distance between God's perfect plan for the world and the way things have actually turned out. The incarnation declares that this desperate brokenness requires desperate measures.

The incarnation demands that we regard the suffering in the world with utmost seriousness. God created human beings with freedom and responsibility; and we have used it to hurt one another, neglect one another, and harm the earth. Christians refuse to define suffering and evil as simply a matter of wrong thinking, primitive impulses, an illusion, or anything else that we can fix by adjusting our thoughts or trying harder. What is wrong with this world is quite real; and we carry the dignity and shame of responsibility for it, as individuals and as the human race. The conditions human beings have created in the world and in our own hearts are so terrible, Christians believe, that we cannot repair them on our own. God must come and do it for us.

Certainly there is an element of judgment in this. Why should God *not* be angry over what we have done to each other? We feel anger ourselves as we listen to the news and endure the daily litany of human corruption, exploitation, and failure. Anger, good anger, is always a by-product of compassion. It rises in defense of a person's true value against what a person is doing to deny her own or another's value. The incarnation, as a response to sin, assures us that God's anger over sin is the roiling surface of unfathomable compassion. God is holy, powerful, and entitled to his anger; but God is so fierce in defense of our true value, so committed to our well-being, that he is willing to suffer with us, suffer for us, in order to rescue us from the mess.

When God suffers with us in the person of Jesus, we see that God is not ultimately against us but *for* us. Jesus first appeared not as a king descending on a cloud to strike terror on the earth but as a helpless infant, born in a barn, welcomed by shepherds. The crazy upside-downness of it, the humor even, assures us that we can set aside our fear and trust this one. When he grew up, Jesus taught wisely, contending with the most elite scholars but also telling earthy stories about planting grain and hiring workers and throwing parties. He had compassion on the least desirable people and healed people of physical and spiritual ailments. He endured ridicule, hunger, homelessness, and conflict. As the author of the New Testament book of Hebrews (4:15) writes: "For we do not have a high priest who is unable to sympathize with our weaknesses, but we have one who has been tempted in every way, just as we are—yet was without sin."

Jesus was no sap, no weakling; he called people to account for their wrong deeds, their negligence, and their cold hearts. But he never did violence to another. Instead, he suffered violence and even death, demonstrating to us that God is not indifferent to human brutality and pain. Quite the opposite: the crucifixion and resurrection demonstrate that God engages the power of evil and death and overcomes it through an explosion of creative love. Paul summarizes it this way: "If God is for us, who can be against us? He who did not spare his own Son, but gave him up for us all—how will he not also, along with him, graciously give us all things?" (Romans 8:31–32). Jesus now "is at the right hand of God and is also interceding for us" (8:34). The gospels tell of Jesus, after his resurrection, appearing to the disciples for a while and then being "taken up into heaven" (Mark 16:15–20; Luke 24:50–53; Matthew 18:16–20). Christians often understand this ascension as something of a coronation; Jesus returns to heaven in order to rule over all the world with love and justice, to release his presence to all who seek it. The humble one has become a king indeed, wielding a power even greater than death but wielding it on our behalf.

If you can accept that Jesus is God, then you can begin to receive the ultimate assurance that God is *with* us and *for* us, that the repair of this world has begun, and that it will be completed by the same one through whose power it was first created. The only thing left to fear is keeping ourselves outside this process, resisting the very purposes of God. As Paul writes (Hebrews 1:3), in Jesus we see "the radiance of God's glory and the exact representation of his being, sustaining all things by his powerful word." We have only to throw in our lot with this glory and this word.

THE BINDING POWER OF LOVE

All the world's great religions posit that the divine is closer than we at first perceive. Christianity, in my view, gives the clearest picture of a God who is both beyond and very near, a God whose name is being and whose being is love. When we observe the noblest things about human existence, Christianity teaches us to trace those essential elements back to their source in the nature of God.

God, first of all, is not a philosophical idea but a person. One of the noblest, most distinctive elements of our existence is the quality of personhood, our individuality. Some cultures value individuality more highly than others, and I have been raised to value it probably to an unhealthy extreme. But even the most communitarian of cultures hardly deny individuality; they seek to shape it toward the good of the group. I take human personhood to be not a misfortune or illusion but a reflection of a much fuller personhood. We display personhood because God, who makes us, is the source of personhood. God wants us to be persons too, because God wants a relationship with us. As the English journalist G. K. Chesterton observed, "For the Buddhist or Theosophist, personality is the fall of man, for the Christian it is the purpose of God, the whole point of his cosmic idea."[8]

The most surprising thing we do as human persons is to overcome our powerful entrapment in our own minds and reach out to one another, not only in perception but in love. That one person can faithfully (though imperfectly) love a particular man or woman or child or friend—this is a remarkable phenomenon that we ought not to dismiss. Human love may not conquer all, but it points to all; and love too is a participation in God and therefore in the essence of all that exists. We can perceive love written in the universe itself, for the design of the universe is everywhere based on the allure of binding energies that hold together atoms and galaxies. Difference uniting yet retaining its distinctiveness, like the atoms in a molecule, like the tones in a chord, like the living organisms on this earth, like the mother with the baby stirring in her body.

Love by definition binds two things that remain distinct. If the two things cease to be distinct, we are no longer talking about love but about identity. Thus, we see the wisdom of the Nicaean elders who described God as a communion of equal, eternal persons. This picture of God offers the perfect model of difference that is not collapsed or compromised but united—the perfect model of love. The Christian faith invites us to bathe in this lively fountainhead of love. In the eighth century, Christian theologians began describing the relationship among the persons of the Trinity as a dynamic communion, a dance of three persons.[9] God's triune and dynamic presence creates space within that presence, a space into which we can be drawn. The Son, who is both God and human, reaches out to us, taking hold of our hand and welcoming us into this dance, this perfect love of God.

The psalmist, wondering at the mysteries of the universe, asked, "What are we that God would bother with us?" (8:4, paraphrase). Christianity answers this question while fully acknowledging God's distance and nearness, personhood and love. We are infinitesimal but beautiful. We are estranged from God in size and sin, yet loved by God; and God has bridged the gap. We are invited to become little personhoods in relationship with one whose personhood is greater than we can now fully bear.

Nothing invites us into that great energy of the universe, the love of God, better than an understanding of God as, in essential being, an eternal dance of loving persons. Nothing invites us into love better than a God who not only created our flesh but shares it. Not only pities our suffering but shares it. Who is not only merciful and magnificent, a lover of his people, but as close to us as a newborn in his mother's arms.

CHAPTER THREE

𝒢𝒵

ALIENATION FROM GOD

*The Human Condition, Sin,
and Repentance*

HAVE MERCY ON ME, O GOD,
ACCORDING TO YOUR UNFAILING LOVE.
—Psalm 51:1

T he day after the terrorist attacks on New York City's World Trade Center in September of 2001, students, faculty, and staff at my college crowded into the chapel to lay our bewilderment, sorrow, and fear before God. The dean of the chapel stood up to speak, and his first words were: "Friends, today we see so clearly that the world needs a savior."

That day was the first time that many of our students had felt a blow with such powerful reverberations. They had not lived through a world war or the Holocaust or Vietnam, and they had hardly been old enough to pay attention when more recent rashes of genocide surfaced in Rwanda or Bosnia. With the exception of some foreign students or missionary kids who had witnessed relentless suffering face-to-face, these young people knew about sweeping, epic evils only from books and movies. But that day they joined every generation before them and felt in their gut: this world is falling apart.

This world is not the way it's supposed to be. When we perceive this as we do on days like September 11, our revulsion hits us like nausea. On most other days, for comfortable Westerners anyway, what's wrong with the world feels like a pot of familiar ingredients on the back burner at a low boil: theft, rape, abuse, corruption, cancer, AIDS, traffic accidents, illnesses, starvation, racism, prejudice, and all the pettier offenses people routinely commit against one another. We manage to live with it, provided no one stirs up the pot on our own personal stove and raises the stink. Isn't it remarkable that we can even recognize there's something wrong? The world is now as it ever was, it seems. Why should we believe it ought to be any other way? What could inspire alternative visions of peace and rest and goodness; and what prompts us to resist actions, relationships, and events as standing between us and that well-being we seek?

Christians explain the painful dissonance between our best human longings and the worst realities of this world with the concept of sin. In a culture preoccupied with building self-esteem and ensuring perpetual happiness, sin is hardly a popular idea. Those who dislike the idea tend to assume that *sin* is the sort of term religious people use to declare everything fun to be wrong, mostly in order to make the rest of us feel worthless so that they can feel superior. Unfortunately that notion sometimes does describe how Christians, for whatever mistaken reasons, deploy the concept of sin. Many adults leave the church of their childhood because they finally grow weary of church people using sin as a blunt instrument to crush people's spirits. They sense that crushing the spirit is not genuinely what the Christian faith is about, and they are right.

The concept of sin, as Scripture and the center of the Christian tradition presents it, offers not a blunt instrument but the necessary, bracing tonic of honesty and wisdom that makes way for a renewed spirit. Sin refers to every dimension of our alienation from God, every way in which our relationship with a good and loving God is damaged and distorted. We need the concept of sin. We need it because it is both persuasively explanatory and—though this sounds paradoxical—personally liberating.

AN OTHERWISE WORLD

Sin can only be explained, of course, over against a perfection that it violates. So to understand sin, we also have to understand what God's idea of perfection might be. We can find some clues about that in the opening chapters of the book of Genesis. The magisterial poem with which the Bible begins describes God creating the world simply by speaking it into being. That method in itself is significant because it contrasts with other ancient creation accounts in which acts of violence, sometimes sexual violence, engender the world. The Bible's creation account suggests that violence is not inherent in the design. Also unique among creation accounts, the Genesis poem emphasizes design and delight. The created world is dynamic, abundant, luxuriant, yet ordered and patterned. And the Creator's response to it is delight, expressed by repeated pronouncements that it is *good*. Human beings enter creation as the crowning glory—they are creators like the Creator, not villains or fallen god figures as in other accounts. Moreover, the humans, male and female, participate in the world's original, unqualified goodness as responsible beings. God instructs them to go create culture: "Go keep this going," instructs the Creator in Genesis 1:28 (paraphrase). "Have a ball!"

In this story human beings are interconnected with one another and with the earth. When Adam first greets Eve, he composes a little poem: "This is now bone of my bone and flesh of my flesh; she shall be called 'woman' for she was taken out of man" (Genesis 2:23). As in English the Hebrew words for man and woman are based on the same root (*ish* and *ishah*). The "one flesh" idea here is traditionally associated with marriage, but that's only one participation in a much larger truth: human beings are intertwined and mutually responsible. Moreover, human beings, having been formed of the earth's own matter and breathed into life with the Spirit of God, are deeply interconnected with the earth as well. Adam and Eve are not sealed off from the rest of creation in their moral state any more than in their physical. God instructs them to "Be fruitful and increase in number; fill the earth and subdue it" (1:28). The fate of the earth, at least to some extent, is in their hands because their hands are made of earth.

Of course, even devout advocates of the Bible's authority argue a great deal over just how literal this account is. If God created the world in six days, as the creation poem declares, what exactly is a day? Were Adam and Eve really the only two progenitors of the whole human race? What about dinosaurs? There's no urgent need at the moment to figure out how the Genesis account could be literal. Instead, it's more important to get to the big point of the text, which is that God's intention for this world is ordered fullness and harmonious delight, a dynamic perfection. The Hebrew word for this state of affairs is *shalom,* often translated simply as "peace," although it means so much more than calm or cease-fire. It points to wholeness and health—vibrant, flourishing life.

Many other religions and mythologies posit the idea of a golden age or realm of perfection from which human history somehow fell. A Jungian psychologist might say that such archetypal correspondences among vastly different mythologies are evidence of a collective unconscious memory: as a species we remember that things used to be better. If it seems too simplistic to imagine that once upon a time the world really was perfect, we can consider such a scheme of history an appropriate accommodation to our necessarily linear habit of thinking. We inhabit time, so we can hardly help organizing realities in a before-and-after scheme. God, on the other hand, is not limited to a linear view of history in which things move from one state to another in sequence. God exists outside time itself and therefore perceives the entire timeline of human history simultaneously. In God's mind, therefore, the original state of perfection always exists. If that seems too bizarre, you can still comprehend that, in some true sense, God created this world perfect. That is the Bible's explanation for our intuition that the world is not the way it's supposed to be. This sense of something better derives from our participation in God's eternal vision of shalom for this world. We wish the world were otherwise because God designs it to be otherwise.

FREE AND FALLING

Well, then, why isn't it otherwise? Where did sin and evil come from? How could a good God let this happen? The story of the fall in Genesis is the Bible's basic answer to that question. Wise people have meditated on this story for thousands of years and still not exhausted its meanings. Here again we need to acknowledge that the Bible is presenting mysteries in the form of stories that are simple on the surface while pointing to unfathomable things beneath.

The jubilant account of the world's creation lasts only two chapters in Genesis. By the end of the creation account we read that Adam and Eve are given responsibility for the care of creation and complete freedom to discharge that care, with only one exception: they are not allowed to eat of the tree of the knowledge of good and evil. In chapter three a serpent—a "crafty" beast (verse 1)—comes along and suggests to Eve that God, by forbidding them this one thing, is only trying to keep them low. Eve falls for that temptation, and she and

Adam both eat of the forbidden tree. They immediately see that they are naked and feel shame for the first time. God requires them to explain why they have made this choice. Adam blames Eve, and Eve blames the serpent—behavior that strikes us as distressingly familiar. God then curses the serpent and predicts pain and suffering for Adam and Eve. Offering mercy as well as judgment, however, God predicts that the woman's offspring will defeat the serpent (Christians see this as a prophecy about Jesus). God makes clothes for the couple and then leads them out of the garden lest they eat from the tree of life and prolong their suffering forever.

Again we need not settle the question of historicity before allowing the Genesis account of the fall to yield its primary observations about sin. First, we can see that God's intention for human beings is that they be free and responsible. The single prohibition concerning the fruit of one tree is not so much a test as a signal of their freedom. The story presents the tree as a concise signifier of humans' freedom to work with the grain of God's design for the world or against it. One line of objection to the Genesis story is the question of why God gave Adam and Eve this freedom, especially if he knew—because he has foreknowledge—that they would choose wrong and suffer for their choice. The Bible does not explain God's thoughts on this matter. But it's not difficult to see why God would give some of his creatures self-consciousness and free will. God, whose nature is love, wished to create beings who could also love. Love is not love if it is compelled or forced. Therefore, God could not create puppets or automatons. Humans had to have the latitude to make choices, to love God freely or not love. Once God set creation in motion with these parameters, he could not compel Adam and Eve away from the tree, even if it meant allowing them to make the wrong choice. To compel would be to compromise their nature, to diminish the value of their free status.

INEVITABLE REPERCUSSIONS

But why did Eve and Adam make the wrong choice? That is a far more difficult question. When my students read *Paradise Lost,* the great English poet John Milton's epic expansion of the Genesis story, I ask them whether they think Milton's Adam and Eve are fallen before the fall. We always have a good discussion on this topic, because it is difficult to decide. Is Eve already vain and ambitious before she eats the fruit, so that the serpent's subtle argument appeals to her? Is Adam too easily "fondly overcome with female charm," as Milton puts it? Milton insists that Adam and Eve were "Sufficient to have stood, though free to fall,"[1] but Milton's portraits of the pair before the fall do not always convince us. And what about the serpent? How is a deceptive, malicious creature possible in a perfect creation? The Bible elsewhere identifies the serpent as Satan, a being of great power who opposes God (see Revelation 12, for example). But where Satan came from is another matter of speculation. An angel who was created good but who chose to rebel against God? The book of Revelation suggests this explanation, and so much imaginative literature follows this view that it has become a commonplace notion.

The Bible says very little about the origin of evil. Perhaps it is enough to say here that when God makes room in the realm of existence for beings that have will, then opposing God becomes possible; and evil, defined as that which opposes the good and loving God, exists at least as a theoretical possibility. This does not mean that God creates evil or intends it. It's a little like the family that decides to adopt a dog. The children love their stuffed animals, but the fuzzy tigers and bears are not living creatures and can't truly return human affections. Of course, they never cause any trouble either. When the family decides to adopt a living, breathing puppy, they are hoping to gain the love and joy of a real creature, but they are also allowing potential trouble into their household. The puppy has a savvy little nose, and that nose might lead him to get into the garbage can. That's not what his nose is for; he needs it to read his surroundings and help him find real food. Nor does the family *want* him to get into the garbage, and they take precautions to avoid it. Nevertheless, when they find the can overturned on the kitchen floor and spaghetti sauce on the pup's muzzle, they have to understand that this was always a potential outcome of inviting Scooter into their lives.

I don't mean to trivialize the fall by comparing it to a puppy getting into the garbage; I only mean to illustrate that trouble is a necessary *theoretical* by-product of freedom. The Genesis account explains that in the case of our world, trouble is an *actual* by-product of freedom, too, and a grave one. Although eating a piece of fruit seems trivial, we have to recall that we are dealing with emblematic material here. It's not so much that the eating itself is terrible—in fact, the text suggests that Eve's motivations were the beauty of the fruit and the desire for wisdom. Adam and Eve were exercising their God-given faculties, but they were exercising them against God's instructions. They were violating the operating instructions, ignoring the warnings, and throwing a wrench into God's perfectly humming universe. Part of the point here is that obedience often has to depend on trust in God more than on a thorough understanding of the stakes involved. Children don't like it when parents say, "Do as I say because I told you so," but sometimes the whole situation is too difficult to explain to a child. I know I've used that line myself occasionally with my own children, not because I had no decent reason for my instruction (which is what people sometimes assume about God) but because it's impossible to explain to an inexperienced child the possible outcomes of his disobedience. God does give an explanation when he instructs Adam and Eve not to eat of the tree: "for when you eat of it you will surely die" (Genesis 2:17). The trouble was that Eve and Adam believed the serpent, who told them that this was a deception on God's part. They ought to have trusted God's word, even though they may not have completely understood.

The text says that the result of Adam and Eve's choice is death, which we can understand in several ways. Their innocence has died, because they have experienced what it feels like to divide themselves from God's will. In a more literal sense, the text indicates that their lives will now end at some point. Death also becomes a shorthand term for all the ways that the first human couple and their world now fall away from God's design.

In light of this story we can make a number of further observations about sin, observations that we recognize as persuasively descriptive of the world as we experience it. First, we notice in the text that a single act has serious repercussions because Adam and Eve are deeply interconnected with each other and with the rest of creation. And isn't it true that our individual acts, whether merciful or cruel or somewhere between, affect others? We enter existence connected to our mothers' bodies, and interconnectedness—our power to help and hurt others, to *be* helped and hurt by others—lasts all our days and beyond. Our moral choices affect the rest of creation as well. We don't usually think of Milton as an environmentalist, but at the point in his poem where Eve makes the fatal choice, the very first result is the suffering of creation:

> She pluck'd, she [ate]:
> Earth felt the wound.[2]

The wounding of the earth by our human moral choices certainly is supported by historical evidence.

Our interconnectedness is further suggested in the Genesis account by the fact that once Adam and Eve know alienation from God by experience, they must leave Eden. Perhaps it's just as fitting to say that Eden, as a state of perfect harmony, leaves them. It may seem unfair that the choices of two primitive humans ruined everything for everyone else, but the story's essence is to affirm what we already know from observation: no one's moral choices occur in a vacuum. As a species we are in this together. We are interconnected with each other and the earth, across the generations.

Not So Free Anymore

The text yields another crucial observation about sin: once the door to sin is open, it is not easily shut. The fall *expressed* our free nature; but by expressing it against God's instructions, the fall *created* our sinful nature. In other words, sin has its own powerful momentum. Once Adam and Eve choose against God, their free will isn't so free anymore. Sin clamps on like dead weight and drags their will down. Once this happens, the weight of sin becomes part of the system and affects Adam and Eve's children and their children's children and so on. Christians have different ways of defining this phenomenon. In the fourth century, Augustine and another theologian, Pelagius, argued over how much free will human beings have. Both agreed that people make sinful choices all the time. But Pelagius argued that we are born innocent and have all the free will we need to choose right; it's just difficult, that's all. Augustine disagreed, arguing that we are born in a state of sin simply by being human, and this corrupted nature bends us toward more sin all our lives. We do not have the power to choose right on our own, ever. He called this idea original sin. Both agreed that God's grace helps us out of our trouble but disagreed on our starting point.

Pelagius officially lost the argument, and the doctrine of original sin has been the orthodox Christian position ever since. But Pelagius certainly lives on in many people's minds. We like to believe that we are basically good and simply make mistakes along the way.

Does that theory fit the evidence? Augustine derived his doctrine of original sin not only from painstaking observation of his own soul but also, possibly, from observing his baby son. (Pelagius, not incidentally, had no children.) Augustine kept a mistress for many years before his final conversion to Christianity, and when their little boy was born, Augustine named him Adeodatus ("gift of God"). Augustine evidently observed his son's babyhood carefully, judging from the detailed descriptions of infancy in Augustine's *Confessions.*[3] As Augustine knew, small children amaze us with their trust and curiosity but also with their innate desire to resist even the benevolent care of their parents. Any parent who has dealt with an exhausted child who nevertheless refuses to go to sleep—exacerbating everyone's exhaustion—knows what I mean. Children exhibit sweet affections but also a desire to hit other children, destroy things with evident relish, and take everyone around them on a roller-coaster ride of volatile emotion. Long before they reach an age of moral decision making, they are full of inner conflicts.

Grownups may learn to manage their inner conflicts—more or less. But clear-eyed observation of the world and honest self-examination bear out that inner turmoils and their outward results torment us all our lives. Our mistakes hurt ourselves and others. These mistakes result infrequently from carefully weighed choices that display the free exercise of will; far more often they arise out of a maelstrom of motivations and desires that we can barely understand and hardly control. Modern people may object to the old term *original sin,* in part because we usually associate *original* with positive qualities such as creativity. But we do recognize that people carry within them a dark chaos that they neither choose nor, even under the best circumstances, completely control. Others might identify this chaos as the id, the dark areas of the collective unconscious, a basic human drive for power, an illusion, or something else. Original sin is simply a traditional Christian way of pointing to the internal chaos with which we all wrestle as part of the human condition. G. K. Chesterton thought that original sin was so obviously an accurate description of the human condition that he once declared it "the only part of Christian theology which can really be proved."[4]

A Tangle of Fault and Result

In the sense that perfect goodness was our original design and remains God's intended purpose for us, human beings are indeed basically good. However, Christianity invites us to be quite honest about the power of sin. Insofar as we experience ourselves as having free will, we are participating in God's intention for human nature. However, we also experience ourselves as helpless to participate consistently in that design. We remember or perceive the Creator's dynamic, harmonious, abundant design for the world and long for it with our best desires; but we also battle a strong pull toward damaging or resisting that design. *Sin* as a term refers to both components of the problem: not only individual acts that counter shalom and thereby alienate us from God but also an innate tendency toward those acts.

Sin also explains what is wrong with the world apart from human acts. Because we are tied to the rest of the created world, because we are responsible for God's creation, our alienation from God means that all creation, as Paul puts it, is "subjected to futility" (Romans 8:20 RSV). Natural disasters, diseases, and genetic disorders can happen apart from anyone's direct fault. But these things are nevertheless part of the pattern of sin weaving itself into the world. They are evidence of the world's separation from God's intended, delightful order. If you consider Eden a moment in history, the moment in which humanoids had evolved and God placed them like infants in a cradle of perfection, then breathed into them a genuine soul, it doesn't matter that this occurred after dinosaurs. God sees the timeline all at once, so the results of one moment in time can run down the timeline, so to speak, both backward and forward—a sort of ripple effect. At any rate, death and destruction in nature have become part of the routine and settled into a different order (by God's mercy, you could say), so that death becomes part of the cycle of life and the world is sustained in a fragile equilibrium.

Nevertheless, the Bible persuades us that this too is not God's ultimate design. Although we often speak of the balances and cycles of nature with appreciation, it is sometimes difficult to observe nature and suppress our impulse to protest. Watch any nature show on TV with an animal-loving six-year-old, and see if you can dispassionately defend nature's way to the child as the cheetah rips the skin off the baby impala and chomps into its guts while it's still breathing. It's not mere sentimentality to object that something so delicate and graceful should be violently destroyed as a matter of course. Something in us wants to cry out when beauty tears beauty apart.

Sin is a shorthand term for our common tragic condition, constantly exacerbated by our own malice and folly. Any day's newspaper offers ample record. Today seven people drowned in Lake Michigan. Another suicide bomb in the Middle East killed seven. Leaders of other nations are struggling to relieve an African nation of the warlord who has terrorized his country and who still refuses to leave power. Judges and officials in "sobriety court" listen wearily to the offenders' repeated lies and rationalizations. A new study further defines the link between pollution and cancer.

Sin is a wearisome, fearsome tangle of fault and result. We commit sinful acts because we were born into a fallen world, and our sinful acts perpetuate the condition. How easy it is to observe that sin is persistent and gains momentum. It has a way of replicating itself: it progresses; it reproduces; and it intertwines itself in individuals, families, societies, nations, the environment. It takes on a life of its own.

The Christian view of sin retains two seemingly contradictory ideas: on the one hand, we are responsible for sin; on the other hand, we are helpless in its grip. We need both halves of this tension. We must retain our responsibility because if we relinquish all responsibility, we cease to be human, responsibility being a necessary component of our dignity and nature. To concede our helplessness, however, honestly accounts for what we observe in others and ourselves.

Downward Spiral

We spend a great deal of energy in contemporary Western culture promoting self-esteem, working through issues in therapy, improving lives through technology, and generally reassuring ourselves and one another that we are good enough and smart enough and that we can all just get along if we try. And indeed, even those who insist most grimly on sin's power have to agree that human beings and the rest of the natural world carry recognizable traces of the way God intends things to be. People act to heal and help one another. The same newspaper section that carried all the terrible news I listed earlier also reported that doctors can successfully separate conjoined infant twins, that firefighters volunteer out of civic pride, and that some of those drunk drivers are eager to get help, recover, and leave their old life behind. I know from a lifetime of visits that the lake in which those people drowned, Lake Michigan, on calm summer evenings flashes with a thousand diamonds of light.

The sun continues to rise and set; the seasons come and go; children are born strong and healthy; people fall in love; the world is full of beauty and kindness. All this, Christians say, is God's sustaining grace, holding back the powers of sin to preserve the beloved creation and to point us to a possibility beyond what we now can clearly see. Some Christian theologians attribute the common good in the world to what they call common grace—the continued sustenance of the Spirit for all people and all creation so that we might not be left without glimpses of the world's intended design. The glimpses evoke a longing in us, all the more so because we catch them through pain and darkness in a life bordered all about by death.

In order for the world to go on, God must sustain any goodness—underwrite it, so to speak—because the tendency of the fallen world is to keep falling. The allure of stars for their planets and atoms for one another is a template of love, but the entropy of the galaxies—their tendency to spin away from each other unless gravity draws them together—is an emblem of our moral state as well. Sin is easy, the default; goodness requires a contrary energy. Strong leaders need very few examples to learn to dominate and destroy. Reining in a tyrant, however, requires enormous effort and sometimes terrible cost: constitutions, diplomacy, massive popular resistance, even armies and ugly wars. Ordinary individuals do not need courses or therapy to become selfish and irresponsible. But for honesty, kindness, and faithfulness to flourish, people need good models and hard work. It takes a village to raise us to our best potential. And even then we so relentlessly fail. This is simply the way it is. A child is born crying; only a great effort of love will teach her to smile.

To imagine that what's wrong with the world is a little error here, a bad choice there, maybe some unjust systems and false ideas scattered about—such an account of things fails to respect the extent of sin and the power of that entropy toward annihilation. It insults all those who have most deeply suffered. Only a robust view of sin takes into account all the evidence.

To be convinced of the power of sin, we can examine the extreme cases, the kinds of things even the most optimistic lovers of humanity must name evil. The story of the fall explains that what's wrong with the world is both a matter of human choices and at the same time influenced by a power that somehow exceeds the sum of human choices. The serpent in the story represents this power, the will that sets itself against the loving God. Sin is letting that power pull you against God's desire, even in small ways. So we could say that even the smallest sin participates to some extent in evil. Generally, though, we reserve the word *evil* to describe a full assent to that power, a succumbing of the will to all that is anti-God.

Despite a persistent, popular optimism about human nature, we citizens of the twenty-first century may be more prepared than recent generations to understand how we can get caught in a powerful undertow until we find ourselves helpless against powers we cannot control. As several perceptive Christian writers have recently observed, the prevalent phenomenon of addiction serves as both a case in point and a metaphor for the way sin operates. Why did my friend Claire's husband, a former teetotaler, start drinking? Why did he continue to drink when his drunkenness led to an affair, a broken marriage, estrangement from his four children? Why did he let alcohol ruin his life and shatter the lives of people he formerly professed to love? For that matter, why does a college student become addicted to porn? Why does a young girl become bulimic? Why does a mother weep with misery over her brain-damaged infant and then go right back to the crack dealer? One of the curious and frightening things about addiction is that it begins with bad choices and after a while removes a person's ability to choose. He is no longer in control. She is spiraling downward but can't stop it. And the misery and shame of addiction only drives the addict back to whatever addicted her, which numbs the pain at least for the moment, until the shame and misery drive her back again. And the cycle repeats.

Addicts of whatever variety watch their own destruction like train wrecks in slow motion. Experts can muse about various causes: genetic predispositions; patterns established in the family of origin; the desired benefits of pleasure, control, or escape; media influence; economic disadvantage. But no amount of analysis fully explains why people choose to hurt themselves and others, let alone what kind of power takes over and begins to control them. Professionals who work with addicts will attest that recovery and healing are not simple matters of the right pill, some hours of healthy chat, and the desire to get better. People I know who have recovered from addictions tell me the addiction starts to resemble a beast whispering lies in the ear: "It's OK. Have another drink. You're fine." They wrestle with the beast, but the wrestling is both a resistance and an embrace. Call it a beast, a demon, a disease, rebellion against God, a skewed bit of brain chemistry, or socially reinforced behavioral patterns combined with genetic conditions. Whatever you call it, something mighty is operating here that exceeds the sum of our biological and sociological descriptions.[5]

AN EXCESSIVE AND SENSELESS FORCE

Only a minority of us are addicts in the clinical sense, but the pattern of addiction serves as a useful analogy for sin in that it describes how a series of choices—our own, other people's, or both—can lead to a diminished capacity to choose, a helplessness. Christians believe that the helplessness of addiction is simply an extreme manifestation of our common helplessness. These days we are less likely to face the truth of our helplessness by taking account of our individual peccadilloes; we are quite happy to excuse or overlook them. However, we have more reason than any generation to feel our helplessness on the grandest scale as the news media treat us to a daily, global view of human failing, folly, and cruelty.

The myth of progress propagated during centuries of optimism about human reason, science, and engineered societies still works powerfully on us. We still try to reassure one another that "Things are getting better!" or as my mother says, expressing her confidence in experts everywhere: "*They'll* think of something!" However, reality, when we look it in the face, overwhelms optimism: the proliferation of terrorism, the inescapable cycle of brutal vengeance in the Middle

East, the international sex trade, remorseless drug trafficking, greedy corporate expansion into new markets so that more people will buy products that destroy their health, massive waves of starvation and displacement caused by pointless wars and petty dictators. And perhaps worst of all, that ultimate nightmare continually whispering beneath it all: humankind now has the power to destroy itself completely. After centuries of so-called progress, are we better? Or are all our advances offset with more expansive evils, so that good and evil make up the same old zero-sum game—only with expanding numbers?

When I read Shakespeare's play *Othello* with my college students, we consider the question of why Iago sets out to destroy Othello. The play itself suggests plausible explanations: racism and misogyny in Venetian society, Iago's frustrated ambition, or his sexual jealousy. The English poet Samuel Taylor Coleridge described Iago as a character of "motiveless malignity,"[6] but my students observe that Iago does have motives. What's frightening is the way his brutality exceeds those motives. He pushes his psychologically brilliant plan beyond any measure of his own frustration or prejudice. Shakespeare understood what we also must recognize: evil is characterized by excess. When we observe the great horrors of history or of today's news, what amazes us most is the way human sin exceeds any motivation, explanation, or purpose.

Evil is excessive and also senseless. The grand social machineries of the nineteenth and twentieth centuries were supposed to engineer stability and prosperity for whole societies, but those measures toward this vision that Lenin and Stalin and Hitler propagated as sensible instead became senseless horrors—whole populations cowering in mind-bending fear, gulags and concentration camps, torture chambers and mass graves. In this century so far, we have seen evil more often without the sophisticated mask of major nationalist movements. Terrorism wears a construction-paper face of grievance, but beneath that we recognize destruction mostly for its own sake, hit-and-run evil. As Christian philosophers have observed since ancient times, evil is merely parasitic. It can never create or build, only twist and destroy what already exists. It uses human brilliance and creativity as well as folly and ignorance toward heinous ends.

In books and movies, the villains reveal their terrible plans at the last second, before the hero barely defeats them. It's a satisfaction we desperately want as an audience, and fictional villains typically deliver it, saying, "Here's what I was going to do. And I would have succeeded too, if it weren't for you meddlers." In life evil does not typically explain itself. What went on in the household of a family in Texas that would drive the mother to drown her five children? We will never know. People in the grasp of evil have often lost contact with reality. They themselves do not know what happened.

When we encounter the horror and mystery of evil, we begin to recognize the possibility of a condition or place usually termed hell. Hell is where sin, by definition, eventually leads; it is the endpoint of the path away from God. The Bible speaks of hell in a variety of metaphors and pictures (none of which includes devils with pointed sticks) but always as a state of being outside the presence of God. Christians have argued over whether hell is an eternal or temporary place of punishment, whether it is physical or only spiritual, whether hell has flames or ice, whether it is a place in any sense we could recognize. But when we see the worst of what goes on in this world, we can see that hell is not only a place people might go after death but the condition of destruction and utter misery in which people can find themselves here and now.

HOW GOOD ARE GOOD PEOPLE?

Even if we are willing to concede the existence of some power we can name as evil, we would like to believe that this power is somewhere out there and that if enough good people work together, by golly, we can conquer it. Perhaps this is why we adore the popular mythologies of *Star Wars, Star Trek, The Lord of the Rings,* and Harry Potter. Sure, the good guys have their faults and foibles, but it's easy to see who the villains are. And although the heroes might get pretty scratched up or even turned temporarily into newts in the process, they will definitely wind up defeating the villain. I love all this stuff too. It's exciting and reassuring and in some cases insightful. We love to enter these imagined worlds in which good and bad are nicely sorted out, because in our lives it's not always so easy to discern.

Particularly in ourselves. Some people dislike the Christian view of sin because it seems so petty. Why should I worry about every little random offense when overall I'm a pretty good person? I agree:

the Christian view of sin is relentlessly picky. It's even pickier than the Jewish view, which is extreme enough. The ancient Hebrew psalmist, entirely familiar with the Jewish law, realized that keeping the law perfectly required impossible feats of moral bookkeeping. In the midst of what amounts to a love song to the law, the psalmist writes, "Who can discern his errors? Forgive my hidden faults" (Psalm 19:12). Even in the most thorough self-examination, one is bound to miss some things. But the psalmist knows that God desires more than law-abiding deeds and words. In the great poem of confession, Psalm 51, the psalmist acknowledges to God: "You desire truth in the inward being" (verse 6). Jesus, an excellent student of the law and of the Psalms, explained this concept to people by turning their intuitive rankings of wrongs upside down. "You know enough not to murder," he said, "but even being angry with your brother will put you in danger of hell." "You know it's wrong to commit adultery, but looking at a woman lustfully is really the same thing" (Matthew 5:21–22, 27–28, paraphrases).

I imagine that Jesus' first listeners felt as indignant about this as many modern readers do. "This is impractical exaggeration! Lustful thoughts are only natural! And besides, I never act on them!" Fine, but let's think about what it takes to maintain such a view of one's own goodness with the slightest of examples. Let's say I'm taking a walk down my street and three teenage boys are approaching on their bikes. I notice that these boys are darker-skinned than I am, that they do not live on my street, and I immediately become suspicious that they might be threatening. Even if I don't act on these thoughts, my racist (and perhaps sexist and ageist) assumptions dishonor these boys. I would not want someone to have such thoughts about me or about my sons. Maybe I couldn't help having the thought at that moment, and maybe I didn't act on it by running into my house. But thinking I'm still a good person means excusing my thoughts, and excusing them would have to be premised on a diminished calculation of these boys' value: they're just teenagers; I don't really owe them my respect. So I'm assuming now that it's all right to diminish the value of some people, and I get to decide whom I devalue. Do I really want that as a moral starting point? It assumes the possibility that others can also diminish the value of me.

Or how about a scornful thought about a man who is very overweight? Same thing; excusing it diminishes his value. Or let's turn it around and consider the poverty even of good intentions. Say you have sympathetic, vaguely outraged thoughts about children suffering from AIDS in Africa, but you do nothing particular about it. You can only justify doing nothing based on the premise that they really aren't that important. Besides, it's not your responsibility. *They'll* think of something.

When you start thinking about it, the poverty of our goodness is truly appalling. We spend our intellect and energies shoring up our own financial security and give only a pittance away to those who do not have enough food to keep their children alive. We say we care about corporate justice but continue to buy cheap goods even though we have no idea who might have been grossly underpaid to make or grow them. We use each other socially by maneuvering to sit with the successful people at a conference, asking after their family when honestly we only care about sealing the deal. We use another person sexually in the name of self-expression and a shallow, temporary intimacy. We avoid even our own friends and family when they need us because helping them might interrupt our all-important work schedule. Fill in your own examples here; it won't be that difficult. How do you fail to honor the miracle and value of each person's life, including your own? How do you look out for your own welfare and disregard the welfare of others or the earth? The form for confession of sin in the Book of Common Prayer, which has guided Anglican worship since the sixteenth century, tries to cover all our failures in a simple summary: "We have left undone those things which we ought to have done, and we have done those things which we ought not to have done, and there is no health in us."[7]

Sometimes our sins are fully voluntary choices, and sometimes our culpability is qualified in one way or another. A child with racist ideas, for instance, has been enculturated into his racism. A person who steals may have a genetic tendency toward risk-seeking behavior. A woman whose father beat her has deep wounds that diminish her own capacity to love. We do cope with some conditions that are not our fault, and in some situations it's worth trying to discern the level of blame of the parties involved. Our human dignity depends on retaining our status as responsible creatures after all. At this point, however, I'm not much worried about the taxonomy of sin nor about tracing out where culpable sin ends and involuntary failings begin.

Whether we intend to do it or not, whether we are perpetrator or victim or both, sin is a burden on our lives. The sins of others hurt us, and our own sin weighs us down; we are caught inescapably in its web. Whether you have cheated on your spouse or only indulged in petty resentments, either way, you've gone over to the dark side. Moreover, how your own indulgences, betrayals, follies, and victimizations stack up against anyone else's is not the point. The point is that your inward being is not whole and healthy. No matter how well adjusted or high functioning you are, every bad thought or word misses the mark, to use an old metaphor for sin. It is a barrier between you and God and between that shalom that God wishes for you and for everyone.

One of the best illustrations I know of recognizing our true condition before God is in C. S. Lewis's great novel, *Till We Have Faces*. The novel's protagonist, Queen Orual, is queen of a kingdom called Glome, where people worship ancient and mysterious gods. Orual spends her life protesting the gods' injustice, mostly because they stole her young, lovely, innocent sister Psyche. Orual vows to write out her case against the gods, most particularly against the brute earth-goddess Ungit. But once she finishes the document, a series of events and visions reveals to her that she herself has loved the people in her life with the same kind of devouring, destroying greed of which she has accused Ungit. At last the gods allow her to state her case, and as she stands before the court of the dead, she describes herself truly for the first time: "Hands came from behind me and tore off my veil—after it, every rag I had on. The old crone with her Ungit face stood naked before those countless gazers. No thread to cover me, no bowl in my hand to hold the water of death; only my book."[8] Orual's nakedness and physical diminishment and her resemblance to Ungit symbolize the ugly self-pity and self-justification that she has cherished at the core of her soul all her life. Now these are all she has left. She begins to read her book aloud, but it comes out all different from how she thought she wrote it. Her accusation against the gods becomes a childish rant in which she simultaneously discovers and admits that her love for Psyche was not love at all but a fierce, possessive jealousy.

In a later vision, Orual is reconciled with Psyche; the two stand together and await the approach of the true god, who is coming to judge Orual. This god is not ugly and devouring like Ungit but inexpressibly beautiful. Even at the promise of his presence, Orual feels "terror, joy, overpowering sweetness." Instead of imminent condemnation, Orual experiences a paradox, a disappearing and reappearing. "I was being unmade. I was no one,"[9] she says, and yet she feels genuine love for Psyche and sees a vision of herself as whole and beautiful for the first time.

Loved Enough

Maintaining a robust view of sin, paradoxically, is the best thing in the world for self-esteem. If we truly value ourselves, we will not be satisfied with some mild, namby-pamby version of good enough. The highest standard of goodness is the one that most highly prizes our humanity, most fiercely insists that we were designed to be something so much greater than what we are. Christianity is picky about sin because of the magnificence of its goal: full reconciliation with God—perfect peace, perfect shalom. Nothing less can satisfy the longings in our hearts and God's.

You may readily acknowledge that the great forces of evil in the world can be countered only with a lever of goodness that exceeds their force. It's harder to admit that the situation is precisely the same in your own soul. But the wisdom of Christianity is to come right out and say it. Recovering addicts know this: the first step, the one that no one can ever skip over, is to admit you have a problem you can't solve yourself. (The twelve-step system is derived from Christianity, after all.)[10]

Christians call this step repentance—a process through which we recognize that we have sinned, feel sorrow for sin, and resolve to change by the Spirit's power. The Greek word for repentance is *metanoia*, "change of mind," where mind includes all our capacities of intellect, emotion, reason, and will. Repentance is a step in a cycle that leads to other steps; you don't want to stay there forever or let someone trap you there. But you can't skip over it either. Because if we refuse to be accountable, we get nowhere. We remain in the state of what we now call denial.

We all know people who have no idea how to say they are sorry. They think they are always right: a domineering father, a high-ranking

administrator who feels she is above the rules, a roommate who bor-
rows your clothes and then denies it. If you live or work with such a
person, you know how maddening it is, because there is no one to
whom you can appeal. The person acknowledges no higher authority.
If you tell the person off, she will definitely turn it around and blame
you. Without a higher authority, such people create their own cozy
reality in which they never need to change. Alas, this is an age-old
pattern. The sixth-century abbot Dorotheus of Gaza wrote: "The root
of all disturbance, if one will go to its source, is that no one will blame
himself."[11] And he was talking about life with fellow monks.

So the concept of sin, paradoxically, frees us to escape the cozy
realities we like to construct, skip the denial, and get a clear view of
our predicament: we are far from the beautiful vision God conceived
for this world. We bear the burden of our own sinful hearts; we are
damaged by others' sins; and we feel the world's great wounds. If we
are not subject at the moment to the worst evils, we still, every day,
live with the poison of fear. We long to throw off these burdens and
be free of the poisons, but we cannot do it alone. Without God we
cannot fix the world's problems. As a member of the Christian social
justice community based in Iona, Scotland, put it: "Evil is not disposed
of by positive thinking and holding hands."[12] We cannot fix ourselves
either. We might be able to lose weight and manage stress, but we
cannot remake our souls or escape death, sin's final result. We might
be able to tread water for a while, but we will never get to shore on
our own. We need a rescue. And we need to understand our need for
rescue.

This posture of humility is indispensable. As long as you think
you are good enough right now or could be soon, you limit yourself
at best to a dim shadow of goodness in this life. Christians believe that
even the brightest of these dim shadows is still a shadow, still an
address in the neighborhood of sin. But you could have something
infinitely better: an entirely new kind of life, made possible by God's
power. Sin is the lock on the door to this life; you can't open the door
unless you recognize that there's a lock and that you need a key. This
is not a reason to be discouraged but a reason to be glad. Now you
know what kind of problem you're facing.

People are often afraid to use the language of sin because they
think it isn't cheerful or encouraging. But who wants a false cheer?

I get tired of putting forth all kinds of effort to paper over what's wrong with me and the world. I'd rather see things straight on, "see life steadily and see it whole," as the English novelist E. M. Forster liked to put it.[13] As Jesus pointed out, "the truth will set you free" (John 8:32).

The Christian view of sin declares that you are not good enough. This leads to the good news: you are *loved* enough. You are loved enough that God will see you exactly as you are; and if you are willing, God will take it from there. God will begin to remove the burdens and distortions of sin, rescue you from the powerful downward forces of sin, recreate you into the person you were designed to be, and draw you into the kind of communion with himself that is our true life, our highest purpose.

CHAPTER FOUR

☙

RESCUE AND RESTORATION
God's Saving Grace

THE LORD HAS DONE GREAT THINGS FOR US,
AND WE ARE FILLED WITH JOY.
—Psalm 126:3

I n one of Jesus' most famous stories—often referred to as the parable of the prodigal son—a son asks for his inheritance from his father, then goes off to squander it in a "far country" (Luke 15:11–32). The son lives the party life for a while, but after a famine hits, he eventually ends up slopping pigs. This was perhaps the worst profession imaginable for Jesus' Jewish audience, who considered pigs unclean, never to be touched or eaten. Starving and broke, the son finally decides to go home to his father, beg forgiveness, and offer to work for him as a servant. But as he walks down the road toward his father, "while he was still a long way off" (verse 20), his father comes running toward him and embraces him. The son admits his foolishness, but before he can get to the part about working as a servant, the father gets busy preparing a party to celebrate his homecoming.

The story is sometimes called "the prodigal father"—a more apt title because the best moment in the story is when the father runs down the road to meet his wayward son, offering us a compelling portrait of rashly extravagant, forgiving, prodigal love. Christians have always treasured this story because the father's love for the child who has wronged him is one of our clearest images of God's love for us. God's forgiveness and love runs out to meet us even before we make it home to him. Christians believe this kind of love is what Jesus himself most clearly demonstrates. In becoming human, Jesus reached out to us first. In suffering, dying, and being raised again, Jesus healed the alienation that sin had created between us and God. We could not do this ourselves, so God has done it for us. This is at the center of what Christians mean by grace: God reaching out to us first with the gift of forgiveness and reconciliation.

It's true that we can't receive this gift unless we recognize that we need it. An alternative version of the story might have had the father traveling all the way to the far country and finding a son who would rather remain with the pigs than admit he needed his father. In the story as Jesus tells it, the son desires reconciliation, but even so he can't make it happen through his own merit. His restoration depends on his father's open arms. In the same way, we don't earn the gift of God's grace by cleaning ourselves up, offering an eloquent apology, and behaving perfectly. Yet God is eager to grant it, and the party things are all prepared. We have only to turn toward home.

RESCUE AND RESTORATION

When Christians use the word *salvation,* they are referring to a rich, multidimensional experience and a promise of that experience's fulfillment. For Christians salvation means both *rescue* from sin, death, and hell in their many manifestations and *restoration* to perfect relationship with God, each other, and creation. We feel this rescue and restoration happening here and now, and we are promised that it will be completed in the future.

Amid all the world's suggestions for curing whatever ails us, all its promises of various kinds of salvation, Christianity uniquely combines two crucial elements. First, Christianity insists that we cannot fix what's wrong with the world by ourselves. This is the necessary corollary of Christian wisdom on the pervasive power of sin. Education, good government, wise philosophies, and excellent methods of self-discipline are all good things to pursue; but because of sin, they will always leave us short of the goal. We are both responsible for sin and helpless in its grasp. It's an inescapable predicament—unless God reaches out to us with grace.

The centrality of grace combines with the centrality of the person of Jesus. What Jesus did in his life, death, and resurrection makes grace available; and we receive it through seeking a living relationship with him. Because salvation promises as its fulfillment a perfectly restored relationship with God, it makes sense that this can be achieved only through relationship.[1] Not through a set of rules or practices, a social system, or a philosophy but through recentering one's life on a person.

PAST, PRESENT, FUTURE

The American theologian H. Richard Niebuhr is reported to have encountered a street preacher one day who asked whether Niebuhr was saved. Niebuhr is said to have given this answer:

> I was saved by what Christ did;
> I am being saved right now;
> I shall be saved when the Kingdom comes.[2]

Niebuhr's faceted view of salvation gets beyond the common reduction of salvation to a kind of heavenly fire insurance with a very low premium: Jesus paid the price for my sins, so if I accept the free offer, I will go to heaven. The problem with this view is not that it isn't true, but that it's too anemic: it can leave the impression that salvation is only about life after death and that the world is a place where we simply wait for that great hallelujah day and remind others to do the same. But Jesus consistently explained that "the kingdom of God is near" or even "within you" (for example, Luke 10:8–12 and 17:20–21). Salvation encompasses the past and present too. The hallelujah day impinges on this world, so why wait? We can be gathered up into it even now.

Niebuhr's first facet of salvation refers to the work of Christ in (what is to us) the past, at a particular historical moment. Jesus' life, death, and resurrection in the first century, Christians believe, together constitute a decisive moment for humankind in all ages. The breach between God and humankind initiated by the first disobedience, as described in the Genesis story of the fall, is healed through Jesus. God loved his creatures too much to let the consequences of sin reach their full extent and last forever, so God himself made the way to heal sin through Jesus' life, suffering, and death. God tore apart his own nature in a way, in order to put ours back together. This part of salvation is

God's work, not ours. It is already done. We don't earn this salvation; Jesus has earned it on our behalf.

This work of Christ then is the central act of saving grace that opens the floodgates to all the more ordinary blessings we might receive from God. But how exactly does Jesus' life, death, and resurrection accomplish this correction of the fall? This leads us into various explanations of how Jesus' work restores our relationship with God, an area of theology called atonement theory. Although people can be more or less curious about this question, it's worth exploring a little because it can shed further light on how people experience salvation in that second of Niebuhr's dimensions, the present life.

CHRIST ATONES FOR OUR SINS

One of the most common and influential formulations for how atonement works—though a troublesome one—is called substitutionary atonement. This is the explanation I learned in catechism class as a teenager. Our textbook was the Heidelberg Catechism, a sixteenth-century document composed as a teaching tool for Protestant churches. The Heidelberg's formulation of atonement follows the basic outlines of the medieval Roman Catholic theologian Anselm, who was archbishop of Canterbury at the turn of the first millennium. Anselm, in his treatise *Why God Became Man,* explains that human sin offends the honor of a perfect and holy God, the one who created the universe and whose laws we therefore must obey. As with an earthly king, who cannot simply overlook an offense without damage to his honor, so God's honor must be satisfied. No human being can do this because every human being already has offended God by sinning and therefore can't cover for anyone else's sin. Besides, the offense of human sin is so large that nothing short of infinite satisfaction will do. On the other hand, a human being *has* to do it, because human beings are the ones who have offended God.

The Protestant Reformers took Anselm's emphasis on God's honor, a principal category of concern in the medieval period, and shifted it to questions of justice. We humans have broken God's law, they said, and God must punish these offenses because God is just. Therefore, we all deserve death. The Heidelberg carefully explains, as Anselm also does, that the only possible way out of this predicament

is for someone who is fully God and fully human to suffer the punishment for all humanity. That someone is Jesus Christ. Jesus' incarnation gives him that dual nature, divine and human, that makes him
the perfect satisfier of God's honor and justice. He is uniquely qualified to take the punishment for our disobedience. All we have to do
as helpless sinners is accept this fact. We simply trust that Jesus is our
Savior. When we do that, his death is applied to our column, as it
were—his surplus to our infinitely debited account.[3]

All this was heady stuff for a teenager, but it appealed to my
logical temperament. And these neat formulations were espoused by
the people around me, who were obviously a living community of
Christians, so I reckoned the explanation was sufficient. It worked
well enough. I read over this explanation now, however, and it seems
rather stiff. Not that God should overlook sin. I can see that sin is too
serious to be dismissed by a nice God saying, "Oh, never mind. There,
there." But substitutionary atonement theory presents our relationship
to God as a matter of accounting with God as fastidious CPA. When
stated as a shorthand summary, the theory does not convey the totality of God's nature, the wonder of Jesus' work, nor the mysteries either
of sorrow or liberation that help compose the fullness of salvation.

Substitutionary atonement also leads people to wonder what
kind of God would make his own son undergo a terrible punishment.
This concern arises from the way the substitutionary explanation
seems to separate the Son and the Father: the Son pays a debt to the
Father on behalf of humanity. However, centuries of Christian theology before Anselm emphasized the Son's free offer of himself out of
love. The Son was not compelled to do this; after all, the Son and the
Father are one and thus cannot have separate wills. The Son's sacrifice
is an expression of the Father's love.

I have come to believe that substitutionary atonement theory
works primarily to keep Reason satisfied, that imperious figure with
the crown. It's a mathematical, debit-credit business that makes sense
to that side of our nature; and it is in that capacity both useful and true.

The formulation is predominant enough in the Christian world
to suggest that for many people it does have resonance. Though so
often we make excuses for our faults and cover up or defend our hurt-
ful actions, there are times when the truth is laid bare and we can't help
but see its ugliness with terrible clarity. Only when we feel our offenses
in the pit of our gut can we call them by their right names, and only

by naming them can we begin to release their grip on us and others. I heard a radio program once about a professional theater director who was working with high-security prisoners to study and perform *Hamlet,* one act at a time. The prisoner-actors had no experience on stage, but they had other kinds of experience that made their performances frightfully genuine. When Hamlet's uncle Claudius attempts, in a solitary moment, to ask God's forgiveness for murdering Hamlet's father, the lines take on powerful immediacy when spoken by an actor who has actually killed another man:

> O my offense is rank! It smells to heaven.
> It hath the primal eldest curse upon 't,
> A brother's murder.[4]

One needn't commit a felony to feel the offense of one's sin, however. When we manage to perceive clearly both the preciousness and beauty of all things and the various kinds of damage we have caused to others and ourselves, then we can feel some version of that same awful conflict: we want justice done because we don't want to betray the value of what we have damaged, yet we fear the pain of that justice meted out to us. We name the ugly deeds, yet we don't want to claim them as our own. It's at such moments that substitutionary atonement comes as a relief: the strong love of Jesus, expressed in his taking punishment on our behalf, satisfies justice yet takes the force of the blow. The ugly deeds are truly named, but our name is removed from them.

CHRIST SACRIFICES FOR OUR SINS

Another way of looking at salvation is deeply rooted in ancient Jewish culture, in which sacrifice was a familiar concept and practice. Sacrificing animals to please and placate the gods, an almost universal practice in the ancient world, was based on the idea that gods considered blood a potent currency of exchange, a way to purchase favors from them. Blood, after all, is both the substance and symbol of life. Offering blood to the gods demonstrated that you meant business; you were willing to do something serious to please them. The Jews adapted and codified sacrificial practices to connect with the law that God gave through Moses to the children of Israel. The ancient Jews regularly offered the blood of animals to God in order to pay for their offenses against God's law, including unintentional sins. The idea was that the Israelites owed God their lives—not only because he created all things but because God rescued them from slavery in Egypt—so they had to pay for any offenses against God with life. They offered the animals' blood-life as a substitute for their own blood-life.

However, a persistent thread within Hebrew Scriptures makes clear that animal blood is not what God is after ultimately. What God wants is the law written on the hearts of the people so that they practice justice and mercy without the prodding of rules. Ritual sacrifice was not an end in itself but designed to teach God's people to take God's holiness and their own sin seriously. When the rituals were performed as a matter of rote, without the accompanying inward desire to please God and the outward practices of justice and mercy that God demanded, then all this blood became in itself an offense. In the book of Isaiah (2:13–17), for example, God speaks to his people:

> Stop bringing meaningless offerings!
> Your incense is detestable to me. . . .
> Your hands are full of blood;
> wash and make yourselves clean. . . .
> Seek justice, encourage the oppressed.
> Defend the cause of the fatherless,
> plead the case of the widow.

The blood of animals never truly paid for human sins because it had no power to change the human heart. Jesus' early followers, Jews for whom blood sacrifice was part of their heritage and culture, came to understand Jesus' death as the ultimate sacrifice to end all sacrifice. All those centuries of ritual slaughter were ended and fulfilled with the blood of Jesus, the perfect offering. The original sin of Adam and Eve, and all that followed from that sin, had been paid for at last. Therefore, Jesus was the one through whom not only God could be appeased but their own hearts could be changed—the results of the fall corrected. This connection between Jesus and sacrificial animals is why one of Jesus' titles is the Lamb of God.

The sacrifice-atonement metaphor has perhaps less relevance to people for whom ritual sacrifice is completely unfamiliar, who have never in their lives seen an animal slaughtered—not even for the supermarket, let alone for religious ritual. But the prevalence of blood imagery in contemporary Christianity suggests that it still has explanatory power. I know of a CD recording of worship songs titled "Celebrate the Blood." It sounds terrible, but what's going on here is that the word *blood* is serving as a shorthand way to honor the cost of Jesus' death. When people sing, "What can wash away my sin? Nothing but the blood of Jesus," they are recognizing that the power of sin requires a high price to defeat, and that Jesus' love led him to pay that price on our behalf.[5]

Even without animal sacrifice, it's possible to understand the high cost of defeating evil, a cost sometimes paid in blood. Americans were reminded of it again in the sacrifices of those rescue workers who were injured or killed trying to evacuate people from the World Trade Center after the attacks of September 11 or of those passengers who wrested a plane from hijackers to prevent it from crashing into the White House. In a less dire and violent way, one can also recognize that the sacrifice of blood as a life substance is required to create new life. I thought of this often during my three pregnancies: how women's monthly bleeding is the way our bodies prepare for the welcoming of a child, how my body literally created an increased volume of blood in order to nourish each child growing inside me, and how each child's birth was marked with the loss of my own blood on the child's behalf. In the same way, Jesus gave his blood freely in order to enable us to be born into a new kind of life, a life of restored relationship with God.

For this reason, when people dismiss Christianity because it has a cross and a broken body at the center or when Christians themselves subdue the image of the cross and the blood, they're succumbing to a serious misunderstanding. The cross as a symbol does not glorify violence; it frankly acknowledges the reality of violence in this world and expresses our dependence on the greater power of God's love to defeat everything that leads to violence. Even if I happen to live in relative safety, many people in the world know violence as an everyday threat; and that greater power of love is desperately needed in more than a metaphorical way. The cross and the blood of Christ remind us that the path of salvation is not only a spiritual path of mind or feeling. Matter matters. Jesus gave of his body so that our bodies too can be caught up in the new life of salvation.

CHRIST WINS THE VICTORY OVER SIN

Another way of looking at salvation is to see Jesus as victor over evil, a kind of cosmic superhero. Jesus suffered the worst that evil has to dish out and emerged triumphant, winning the victory over sin and death for us. Unlike with other hero-gods, however, Jesus' heroism is accomplished through humiliation and weakness, a paradox that takes some getting used to. However, it's an explanation that offers hope to anyone who has felt overwhelmed by fear, who has looked death in the face, or who is beset with troubles and sorrows beyond his control. No place of sorrow or fear is beyond Jesus' power, because Jesus suffered and died. He has visited those places of darkness. Two gospels describe Jesus on the cross, crying out in the words of Psalm 22: "My God, my God, why have you forsaken me?" (Mark 15:34; Matthew 27:46). Christians take this as a sign that Jesus suffered the ultimate pain—abandonment by God the Father. You could say that in the incarnation, God stretched himself wide; and in the death of Jesus, God allowed himself to be torn apart. All this so that God might bind himself to us and never forsake us.

In the ancient summary statement of Christian belief called the Apostles' Creed, Christians acknowledge this part of Jesus' work by professing that he "descended into hell." Because Christ has suffered the final affliction, in any place of affliction we find ourselves, we can also find the presence of Christ. Christ has experienced hell, so no hellish places are beyond his reach. And because of the resurrection, no suffering—not even death—is beyond hope. Jesus came out the other side so that he might reach back and pull us out too. "Death has been swallowed up in victory," wrote Paul in his first letter to the Corinthian church (15:54), quoting and confirming the prophecy of Isaiah (25:8): "he will swallow up death forever."

Related to the victory theory of atonement is the ransom theory, which characterizes sin as a captivity to the devil, and in which Jesus pays the ultimate price to ransom us. This description might seem especially meaningful to people who keenly feel their own entrapment in sin or who have some experience with political imprisonment or oppression. In the twentieth century, theologians connected with poor and politically oppressed people in Central and South America explained the cross as the ultimate sign of God's solidarity with suffering people. Here the emphasis is on Jesus saving not only individuals but whole races and nations of people. He meets them in their suffering, has won their ultimate freedom through his own suffering and resurrection, and leads the way out, not just spiritually but practically and politically, in the here and now. People who struggle daily for survival, for justice, for dignity, see in Jesus a savior who intimately understands their condition.

The workings of salvation have preoccupied Christians for centuries, and new interpretations continue to emerge. C. S. Lewis outlined a theory of Jesus as the "perfect penitent," offering with his life and death the perfect apology for sin that no human can ever muster.[6] I have often heard theologian Cornelius Plantinga Jr. remark in his sermons at our college chapel that Jesus is the only person who could absorb evil without passing it on. Jesus breaks the cycle of sin; it stops with him. And our therapeutic culture has given rise to an emphasis on Jesus as the healer of all our wounds and diseases of every variety, a view firmly rooted in the gospel accounts of Jesus' acts of healing.

All of these explanations express a true dimension of salvation, whereas none on its own expresses the totality of how salvation works. However, one important pattern winds through all the theories, a pattern necessary to express the fullness of the matter. Jesus is more than a wise teacher or a world-class moral example. Jesus' miracles and teachings show us the character of God and signal the coming of God's kingdom. But the teachings and miracles in themselves are *not* how Jesus saves. Jesus' work for our salvation would not be complete without his dying and rising from the dead. Few people have a problem agreeing that Jesus was a moral teacher, but that less palatable business involving blood and death and a dose of the supernatural often makes people stop short of seeking any sort of personal connection with this Jesus. Paul acknowledges the strangeness of accepting salvation on these terms: "Jews demand miraculous signs and Greeks look for wisdom, but we preach Christ crucified: a stumbling block to Jews and foolishness to Gentiles, but to those whom God has called, both Jews and Greeks, Christ the power of God and the wisdom of God" (1 Corinthians 1:22–24). All of us are what Paul here calls Jews and Greeks. We want impressive displays of divine power or reasoned argument, preferably both. Instead, what Christianity offers is a God-man bleeding on a Roman instrument of torture and improbable stories about his subsequent resurrection from the dead. The world has always had its share of good moral teachers. But Christians believe that the dying and rising of Christ are the ultimate conduits of God's power. These events changed the world, and they can change each of us.

SALVATION SOMEHOW

My friends Trevor and Linda, both Princeton Seminary–trained pastors, are forming a church in Jersey City, New Jersey, made up entirely of children and teenagers, a generation navigating the perilous terrain of inner-city despair. Trevor and Linda preach Jesus as savior every day, in word and deed, and they have many stories to tell about young people for whom a commitment to following Jesus Christ means daily resistance to powerful forces like gangs and drugs. The peril from which Jesus saves is real and immediate. Although Trevor sees dramatic demonstrations of salvation's effects, he confesses to me that he still struggles with what he calls "the mechanics of salvation." He still wonders exactly how what Jesus did way back when saves us *now*. He knows all the theories. But he's left, in the end, with the *somehow*. My friend Leanne Van Dyk, a professor of theology, offers a wise observation: "It is important, at this point, to remember that the cross and the empty tomb do not acquire their saving reality by theologians and thoughtful Christian believers. Our brilliant insights or hard thinking about these events is not what conjures up their saving power."[7] The cross and the empty tomb are the central mysteries of the faith; and as mysteries their power does not readily yield to explanation. For some people the somehow is enough. For others, like my friend Trevor, the somehow continues to nag them, primarily because questions of "how exactly" are at heart questions about the nature of God. Is God a punisher, a lover, a rescuer? We can attempt to explain and reason and satisfy our need for sense, and we should do so. But ultimately salvation's operative mechanism remains supra-rational.

The supra-rational quality of the atonement has been a common obstacle for people's acceptance of the Christian faith, especially since the eighteenth-century period in the West that we call the Enlightenment. During that period, in which rationality and decorum were the salient

virtues, the cross and resurrection seemed nonsensical and embarrassing. As a result some Christian theologians tended to focus on Jesus as a
social reformer, a great moral example. Certainly this kind of rational
embarrassment persists. But these days, particularly among the young,
the atonement's supra-rational quality may be more an asset than a
problem. Karen Ward, a Lutheran missionary working in Seattle, is part
of the alternative worship movement that seeks to relate Christianity
to the next generation of young adults. One critical quality of the so-
called postmodern sensibility among young people, Karen says, is a
keen awareness of pain, their own and the world's. In one of her pre-
sentations on her work, Karen quotes a young man who says, "This
generation is dying to die." This means not only that a shocking number of young people contemplate suicide but that young people are
seeking something meaningful amid the meaninglessness. They desperately want something worth surrendering their lives to. Jesus on the
cross makes sense to them in a way that defies rational explanation.

My own attempts to comprehend the atonement also focus on
this place of suffering and surrender. To me the problem of suffering
is the critical problem any view of the universe must answer. More
persuasive than any method or philosophy or theological system—
even Christian ones—is the image of Christ on the cross. In that image
God says to all of humanity, "I have not forgotten you. I hear the cries
of your suffering and have come to suffer it with you and for you."
The crucifixion eloquently expresses about the nature of God this
critical truth: that God loves us enough to do whatever it takes, including suffering the ultimate affliction, to restore us to himself.

THE REAL HOPE OF RESURRECTION

Theories of atonement articulated and elaborated over the centuries
all have their roots, of course, in those remarkable documents developed in the early period after Jesus' earthly life and gathered in the
New Testament. The New Testament writers, particularly Paul, laid
the foundations for later Christian thought by sorting out Jesus' relationship to God and making sense of his death and resurrection. In his
letter to the Philippians (2:6–8), Paul is either quoting an early Christian
hymn or composing one when he describes the incarnation:

Jesus, being in very nature God,
did not consider equality with God something to be grasped,
but made himself nothing,
taking the very nature of a servant,
being made in human likeness.
And being found in appearance as a man,
he humbled himself
and became obedient unto death—
even death on a cross!

Paul also sorts out why the resurrection was necessary and how it fits
with the Jewish understanding of a wider resurrection. He insists, first
of all, that belief in the resurrection is not optional but essential to the
new faith: "If Christ has not been raised, our preaching is useless and so
is your faith" (1 Corinthians 15:14). The resurrection completes what
the incarnation began. In the incarnation Jesus enters the place where
we are, trapped in sin, and satisfies the justice of God. In the resurrection Jesus reverses the ultimate result of Adam and Eve's disobedience—
mortality—and blazes a new trail, going before us into a life that is
beyond the power of death. He is the "first fruits," as Paul puts it, and
we will eventually follow (15:23). If this new life is to be real for us
in our bodies and souls, then Jesus' resurrection must also be physically real and not merely a pleasant symbolic concept. Otherwise,
Jesus' death was a noble sacrifice that accomplished nothing, and Jesus
a great fellow who is now quite dead. The resurrection is what completes the process of wrenching the world's pain toward redemption.
Without it we have only pleasant ideas; with it we have real hope.

Of all our fears, death is the centerpiece; yet many of us find the
promise of the resurrection too good to believe. People die; and when
we see their bodies and feel their absence, death seems entirely real
and final. To believe in anything beyond that simple finality seems
unscientific—a fond dream, a wish-fulfillment fantasy. However, science may offer us something other than skepticism as scientific study
continues to reveal that the universe *is* full of wonders. The movement
from death to life is not so foreign; it is written in the patterns of
nature. As Jesus pointed out, "unless a kernel of wheat falls to the
ground and dies, it remains only a single seed. But if it dies, it produces
many seeds" (John 12:24).[8] That's just one example. God, I believe, has

shaped even the fallen creation to point to the hope of new life. I have experienced in my own body the miracle of a human life's improbable beginnings. Each of the three small people now running around in my house began with a single cell. Incredible! That ordinary process of pregnancy and birth—which you have to admit would seem too bizarre to believe if it didn't happen every day—helps convince me that for the God who created and continues to sustain a universe, a resurrected Jesus is entirely possible. And so is a resurrected *me*.

A Change in Direction

Niebuhr's second facet of salvation—"I am being saved right now"— speaks to the way in which the saving work of Christ is applied to people here and now in their everyday lives. This dimension of salvation is often called sanctification, the process of becoming holy, being made an everyday saint, experiencing that restored relationship with God. People come to the faith most earnestly seeking this part. They want their lives to change. They want not only to *know* that they are reconciled with God but to *feel* that and see results in their lives.

Explaining this process of salvation in the present requires that we expand our definition of grace. Salvation is initiated for anyone by God's big act of grace in sending Jesus, but it is fueled for each of us by a million little acts of grace tailored to us in each moment. God reaches out to us in the big story of history but also in the details of life. This happens through things people say to us, words we read, constellations of events, our thoughts and feelings. God can use just about anything as an opportunity to work out our salvation in the here and now.

The Christian life begins at some point of change and becomes a long process of change. It's a little like driving along on a country road somewhere in, say, Illinois. You're not entirely sure where you're going, but you've heard it's a good idea to head west, so you're trying to keep the sun behind you in the morning and ahead of you in the afternoon. You have several maps: one of ten counties in southeastern Illinois, one of New Jersey for some reason, one of the Mississippi River, and one of the entire globe in very small print. Eventually, fed up with winding roads and feeling very tired, you stop at a diner for coffee. There you casually ask your neighbor at the counter what he knows about going west.

"Well, what do you mean by west?" says the fellow.

"I'm not sure exactly where I want to end up," you reply. "West. You know."

"Maybe you're looking for California," says the stranger, and he proceeds to describe the mountains, the fertile land, the prosperous communities, surfing.

"Yes, yes! That's it! That's where I want to go!" you say.

At this point the fellow not only offers you a decent atlas of the entire United States and writes down suggested routes, but he also installs a global positioning system (GPS) in your vehicle in a matter of minutes—all for free. (He's quite a clever and generous fellow.)

Well! When you get back in the car, things are entirely different. Of course, you haven't reached California yet, but at least you know where you're going and how to get there. It takes a while to figure out your current location on the maps in the atlas, and it takes even longer to get the hang of using the GPS. You still get lost occasionally but not for long. And you discover lots of other people are headed to California too and are willing to keep you company. Many of them are happy to give directions, point out landscapes that show what California will be like, and warn of dangerous or difficult places on the way. You become a part of a rather grand caravan. You have a long way to go, and you know you'll face some troubles; but having a plan and some traveling companions means that now you can start to enjoy the ride.

This story is, of course, a variation on an old metaphor for the Christian life: the pilgrimage. California stands here for shalom in the kingdom of God; the atlas is the Bible and Christian wisdom; and GPS stands for the guidance of God, especially as experienced in prayer. Grace is every kind of energy that makes the trip possible. It inspires the fellow in the diner to help you; it enables you to take his advice; and it's the fuel in the tank too. The whole analogy, I know, is quite a stretch. But I hope it serves to illustrate that when Christians talk about being saved, they're talking about two related things: first, that moment when it finally becomes clear where your longings are leading and how to get there; and second, the journey itself, the daily process of getting closer to that destination. Faith is the trust that all this is going to work.

Some Christians put great emphasis on that first moment of turning toward the right direction, describing it as the moment of conversion. They advocate marking that moment with a certain kind of prayer, one that acknowledges your sin and accepts Jesus as the one who saves you from it and puts you back on the right path. There's wisdom in marking such a point, because it emphasizes the humility and trust required to change one's direction. Faith is premised on humbling ourselves before God and putting ourselves in God's hands, and such humility and trust is not always easy to muster. I know people who have all kinds of knowledge about Christianity and no particular objection to it, intellectual or moral; yet they can't seem to throw their inner faith switch from the off to the on position. Or to put it in the context of our story, they keep driving around without following the map.

Christians with any experience in the faith know, however, that a first moment of conversion is only a start. Some people never have a particular moment they could put a date and time stamp on, no encounter in the Illinois diner marking the beginning of their new travel plan. Some of us have been moving along in this direction for as long as we can remember and have always had the maps handy. Others begin with a series of odd feelings and incidents that lead them down a few new roads, and eventually they find themselves on the highway headed west. They go along for a while not knowing why, then increasingly they are willing to say, "I guess this is where I'm going. Yes, I'm glad to be going there. I'll stay on with you others." The exact nature of the starting point is not nearly as important as the destination, because conversion is never only a single turning point. Conversion is a lifetime of turnings, according to God's map and with the help of God's continued guidance.

A CONSTANT TURNING

How do we make any kind of first turn? Is the faith to get on the way only an assent of the will? An effortful activity in which you close your eyes, clench your fists, and try very hard to believe that Jesus is the Savior? If faith were only that, we would be in trouble, because many of us can't muster a constant level of willed belief. Fortunately the faith through which we receive salvation is more like an overall leaning, with more and more of oneself, in more and more areas of one's life, in the direction of God. Faith encompasses a number of things, any one of which can be, at a given moment, the forward edge of that leaning.

The here-and-now process of salvation is not merely a matter of one's spiritual life as we commonly think of it. If we are to be saved, we must be saved in our wholeness as physical, spiritual, and social beings. That means a reorientation of our fundamental purpose and identity. Our purpose becomes a restored relationship with God and a participation in God's purposes for the restoration of all things. With this as our greater purpose, we begin to identify ourselves with all those who are being saved.

The Christian life therefore places all its elements under the headings of that purpose and that identity. It involves the intellect in the form of assent to a set of propositions. It involves the heart and will in the form of a continual inward turning away from sin and turning toward God. It involves our ethical selves, our deeds and words, through which we seek to turn away from sin and establish new habits that reflect God's law of love. It involves disciplines—such as prayer, Bible reading, and worship—that nurture relationship with God, sustain an inward attitude of turning, and promote new habits of life. It involves the social self, joining the Christian community and participating in its formal practices of worship and informal practices of mutual support. And finally the Christian life involves receiving the Spirit's particular gifts to each of us, through which we are enabled to serve God's purposes for ourselves and others.

Of course, we can do none of these things perfectly, even after being saved. The central work of Christ's atonement is done, but the work of Christ *in us,* the process of rescue and restoration, takes a very long time. Here Christians affirm a wide range of estimations on how much of this ongoing salvation work depends on our willed cooperation. Everyone agrees that God initiates the process of salvation through unconditional love. Everyone gives God at least 51 percent of the credit for the will it takes to make salvation happen in our lives. Some Christians, among them (generally speaking) Baptists, Methodists, and Roman Catholics, give considerable weight to the human will, always assisted by grace, to get the other 49 percent into the equation. They emphasize human freedom and our responsibility to keep leaning by acts of will toward God. Christians whose theological tradition goes

back to the sixteenth-century theologian John Calvin and his followers, on the other hand, give God about 99.5 percent of the credit and
dislike talking about that last half percent. Calvin barely wanted to
retain human freedom because he found that human will was a wild
card. The more comforting view was to put virtually all the work of
our salvation in the hands of God, who is utterly faithful.

Both a strong view of the role of human will in salvation and a
view that diminishes it almost to a vanishing point find support both
in Scripture and in people's experience of faith. It's probably a good
thing that we hear among Christians a kind of dialogue between these
views:

> *Christian 1:*   You have to try.
> *Christian 2:*   Yes, but God has to give me the grace to try.
> *Christian 1:*   Yes, but you have to try.
> *Christian 2:*   Yes, but I need grace.
> *Christian 1:*   Yes, but . . .

It's less important to settle on a precise calculation of human and
divine contribution than to acknowledge that insofar as we experience ourselves as having choice, we ought to exercise that choice. On
the other hand, we ought to trust in the comforting assurance that
God will do the work of our salvation. If our salvation depended on
our own effort, ability, and will, we would have reason to despair. It's
too difficult! My own way of sorting it out is to observe that the tiniest leaning of the will seems to be enough to get started; God will
give (has already given) grace for another leaning, which will open
the door a little wider, which we can respond to with another leaning, which will open . . . , and so on. The great and perfect will of God
and the small and imperfect will of an individual can work together,
even if the effort involved is laughably and blessedly asymmetrical. Sin
has momentum, but so does salvation. God increases what we truly
offer by the exponent of his infinite grace.

God is in the salvage business. God salvaged the fallen creation
through Christ's atonement; and God is salvaging our lives, making
use of every scrap we offer, even turning our wounds and our failings
into the tools of his gracious repair. So it's all right that we stumble
quite a bit on that salvation path. We continue to rely on Jesus' saving

work to make up for the ways in which we fail. The Spirit lifts us up and keeps us walking or running (or driving) or crawling in the direction of God.

DYING AND RISING IN BAPTISM AND DAILY LIFE

Christians have always publicly marked the entry into the life of faith through baptism, in which a person is sprinkled with or dunked in water in the presence of other Christians. Baptism ritually connects the person to the saving work of Christ. To save us, Christ died and rose—down and up. We die in the waters of baptism and rise out of them to new life. Baptism beautifully conveys how Christ has transformed our peril: water is both perilous and life-giving; and Christ has transformed the peril of drowning in sin into the gentle, cleansing bath of salvation.

Baptism signals to us that the process of salvation in the Christian life takes on the contours of this dying and rising with Christ. The New Testament writers often use the phrase "in Christ" to describe someone in the midst of this process: "anyone who is in Christ is a new creation," writes Paul (2 Corinthians 5:17, paraphrase). All the elements of faith described here are ways Christians try to be in Christ—nurturing belief by study, living in community with other Christians, worshiping and participating in the practices of the church, communing with Jesus through the disciplines of prayer and Bible reading, imitating Jesus in one's actions, and seeking to discover and use one's gifts. These are the particular forms of that relationship with a living person necessary for receiving grace. The idea is that in seeking communion with Jesus through prayer, worship, and ritual, one experiences more and more the transforming results of Jesus' saving grace.

The daily dying and rising of this salvation process turns up in all kinds of ways, both dramatic and subtle. Some people experience an obvious turning point in their lives that begins their transformation outward and inward. My friend Sean, for instance, besides becoming a leader in his church after his brush with the criminal who robbed him, tells me that he also is more and more free of the materialistic envy he felt in earlier years. He just doesn't care as much about other people's cars or houses or incomes. That part of him is dying away to make room for a new contentment. Often we experience dying and rising in ordinary things like putting away selfish resentments toward others and putting on forgiveness, care, and acts of kindness. In turning away ambition and thirst for achievement and seeking faithful service regardless of success. In letting go of the shame and mistakes of the past and allowing God to heal and show us new ways to think and live.

None of this is easy. Salvation does not typically feel like instant prosperity and comfort. Sometimes the dying part seems overwhelming. I know of a woman named Sara whose husband, the father of her three college-age children, divorced her a few years ago because he wanted to have a fresh start with a different wife. During the bitter divorce process, it became clear that he had been having affairs throughout their marriage. Sara's Christian faith did not make her terrible pain go away, but it gave her a way to endure the dying with the hope of new life. She eagerly sought Jesus' presence through prayer in the midst of this devastation, pleading with him to show her how she could be healed. She asked others to pray for her. She sought advice from friends, clergy, and counselors about how she might have contributed to the problems in the marriage and where she had been dishonest with herself, her husband, and God. Sara has emerged from this experience with wounds, surely, but she has also found healing. She is more at peace now than she ever was in her marriage. She continues to ask God to teach and heal her, and she continues to experience the release and clarity that comes with real honesty before God and others. By submitting this dreadful period of her life to Christ, she has allowed him to bring order out of chaos.

For some people, dying to sin and rising to new life means turning away from horrible behaviors that hurt themselves and others. People make little hells on earth every day after all; and there's a lot to be said for staying out of hell here and now, let alone in the next life. Recovering addicts know all about this. For them—and church pews are filled with them—salvation is an everyday clinging to life in the face of powers that would destroy them and in some cases very nearly have. Trusting in Jesus to help them get rid of destructive behavior may not eliminate all trouble, but it can eliminate a good share of it. Recovering addicts have a very clear picture of where they might be headed if they let certain weaknesses in their character, certain little fissures, break open. Not all of us have this clear picture. But maybe we are aware of temptations toward deceptive investment schemes or extramarital affairs or petty vengeances. Dying means refusing to let those fissures crack open; rising means practicing faithfulness, honesty, and service. All this can happen only when we are continually seeking grace.

Salvation draws us toward greater spiritual maturity. As with children facing the awkward and painful process of adolescence, growing toward spiritual maturity can take us through difficult passages. Christians testify, however, that even when dying and rising feel like hard work, they experience a durable joy, a peace that does not depend on daily circumstances and "transcends all understanding" (Philippians 4:7). The joy of the new life begins to flood into the present. Paul wrote in Galatians 5:22–23 that as the Spirit works in us to bring about our salvation, we begin to exhibit the fruits of this process: love, joy, peace, patience, kindness, goodness, faithfulness, gentleness, and self-control. These come as a gift; and when we see them growing in ourselves and others, we are witnessing the amazing power of God to transform us into the people we were designed to be, living in joyful communion with God and others.

Sin has momentum, but so does salvation. One grace-filled step leads to another. A couple begins to pray together and study the Bible with others, and they soon find themselves taking a delight in their marriage they have never felt before. A man quits drinking and replaces that habit with churchgoing and prayer, and he soon finds himself relishing life again, enjoying his work and showing faithful care to his family. Older people inspire younger people to faithfulness and service; friends encourage friends in acts of kindness; parents teach self-control and gentleness to their children; and communities form and grow and endure down the generations until the fruits are so abundant that they leave little space for weeds.

I feel the joy of salvation most keenly as I rest the confusions and mysteries of my life in a framework that connects me, in love, to the essence of all things. God created and sustains the universe, and this powerful being has reached out in love to me. Because of this, I never feel, even amid the worst frustrations, that my life is futile or my work in vain. In its humble details, my life fits into a broader purpose, my tiny efforts and my constant failures caught up in God's patient and elastic plan. I still wrestle daily with fears and anxieties, but when I look to those who have spent many years practicing the presence of God, I see their peace and radiance. So I am coming to trust over the years that God is present to me, attentive to me, that God holds my life in God's hands. Because salvation does not depend on my goodness and has already been accomplished, I can rest secure that this here-and-now process of salvation will culminate in perfect fulfillment. I know that, as Paul wrote to the Colossians (3:3), my "life is hidden in Christ with God." It is kept safe.

The real power of salvation in the here and now faces its most important test at that moment of ultimate reckoning—death. Christians believe that a life of dying and rising with Christ becomes, at the point of death, a literal dying and rising. That conviction brings a palpable joy, which I have seen powerfully displayed among Christians who are dying or burying the dead. I've been to many Christian funerals; and although I've seen and felt grief, sometimes very deep grief, despair does not win the day. We sing together the comforting words of familiar hymns. We embrace each other and offer once again the promises of Scripture: that God is real, that God loves and preserves us, that what we see is not all there is. Christ's resurrection gives us victory over death, and that promise pierces our sorrow with hope.

WHO'S INVITED?

These precious promises, this palpable joy—is it for everyone? What about people who don't seem to care? Or who seem to be traveling on the right roads but don't claim to be going toward God? What about people who are headed the other way? What about people who really don't know what direction they're going? And how do I know *I'm* on the right road?

Christians have some disagreements on these difficult questions, primarily because Scripture flows in two strong currents on the matter of who is included in the salvation process. One current, generally referred to as universalist, implies that everyone will be redeemed. In Colossians 1:19–20 Paul writes that "God was pleased to have his fullness dwell in [Jesus], and through him to reconcile to himself *all things.*" That ancient hymn from Philippians (2:9–11) finishes like this:

> Therefore God exalted [Jesus] to the highest place
> and gave him the name above every name,
> that at the name of Jesus *every knee* should bow,
> in heaven and on earth and under the earth,
> and every tongue confess that Jesus is Lord,
> to the glory of God the Father. [italics mine]

Of course, you might point out that the line goes "every knee" *should* bow, not *does* bow or *will* bow.[9] But passages like this seem to open the door to every one of God's wandering children. On the other hand, Jesus told stories about dividing the sheep from the goats and the wheat from the chaff. Other of his stories speak of an outer darkness or being *dis*invited to the big party. Certain of the darker passages in Revelation (21:8, for example) follow the same lines. Taken together, these suggest that it is entirely possible to get stuck outside the door.

Christianity maintains that salvation comes through Jesus Christ, but different strains of Christianity mean somewhat different things by that. Jesus as the only way certainly means that except for the work of Jesus, no one could be saved in any sense of that word. It also usually means that a person has to believe in Jesus to be saved. This immediately raises all kinds of questions. What does it mean to believe exactly? That you have said a certain prayer? That you agree to certain propositions? That you feel trust? That you act with mercy, justice, and love? What about good people of other faiths? And people who have never heard about Jesus or only heard distortions of his name? Are they bound for eternal hell because they didn't get the password right?

Christian discussions of this question can be terribly confusing and even hostile. I manage this confusion for myself by believing that both the universalist strand and the outer darkness strand are in the Bible for good reason. The universalist strand tells us that God's love invites everyone, that God wants to redeem every person he has made. This strand ought to (but doesn't always) keep people from declaring on God's behalf that salvation is limited to their own particular race or social class or theological cohort. At the same time, the outer darkness strand keeps us from getting lazy or arrogant about salvation, like the rich kid who behaves like a hooligan because he knows he'll get the inheritance no matter what. Some confusion about who's in and who's out is probably quite healthy.

Certainly none of us is in a position to say that someone is definitely and permanently out, like the eighteenth-century Dutch American preacher Theodore Frelinghuysen, who claimed he could look out on his congregation and determine on sight who was among the elect (in) and who among the reprobate (out). Some people seem by every outward sign to be turning away from God. God will never force someone back to him, turning the person into an obedient robot. Yet God never gives up on anyone either; ghastly murderers are occasionally converted to Christ.

At the same time, many people who do not confess Christ still display a desire for shalom, work for the relief of suffering, show a love for God as they understand God, and perform great kindnesses to others. A Christian way of explaining this is to say that the Spirit of God is on the move among people who do not acknowledge the name of Jesus. And if God wishes to count these things as participation in Christ's faithfulness, as some Bible passages suggest he does, then I am glad. After all, the idea that Jesus is the only way to salvation rests on a key phrase in the original Greek that is beautifully ambiguous. In Galatians 2:16, for instance, when Paul writes that we are not "justified by observing the law, but by faith in Jesus Christ," the phrase *ek pistou Christou* can be translated either "through the faithfulness of Christ" or "by [our] faith in Christ." Greek contains the ambiguity; only in translation do we have to decide. Perhaps the faithfulness of Christ covers anyone who has a genuine spark of longing for God. God's mercy is beyond our understanding and not ours to limit; it may well be that God keeps open doors into his bliss whose passwords only God can find in the secret places of the heart.

Those of us who put our trust in Jesus can be sure we have found the front door, a door unlocked by grace. Seeking a relationship with Jesus comes with unparalleled benefits: an assurance about our salvation, the life-changing presence of the Spirit in our lives, and a vision of hope. Sometimes, it's true, Christians' assurance of their own salvation gets distorted into a superior sense of being in the club and a patronizing (or demonizing) regard for nonmembers. Apparently the sin of pride can be a parasite even on salvation. It's very easy to confuse hatred of sin with hatred of sinners, construed as those people over there. But hatred of sin makes sense only in the context of humility about our own sin and a complementary passion: a deep longing for shalom. It's out of this longing that invitations to others ought to come. We have found the road to that shalom, and in our joy we desire others to join us on the way.

Citizens of Another Kingdom

Like Orual, the queen in *Till We Have Faces,* people who believe in Jesus feel themselves unmade and made again. They are new creations; they have a new identity; and they begin to live more and more within God's purposes. Their here-and-now experience of salvation is a participation in the third facet of Niebuhr's thought about salvation— the last day, the kingdom coming.

The Christian view of the world graciously concedes a linear view of history: history has a beginning, a middle, and a culmination. At least, as creatures of time, that is the simplest way for us to understand it. In public discourse you can often discern a view of human history as a series of terrible events in which the human spirit repeatedly prevails. In the *Star Trek* universe, for instance, humanity is engaged in a long process through which we are slowly but surely evolving into totally just and peaceful beings. Unfortunately we keep running into new, nasty aliens who force us to resort to violence yet again, lasering humanoids and blasting enormous ships to space debris. There's an important difference between this popular view and the Christian view. The view that celebrates the enduring human spirit is essentially a tragic rather than triumphant view of history: in the midst of abundant disaster, a remnant of goodness remains. It's only a temporary victory, a shred of hope with which to carry on. Christianity, in contrast, fully acknowledges the tragic element but considers the drama of history, taken in sum, as something more like a romance. That is to say, from out of the perils *will* emerge a harmonious, healed ending. The cycle of tragedy will eventually end in full restoration, not because we finally get ourselves there but because God will get us there. We live in hope that the saving work God has begun will be perfected.

Reflection on the culmination of history ought to be a matter of looking for signs of the final healing of creation and seeking to *become* signs of that healing with our own lives. For Christians acts of love and obedience are a down payment on the promised fulfillment of a new kingdom. Christians seek racial reconciliation, gender justice, and environmental protections not because they are afraid of the wrath to come but because they see a vision of the kingdom to come. We have seen what it looks like, and we want to show others.

What *does* it look like? In Paul's great poem on this final day, he writes: "Listen, I tell you a mystery: We will not all sleep, but we will be changed—in a flash, in the twinkling of an eye, at the last trumpet. For the trumpet shall sound, and the dead will be raised imperishable, and we will be changed" (1 Corinthians 15:51–52). *Changed* is the key word here. The burdens of sin and fear, the power of death, will fall away completely at last. The struggle will be over. Not only we as individual entities gathered together but also creation itself will be changed. The great visions of God's redemption from both the Old Testament prophets and the book of Revelation reveal that the perfection of salvation will not be a return to the garden or a disembodied gathering of blissful souls but a participation in the new heaven and new earth (Revelation 21:1). The prophet Isaiah describes the new creation as a blossoming desert, a rich feast, or a restored city to which all the nations bring their most precious treasures. Jesus describes the kingdom as a big party. The visions of this alternative reality in the book of Revelation take the form of a breathtakingly beautiful city: "I saw the Holy City, the new Jerusalem, coming down out of heaven from God, prepared as a bride beautifully dressed for her husband. And I heard a loud voice from the throne saying, 'Now the dwelling of God is with people, and he will live with them. They will be his people, and God himself will be with them and be their God. He will wipe every tear from their eyes. There will be no more death or mourning or crying or pain, for the old order of things has passed away'" (21:2–4, altered). In this final reality, joy will have settled in for good; the writer of Revelation echoes Isaiah's prophecy (35:10) that "sorrow and sighing will flee away."

I don't spend a great deal of time thinking about what heaven, the kingdom, the new creation, or whatever you want to call it will be like. Probably we do not have the capacity to imagine it fully, so the Bible gives the sorts of hints we can understand. I tend to imagine it in Sunday school terms, as in the perky old spiritual that goes "I've got a home in glory land that outshines the sun."[10] I imagine trees and

RESCUE AND RESTORATION   87

lakes and beaches of unblemished beauty. I expect there will be dancing and music, feasting and laughing, and bodies that have senses and
abilities about which we can hardly guess now. Perhaps we will know
everything we want to know and speak any language easily. Perhaps
we will meet great historical figures and ask them questions we've
always wanted to ask. Perhaps we can meet our own ancestors, asking
them their stories. Perhaps we will see old friends again, like my
friend Ed, who died of AIDS at the age of thirty-two, and they will
be more whole and healthy than any of us ever was on this earth.

Because this kingdom is eternal, it exists, from our time-oriented
point of view, at the endpoint of the linear time we know. But more
accurately it exists on all sides of linear time, so to speak. To borrow an
illustration from C. S. Lewis, the eternal kingdom is the paper on which
the line of human history is drawn.[11] That means that the kingdom of
heaven exists *now* (by our way of thinking), and that's why the reality
of it can touch our own reality. The limitations of our minds prevent
us from comprehending fully what it might be like. But our protests
over this world's sorrows; over death itself; and our aching longing for
peace, rest, harmony, and joy are not vanities. They are the homing
signals drawing us to our true home.

CHAPTER FIVE

෧

NOT THE LAST WORD

Suffering and Hope

MY GOD, MY GOD, WHY HAVE YOU FORSAKEN ME?
—Psalm 22:1

෧ On the night of November 14, 1940, the German Luftwaffe bombed Coventry, England, burning the city and collapsing Coventry Cathedral, the lovely Gothic mass that had stood its ground since the thirteenth century. The next morning the cathedral stonemason, in a state of sorrow one can only imagine, examined the smoking rubble and discovered that two charred roof timbers had fallen onto the pile in the shape of the cross. He fastened the timbers together and set them up on an altar of rubble; and then, onto the sanctuary wall behind this cross, the provost of the cathedral chalked the words "Father, forgive." When the cathedral was later rebuilt, the ruins of the old cathedral were not entirely cleared away. The new cathedral, rather than replacing what was destroyed, embraces the ruins to create a moving, architectural declaration of remembrance and hope.[1]

Strangely enough a similar incident occurred after the destruction of the once-mighty World Trade Center towers. Construction workers engaged in the terrible task of combing through thousands of tons of rubble also discovered a cross. This time the crossed beams were steel girders, still attached to each other. The president of the workers' union clearing the site, a Roman Catholic, had the cross mounted in concrete and set up as a memorial.

Were these crosses coincidental? After all, structural beams are joined at right angles hundreds or thousands of times in any large building. Chances are good that one of these joints will survive a disaster or that two beams might fall crosswise. Or could these crosses be miraculous signs, messages from God? One atheist organization's Web page scoffs at the so-called "miracle debris cross" at the World Trade Center site, advocates that it be removed, and insists that "a real miracle would have been to stop the attack and save 3000 lives," not leave "two connecting steel beams that any construction worker can create."[2] The remark seems to arise in this writer's case mostly out of scorn, but it nevertheless points to a valid question. In fact, it points straight to the heart of human anguish, to one of the central problems of existence: Why do we suffer? Anyone who believes in the all-good and all-powerful God described in the Bible, or who wishes to believe, must face the question in an even more distressing form: How can an all-good and all-powerful God allow suffering, particularly the suffering of the innocent?

THE CASE OF JOB

The biblical book of Job addresses the problem straight on. There once was a man named Job, the text begins, a thoroughly prosperous fellow who was also so "blameless and upright" before God (1:1) that he frequently made ritual burnt offerings to apologize to God for sins his children might have committed in secret. In the first scene of the story that follows this opening, Satan appears before God and, seeing that Job is God's favorite, poses a challenge. He asks permission to see just how far Job's faithfulness to God will go if Job's happy existence starts falling apart. God agrees to the challenge. In a reversal so swift and brutal as to seem comically preposterous, Job's ten children and fabulous wealth are completely wiped out in a mere seven verses of text. Soon after, Job himself is afflicted with sores all over his body. Then Job's three friends enter the scene in an effort to comfort him. But their comfort consists of long philosophical discourses on the nature of God, evil, and suffering, all of which can be bluntly summarized as "Well, you must have done *something* to deserve all this."

The bulk of the text is an extended dialogue between Job and his friends in which the view of the universe we would all like to maintain—one in which good is rewarded and evil punished—butts against the stubborn counterexample of Job himself, sitting on an ash heap scraping his sores with broken pottery and insisting that he has done nothing to deserve this degree of suffering. Moreover, Job will not, as his wife suggests, "Curse God and die!" (2:9). Amid his anguish, Job grips his belief in God in his disease-plagued hands, declaring, "Though he slay me, yet will I trust him" (13:15 KJV).

At last, after pages of discussion and rebuttal alternating with Job's anguished cries, God speaks "out of the storm." God's lengthy poetic answer begins:

> Who is this that darkens my counsel
> with words without knowledge?
> Brace yourself like a man; I will question you
> and you shall answer me.
> Where were you when I laid the earth's foundation?
> Tell me, if you understand.
> Who marked off its dimensions? Surely you know! [38:2–4]

God then recounts his mighty works of creation in order to make the point to Job that, as a human being, Job understands nothing and that his protests arise from the puny perspective of his own little life. Job responds to this thunderous epiphany in the only way possible. He says,

> I am unworthy—how can I reply to you?
> I put my hand over my mouth. [40:4]

So that's the answer the book of Job gives to the problem of suffering: God is great. You couldn't possibly understand. Be silent.

Not a terribly comforting answer, certainly on first appearances. When my husband, Ron, was in seminary, he heard a lecture in which the professor remarked that the essential question the book of Job raised was not whether Job deserved his suffering but whether such a God deserved Job's faithfulness. Many students left the room murmuring in shock at such an outrageous and irreverent question. But the professor was attempting to point out that the book of Job figures in the Scriptures partly as a text of dissent. Here we do not see very clearly the God of intimate compassion and mercy, the God who is "slow to anger and abounding in steadfast love" (Psalm 103:8 RSV). In this text God seems distant, arbitrary, even sarcastic. At the end of the story, Job is restored to health and lavished with even more children and even greater wealth than before. But one can't help seeing here a hint of a cosmic order in which, as the blinded Gloucester remarks in Shakespeare's *King Lear,*

> As flies to wanton boys are we to th' gods;
> They kill us for their sport.[3]

Nevertheless, people who know suffering from the inside testify that the book of Job is after all a comforting text. Perhaps this is because, although it does not reveal God's full nature, it speaks very eloquently of a not uncommon *experience* of God: distant, inscrutable, and very very great.

We all long to make meaning of suffering, to find some hope despite it and within it. The first step, paradoxically, is to acknowledge honestly that sometimes God seems hidden in the darkness. In a strange way, in the midst of suffering it comes as a relief to give up trying to make sense of it all and instead to allow our pain only to *be.* In the very crush of pain, it can bring relief to acknowledge that the ways of this universe are a mystery, that we sometimes feel like puny insects in the cosmos, and that God's power and thoughts are "too wonderful" for us to comprehend (42:3).

Still, if we keep our eyes open in that darkness, the truths of the Christian faith shed a steady light; and that light helps us see through suffering to meaning and a sure hope.

MORE MESSAGES THAN ANSWERS

The problem of suffering is one of those classic objections to the existence of God, and it is sometimes formulated as a purely logical objection: an all-good and all-powerful God could not permit suffering and still be all good and all powerful. Therefore, God either does not exist or is not all good and all powerful. Christian philosopher Alvin Plantinga has worked out an argument to counter this objection to the existence of God. Plantinga points out, first of all, the premise of human freedom left out of this statement. God's design for human nature affords us the dignity of free will; God therefore accepts parameters on himself, limiting interference with our choices even when those choices are mistaken, foolish, or even evil. Moreover, Plantinga argues, just because we cannot formulate an explanation for how the suffering of the innocent can fit into the design of an all-powerful and all-good God does not mean that there is no possible explanation. We may very well not have all the pieces of the puzzle in our view.[4]

Logical refutations to the problem of suffering may help remove intellectual obstacles to faith, but they do not explain suffering. Logic can only take us to the bounds of comprehension and, unfortunately, abandon us there, still cold and afraid. The confusing reality of suffering challenges any explanation, philosophical or religious. The world is full of examples of suffering that seems randomly distributed, that strikes too hard, and that seems to strike the innocent most harshly. The nonanswer in the storm that concludes the book of Job turns out to be the end of the matter as far as sense and logic go: this is far beyond you. You cannot understand.

We are left to seek answers, not so much in logic or theories of cosmic order as in the experience of suffering itself. Into that experience Christianity carries its distinctive response: the cross. If we imagine that those "miracle debris crosses" are indeed a message from God amid the smoking wreckage of our pain, then what might the message be? Perhaps it is the same message God always sends through the cross: I am not blind to your despair or distant from it but present within it, and I am the reason for hope. To me the miracle is not that certain cross-shaped beams survived but that people set them up in gestures of trust and hope. I have seen both of these crosses with my own eyes, and I can testify that in themselves they are simple, humble things. But they mark the center point of something far more powerful.

Coventry Cathedral, since almost the moment of its bombing, has become an international center of forgiveness, reconciliation, and peace. Today the cathedral sends representatives to places of conflict all over the world to aid in the peacemaking process. The grounds and interior of the cathedral are full of artwork and architectural elements—many of them gifts from other nations, including Germany—that transform the symbols of Christ's suffering into an incomparable setting for prayer. The cathedral and the people who bring its mission to life testify to Christianity's foundational beliefs: that in Christ, God has participated in our human suffering and reconciled the world to himself, so that in Christ, God can guide us into the way of reconciliation with each other (an idea most concisely stated in 2 Corinthians 5:19).

In such a place, where great evil is countered with great hope, skepticism crumbles like brittle mortar. Naturalistic views of the universe hardly explain the depths of human cruelty; even less do they explain our moments of greatest nobility. Is there a God who deserves such trust, such faithfulness amid the blackest devastations? Could it be that the trust and faithfulness displayed by those in the midst of terrible pain are the very clues we need to understand the full nature of God? Where would such miraculous responses come from, if not from the power of God, who may allow suffering but whose mercy and compassion will not allow suffering to have the last word?

WHY?

While living in England for a few months, I had the opportunity to learn a great deal about British history and to visit places filled with historical treasures. As fascinating as British history can be, especially to a lover of British literature like myself, after a while I became weary of all the bloody battles, all the ambitious kings, all the invasions and plots and intrigues, all the armor and weaponry, all the bodies hacked to pieces using ever more clever equipment.

One afternoon I visited the British Museum and walked down long corridors crowded with Egyptian sarcophagi and enormous Egyptian sculptures. Instead of feeling excited to be seeing these rare objects, I felt a numb sadness. Assyrians, Romans, Greeks, Anglo-Saxons—all the civilizations rising over centuries and then passing away, leaving fragmentary histories and scattered remains. What does it all mean?

In the section dedicated to pre-Roman Britain, visitors can view the shriveled but well-preserved body of the Lindow man, who was found in a peat bog near Manchester, England, in 1984. When the man died sometime in the first century A.D., he was about twenty-five years old. He apparently died as a human sacrifice: he had mistletoe pollen in his stomach—a substance commonly used in Druid ceremonies—and he had been hit on the head, strangled, and his throat cut. Looking at the leathery, collapsed remains of this poor fellow, I thought of how his body had formed in some woman's body, how it emerged into the world, how it was slit open in some horrid death ritual. Suddenly the sweep of all those civilizations, their ebb and flow and the thousands of tussles between them, came down to this: bodies formed in women's wombs, bodies torn apart. Beautiful and miraculous things ripped and ruined. Suffering.

I believe that human sin—in general—is the root cause of all suffering—in general. But why are sin's results distributed as they are? If God is all powerful, if God is in control, I do not know why God permits such terrible swaths of suffering to cut across history. I do not know why God permits whole civilizations to rise and flourish for a time, some based on noble ideals, many based on barbaric violence, some based on both. I do not know why God permits floods and earthquakes and fires. I do not know why God permits a petty tyrant to abduct young teenagers, imprison them in his camps, and cripple their souls by teaching the boys how to torture and by sending his henchmen to rape the girls. I do not know why God permits world wars or genocide or terrorism.

I do not know why God permits the infinite varieties of private suffering. I do not know why God permits child abuse. Why Candace suffers from schizophrenia, why Todd's wife had an affair and divorced him, why Mandy died of cancer and left her children without a mother, why Jane must live the rest of her life in a wheelchair because of a car accident, why Sherrie's desperately longed-for baby died at birth.

For those of us who do not suffer much ourselves, the suffering of the world, when we dare to look at it, leaves us bewildered and frightened. We may be sad for others and glad to be spared, but there is no guarantee this situation won't change to our disadvantage tomorrow—so that fear and insecurity are themselves a species of suffering. For those of us who have suffered in direct and awful ways, in the most terrible moments we may share Hamlet's famous musings and wonder whether "to be or not to be" in such a world with such pain.[5] My friend Craig, one of the most faithful Christians I know, felt the vise of suffering crushing him when his younger sister was murdered. When I visited his family at the funeral home, he said to me through his tears that he had two choices now: "the barrel of a shotgun or the foot of the cross."[6] I did not get the impression this was an easy choice.

Faced with such terrible sorrows, how do we find a way to go on? Out of the depths of agonized cries of "Why?" Christian faith invites us to choose against the futility either of retaliation or self-destruction and to lay our pain instead at the foot of the cross. We are invited to shout or whisper or weep out our cries of pain to God because we know that God, having suffered in the person of Jesus, most especially on the cross, cares and understands. Bringing our suffering to God may not relieve the hurt completely, and it may not take the cause of suffering away. But the promise of the cross for the present is that the quality of our suffering will change because we will find the companionship of Jesus in it. That companionship allows our suffering to take on a new shape: the downward slope of death turns to the rising hope of new life. Because Jesus suffered death on the cross, then conquered death through resurrection, our suffering too becomes pliable to hope. Our dark caves can begin to crack open and let in that resurrection light.

THE PROMISE OF GOD'S CARE

I do not know why God permits suffering. But I do know that the Bible reveals a God who sees suffering from two perspectives: the grand pattern of all history and the intimate perspective of a single tear. The prophetic books of the Old Testament describe God overseeing the fates of nations and kings, permitting them their days in the sun, allowing their wickedness to bring terrible consequences but also shaping their histories. At the same time, the prophets bring the words of a God who promises to create "a new heaven and a new earth," and in this new creation "Never again will there be . . . an infant that lives but a few days, or an old man who does not live out his years" (Isaiah 65:17, 20). God's plan for the nations, the prophet declares, attends to and intends to heal the private griefs of individuals so that all "sorrow and sighing will flee away" (35:10). God promises to fulfill our longings for healing and repair in ways that do make sense to us, in ways that answer our deepest longings. This is the greatest promise of salvation: the culmination of all history in which all things will be made new.

In the meantime, however, while the suffering of the present days lasts, we have the promise of God's care to help us find patience and keep trusting God. Jesus assures his disciples, before he sends them out to preach and perhaps to be persecuted, that "even the very hairs on your head are all numbered" (Matthew 10:30); this is a measure, Jesus says, of God's intimate attention to our troubles and fears. Jesus invites his disciples to trust in God's careful and tender attention as well as his power, especially when circumstances look dire.

Trust in God's care is one important way that Christian faith changes the quality of suffering. But it's important to understand clearly how God's power and care work together because it's easy to become confused. Christians often assure one another in times of crisis that "God has a plan." However well intended, this kind of statement can feel like a dismissal of the pain. Sometimes people proffer it less as a comfort for the suffering person than as a protection against their own fear, the fear that someone else's grief always raises about one's own fragility. I know there have been moments in my life where, if someone had said "God has a plan," I would have responded with "Oh yeah? Well, I don't like it!" or "Well, I wish he'd explain it instead of springing these rotten surprises on me!"

To respond to someone's suffering by saying that God has a plan can suggest that God purposely causes us pain in order to . . . what? To force us to turn back to him? To punish us for our sins, however unconnected to the suffering? To make some good come of it? But so often whatever good comes out of suffering does not begin to pay for the pain. It hardly seems fair or explains the ways of a loving God. Did God shake the mountain Eric Wolterstorff was climbing so that he would fall and die, *in order that* his father, Christian philosopher Nicholas Wolterstorff, would gain an even wiser heart and write a moving book about suffering that would in turn comfort thousands of other grieving people? A noble outcome, but it doesn't come close to paying for Eric's death or his family's suffering.[7]

But that's not how it works. To reconcile the bewildering reality of suffering with God's power and intimate care, it helps to distinguish between the permissive and active will of God. God *permits* human freedom and the workings of a fallen creation to cause pain and sorrow. However, God is also *active* in weaving that pain and sorrow into his larger purposes for individuals and all of history, purposes we can't always clearly discern, especially at first. God permits suffering but does not abandon us. By the Holy Spirit, God is always working within societies to challenge the darknesses in them, always moving to call people out of their darkness, always sending his faithful people out to relieve suffering, always available to those who seek him.

For some reason God permitted Eric to fall to his death while mountain climbing. But God was not absent. Whether Eric felt terror or miraculous peace as he fell, God remained attentive to him. God remained attentive to the family too, even when in their grief they felt swallowed up by the black maw of death. It was that active presence of God that enabled them to find meaning in their grief and to maintain their belief that his death was not the end of Eric forever.

Dividing God's will into active and permissive categories gets complicated and at some level is a moot point. What difference does it make? The terrible thing still happened. But the distinction between active and permissive does remind us that God never wishes us to suffer. God's ultimate will for us—*will* in the sense of *desire*—is for our perfect flourishing. So we can say that God permits suffering rather than wills it in that sense. However, if God is sovereign over all things, if God is all powerful, then nothing happens apart from God's control. So suffering, though it is not God's desire, remains within God's active will—*will* in the sense of *control*. God's active will is ready to shape, respond to, and redeem whatever happens by God's permissive will. This active will is the sign and promise of that complete healing to come. Somehow, in ways we cannot begin to fathom because of our limited perspective, God weaves the tapestry of history using even the uglier threads of suffering. For those of us who bring our suffering to God, God can take our sad and terrible threads and create with them, given time and our cooperation, local patches of beauty.

Placing our suffering in the perspective not only of God's power but also of God's intimate care is one way that Christian faith changes the quality of suffering. When people say, whether clumsily or with real passion, "God has a plan," the words point to a comforting assurance at the heart of faith: that even when things seem to be falling apart, God's loving purposes are not thwarted; God still intends our good and still holds out the promise of healing that will transcend every pain.

PROTESTING AND DOUBTING

Christian faith offers promises that invite our trust in God but also invite us to face suffering honestly. My pastor friend Dawn tells me that when people come to her struggling with a dying marriage, memories of abuse, trouble with their kids, or some other serious heartache, she finds herself reminding them over and over: "It's OK to be angry with God. God can take it." People don't know what to do with their anger, she says. Often enough, they don't even know they're angry.

Knowing a little bit about God's justice and holiness, Christians sometimes imagine that God will be offended and turn against us if we do anything other than meekly submit to whatever happens, no matter how awful. So when we feel angry at God or the world, we might believe, half consciously, that we can choose one of two options: we can put on a good front and pretend in our prayers and our actions to accept obediently whatever God dishes out in his almighty sovereignty, or we can avoid God through agnosticism or disbelief. But God is far wiser about us than we give him credit for. He does not want our avoidance, of course, but he also does not want a pleasant, pretended submission. God wants us to bring to him our genuine selves, including the anger, the pain, the doubt, and the ugliness. God knows us intimately anyway. He knows all our weaknesses, all the obstacles and troubles we face. He remembers, the psalmist writes, that we are dust (103:14).

Contrary to much popular belief and practice, Christians, in the tradition of their Jewish brothers and sisters, are permitted their protests. People of mature faith can learn to endure suffering with spiritual equanimity and poise, with increased devotion and trust, with genuine acceptance of all that happens. But as spiritual skills go, that's fairly advanced. Most of us wandering around in the lowly foothills of the spiritual landscape face trouble and suffering with bewilderment and distress; we want to complain.

When we look to the Bible, we can see that the impulse to protest is ancient and that God understands and accepts our complaints. The Bible presents words of complaint and protest that we can use as our own whenever needed. Job may have covered his mouth and stopped complaining by the end of his story, but his is not the only response to suffering modeled in the Bible. Those who first decided the ordering of the books of the Hebrew Bible knew what they were about when they placed the book of Psalms immediately after the book of Job. The Psalms are stuffed full of eloquent protests from amid all kinds of trouble and pain: "My soul is in anguish. How long, O Lord, how long?" (6:3). "Will you forget me forever? How long will you hide your face from me?" (13:1). "My days are like the evening shadow; I wither away like grass" (102:11). If the book of Psalms is the prayer book of the faithful, as Jews and Christians have always believed, then apparently my friend Dawn is quite correct: it's OK to be angry at God. God can take it. God even invites it.

In fact, not only are we permitted our anger, we are permitted our doubts. Psalm 22, from which Jesus quoted while in anguish on the cross, begins with a desperate lament:

> My God, my God, why have you forsaken me?
> Why are you so far from saving me,
> so far from the words of my groaning?
> O my God, I cry out by day, but you do not answer,
> by night, and am not silent. [verses 1–2]

God knows that when terrible things happen, when death or illness or betrayal or violence or war shatters our security, the universe that may once have felt full of beauty and goodness suddenly feels empty and indifferent, "full of sound and fury, signifying nothing" as Shakespeare's Macbeth describes it in his final moment of hopeless resignation.[8] These periods of emptiness can lead us to doubt whether God does have our best interests in mind or whether God exists at all. But if through his incarnation Christ experienced the extent of our suffering, crying out against this terrible nothingness, this absence of God, this traitorous universe—then surely we are permitted to cry out too.

Some people wear their doubt like a badge of honor. They seem to want us to believe that they are somehow more intellectually honest or brave or more sophisticated than people who agonize less over whether God exists or whether God has our best interests at heart. I'm never terribly impressed with this posture. To me doubt is a common condition, very much like, say, the fear of heights. When you are standing on the viewing balcony outside the dome of St. Paul's, high above London, you may feel shaky and dizzy, but you would hardly boast about this to your companions. Making it up that precarious spiral staircase despite your fears—now *that* was brave. Doubt similarly is only a side effect of our distance from God, a condition many of us experience because we have become accustomed to crawling on the ground although we were meant to fly. Like all such side effects, some of us feel it more than others; and it is a matter neither of particular shame nor credit.

Doubts come because although we were created for communion with God, we have lost our head for the heights of God. Our own sins and the sinful state of the world have resulted in our diminished capacity for belief. Another way of looking at doubt is to point to God's otherness and therefore God's hiddenness. Most of the time, believers in God know God through the words of the Bible, through theological teaching, through the companionship and witness of others, through the experience of divine presence in prayer, through the practices of the church—all ways of experiencing God's presence. Those who suffer, however, sometimes come to know God's absence, his hiddenness. Suffering's painful lesson is that we cannot encapsulate God in our statements of belief, our religious practices, our expressions of praise in the most gorgeous cathedrals or cantatas or poetry. Unless we recognize God's hiddenness, we have circumscribed God's fullness within the bounds of our limited understanding. The medieval English devotional classic *The Cloud of Unknowing* teaches that those who are ready for a challenge ought to seek to know God not through prayer or even words at all but through systematically stripping away everything we think we know about God—a cloud, as the writer calls it, of *un*knowing.[9] Suffering can be a shortcut, a painful one, to that antiperception of God, the recognition that we are not in control of what we perceive about God. This understanding is as important in its own way as the deep communion of faith.

If we imagine that belief is a pleasant feeling of conviction, then we will worry too much about our angers and doubts. We will go through all kinds of gyrations to try to achieve some elusive experience of certainty and faith. The Psalms and other scriptural texts suggest instead that the proper medicine for anger and doubt is to bring them straight to God through prayer—even coarse, chaotic prayer. That anguished cry of absence from Psalm 22 is still a direct address to God. The Psalms further guide us in placing anger and doubt in the proper context by inviting us to recall, amid our suffering, God's past care for us. After its opening cry, Psalm 22 continues: "Yet you brought me out of my mother's womb; you made me trust in you even at my mother's breast" (verse 9). And then this psalm, and many others like it, directs our line of vision beyond our own plight to consider the wider picture of God's faithfulness: "In you our fathers put their trust; they trusted and you delivered them" (verse 4). Finally, even when we cannot muster a shred of trust or hope ourselves, the psalms of suffering invite us to listen to their testimony of the faithfulness of God, a testimony that has been on the lips of millions before us whose prayers reverberate with our own:

> For he has not despised or disdained
> the suffering of the afflicted one;
> he has not hidden his face from him
> but has listened to his cry for help. [verse 24]

The model of the Psalms for dealing with anger and doubt is echoed and confirmed everywhere in Scripture. Even in the darkness of God's apparent absence, Scripture instructs us, stay engaged with God. Rant and rail if you must, but stay engaged. Then remember. Remember examples of God's goodness to you and others; remember that God created and sustains the entire universe. And then listen. The words of the Psalms model our own expression of anger, doubt, and pain; but they also, along with the other assurances of the Bible, become the words of God in response to these cries. When we cannot muster our own words of trust and hope, the Scriptures speak words of comfort to us: "The Lord is compassionate and gracious, slow to anger, abounding in love" (Psalm 103:8). And "Those who sow in tears will reap with songs of joy" (126:5).

WHAT DID I DO TO DESERVE THIS?

Christian faith changes the quality of people's suffering because of the conviction that Jesus has already conquered all evil things in his death and resurrection, so that nothing that happens to us can finally defeat us. Jesus reconciled us to God so surely that nothing can now separate us from God, not even the most terrible afflictions. As Paul writes in the book of Romans (8:38–39): "For I am convinced that neither death nor life, neither angels nor demons, neither the present nor the future, nor any powers, neither height nor depth, nor anything else in all creation, will be able to separate us from the love of God that is in

Christ Jesus our Lord." This is a piece of knowledge that we can cling to even when we have lost the *feeling* of confidence in this truth, even when God seems absent, even when our pain leaves us too weak to pray. Jesus has paid a price to make us his own, and he will not let go. It is done. It does not depend on the strength of our grasp but on the strength of God's through Christ.

There's something about faith in this truth that allows suffering, though still painful, to become a receptacle of grace. Mature Christians do not live lives free of all suffering, nor do they welcome suffering. But when it comes, they seem to know what to do. They acknowledge their anger, but they move beyond it. They trust in God's power over all things and care over small things, but they move beyond that too. At some point, perhaps when they're feeling a little stronger, they start to look for how God might redeem their suffering into blessing, into glimmers of that new life that is promised to us beyond all things of this world. "What might God be teaching me through this?" they ask. "How might this suffering become a gift to me and others?"

Sometimes suffering can teach us to recognize sins we have so far managed to hide from ourselves. God often allows our own bad choices to reap their natural results; and suffering can be the big clue that something is wrong, like pain or a fever or bleeding when the body is ill. Self-examination is a regular dimension of the Christian life, and suffering can act as a bracing wake-up call to total honesty: maybe working too many hours has caused a husband to neglect his marriage, and that's part of what's causing tensions with his wife. Maybe a young student is far too concerned with grades and test scores and achievements, and her depression is a signal that she's looking for self-worth in the wrong places. Maybe an older man needs to admit that his loneliness is partly the result of scorn for others and a penchant for exaggerated gossip. When such realizations come, the right thing to do is pray for change.

The Christian faith teaches us to pray, amid dark times as well as other times, that the Spirit will reveal our sins to us so that we can consciously turn them over to God and ask forgiveness. Then we pray that the Spirit will give us the power to change our ways. Of course, there's a difference between healthy self-examination and attempts to bargain with God. My friend Dawn reports that when people come to her with troubles and problems, they'll often say things like, "I know I haven't been coming to church much lately, so I think that if I can just get myself right with God, then my marriage will improve." They want to make a deal with Dawn, as God's official representative: "If I shape up, then will you make God fix my problem?" But bargaining as a strategy for coping with suffering is bound to be disappointing.

People who follow the ethical guidelines in the Bible and who live decent, God-fearing lives do eliminate a lot of potential disasters.[10] But right living does not guarantee freedom from suffering; it does not promise a magically protected existence, free of all dangers and troubles. The most devout and beautiful people still get cancer, die in car crashes, lose children to rare diseases. So to imagine that we can bargain with God is to lapse into a misunderstanding, albeit a tempting one, of God's character. God is not the kind of deity you must constantly appease with sacrifices lest you find the one black cloud in the sky suddenly storming right over your head. Faithfulness does have clear benefits, but these benefits do not come with an insurance policy to eliminate all unpleasantness. Sin does bring bad results; but people get away with a lot too, at least for a while.

It would be easier if we could buy cosmic favor with our good behavior. But in the end, it's better that we depend on grace. After all, we could never sustain enough goodness to earn the floods of grace we need. It's far better that God has transformed the entire cosmic calculus of punishment and reward by enduring suffering himself. That's why it's also important to understand that searching for what suffering might reveal about our sin is not the same as assuming that particular sins cause particular sorrows. It's possible to blame ourselves where we shouldn't. My friends who are enduring the grief of infertility often wonder what they have done to displease God. "Is God punishing me," they ask, "for my sexual mistakes as a teenager? Is God punishing me for my failed first marriage? Is God punishing me for something I just can't think of? Why is this happening?"

The gospel accounts record a couple of occasions when people ask Jesus who is to blame for certain tragic events. In one case some Jews have been murdered by the Roman governor; in another case eighteen people died when a tower fell on them; in a third a man was born blind. In all cases Jesus replies that you can't assume bad things happen as a direct punishment for people's sins. About the tower victims, he says, "Do you think they were more guilty than all the others living in Jerusalem?" He then answers his own question: "I tell you, no!" Then he adds ominously, "But unless you repent, you too will all perish." That last remark is meant to point out to these questioners that they are too eager to blame disasters on the sins of the people who suffer them—a strategy obviously designed to highlight their own innocence. Jesus scolds them for busily searching out other people's sins rather than worrying about their own (Luke 13:1–5; John 9).

Jesus' responses let us know that when bad things happen, we cannot assume that the victims are directly to blame. We should always be ready to recognize our own sins, but that's not necessarily the explanation for our suffering either. As the case of the blind man demonstrates, sometimes God uses suffering not to reveal sin but to reveal his own healing power. When Jesus heals the man born blind, he explains that he does so, "so that the work of God might be displayed in his life" (John 9:3). Suffering invites us to self-examination, but even so we can take comfort in the knowledge that because of Jesus our sins are forgiven. As forgiven people we need not fear the wrath of God and search for ways to appease him. We need only keep praying, "Show me, and help me to change."

WHAT CAN SUFFERING TEACH US?

Resting in the knowledge that nothing can separate us from the love of God, we open ourselves to the possibility that suffering can teach us wisdom and compassion that in turn can transform suffering into blessing. When we are in pain, our senses can be heightened to God's tender care in the little things. We can gain a keener sense of perspective. I know of a woman who, when diagnosed with breast cancer, in her shock and grief wondered whether her faith and her husband's faith would survive. A member of the woman's church, having heard about the diagnosis, spent an evening in tearful prayer for the couple. The next morning she stopped over at the couple's house, carrying a box. "I saw this this morning," she said, "and I knew it was for you." The cancer-stricken woman opened the box and saw that it contained a plaque bearing a beautifully rendered, single word: faith. In her desperation for a comforting word from God, this woman was ready to see God responding to her fears through this simple gesture. She was able to read this small gift as an assurance that her faith was not something she had to keep up by her own efforts but a gift that God would keep safe for her—partly through the encouragement of others. God is present in the grandeur of the cosmos but also in the details, and we may perceive that most sensitively amid times of trouble or pain.

Suffering can also teach us sensitivity to the suffering of others, enlarging our compassion. When we feel most empty, that's when God can fill us with his grace; and we can then pour that grace out in blessing for others. The chaplain at my college, Dale Cooper, has shown compassion and grace to thousands of students over the years. He learned compassion, I think, from watching his parents' grace-filled response to suffering. Dale's mother, stricken with polio when Dale was three years old, was paralyzed from the neck down. The doctors expected her to die. His father, a farmer, stayed by his mother's side in the hospital every day, and she didn't die—but she didn't get better either. After four years in the hospital, she was released to live at home. She had to live in an iron lung, able to be free of it for only one hour each day. Dale's father cared for his mother at home, full-time, for the next thirty-five years. Despite these terrible limitations, Dale recalls, they were a joyful family, praising God for his goodness and trusting in God for each day's strength. When his mother died, his father said to Dale, "She was a good wife." This powerful example of grace amid suffering has helped form in Dale the kind of clear-sighted compassion that helps so many students face their own troubles with honesty and trust in God.

Those who follow Christ are invited to do more than endure with grace whatever suffering comes. They are called to enter places of suffering voluntarily in order to become the compassionate presence of Christ to others. At the end of the Gospel of John, when Jesus appears to the disciples after his resurrection, he says to them, "As the Father has sent me, I am sending you" (20:21). Jesus instructs his followers to go out into the world and act as his ambassadors, doing the sorts of things he himself did. That includes offering companionship to those who suffer, carrying some of their burden, bringing comfort, healing, and hope.[11] Thus, Christians, in imitation of Christ, travel to remote villages and live with people who have no fresh water and who are hungry and sick; and they bring technology, medicine, and knowledge that help initiate a new, more secure life. In imitation of Christ's compassion, Christians run homeless shelters and coffeehouses in the worst urban neighborhoods of the world. In imitation of Christ's

love, Christians establish and serve at schools for mentally and emotionally disabled children, advocating for their well-being and patiently
teaching them that God loves and values them. In imitation of Christ's
power and justice, Christians look for the places of struggle and suffering in their own neighborhoods and cities and professions and seek
ways to bear some of the burden through prayer and action.

It might be easier to avoid having to deal with people who suffer; after all, we've all got enough problems of our own. But following Jesus can't be only about solving one's own problems. It has to be
about taking on a little of the world's suffering too, in imitation of the
one whose compassion took on the whole weight of the world's suffering. By willingly entering the suffering of others, Christians become
the conduit of Christ's presence to others. Through us, through our
actions or words or just our silent physical presence, Jesus is still healing and giving people hope.

But it works the other way too. Those who suffer also present
the face of Christ to us. In their suffering we can glimpse the suffering of Christ and receive the mysterious blessing of offering simple
acts of mercy through them to the one whose mercy has saved us. By
seeking the face of Christ in suffering people whom we serve, we
place ourselves directly in the power of Christ's healing presence. In
this we follow the pattern of the women who stayed with Jesus
through his suffering and death and who took responsibility for following the proper burial customs and caring for his body. Because
they rose up amid their own lost hopes to offer simple deeds of mercy
to this Jesus whom they loved, they became the first witnesses of
God's powerful transformation of Christ's suffering: the resurrection.

The Real Presence of God

Suffering can be turned to blessing because this dimension of human
experience is infused with God's presence. God has entered the experience of suffering in Christ; the result is that suffering can become a
place of intimate communion with Christ, and through Christ with
the triune God. In desperate times the experience of Christ's presence
is especially available.

My mother-in-law, Marchiene, tells of a time in her life when,
though she was a pastor responsible for helping others grow in their

faith, she herself felt distant from God and unable to pray. When she told her friend and colleague Father Gus, a Roman Catholic priest, about her feelings, he wisely recommended that she consider whether she was angry with God. If so, then she should try to express that anger as fully as she could. Marchiene took his advice and realized that she was, in fact, terribly angry with God. She thought of her father, a missionary doctor who suffered from a rare, degenerative disease for ten years before he died. She thought of her sister Judy, who had been suffering from multiple sclerosis for years and every day diminished further from her once lively self. She thought of all the disease and disaster in the world, and the more she thought, the more she discovered deep wells of anger inside her.

So one winter day, she went alone into the woods and started walking. After a while she started yelling out loud at God, saying, "You are supposed to be this great king ruling the world! Well, I think you are doing a lousy job! How can you allow all this awful suffering and violence? How can you let people who love and serve you all their lives suffer? I don't want anything to do with you!" After more yelling and stomping and even kicking of trees, she wore herself out and had nothing more to say.

She found her car, climbed inside, and sank into silence. Then after a while, she says, the image of Christ on the cross came to her mind. She felt God saying to her: "*This* is how I deal with human sin and its consequences—disaster, disease, violence—all of it. I am not a God who just intervenes and fixes things. I never force. I take the long, slow, painful way of entering human suffering and redeeming it through divine love. You have to choose whether you are willing to accept me and my way." At that moment, she says, she felt deeply understood, deeply at peace, and deep in the presence of God. Marchiene says that after that day, she has never again wrestled or agonized over the problem of suffering; nor has she felt distant from God. The powerful presence of God, the loving person of God, became the enduring answer.

THINGS NOT SEEN

In that incomparably rich passage on suffering, Romans 8:28, Paul writes, "We know that in all things God works for the good of those who love him." This promise sums up all Scripture: God is love; all things are in his control; and God has our best interests at heart. We turn to this promise so often precisely because life presents evidence to the contrary. How is God working for good with Chris, whose schizophrenia gets worse with every year he lives in its terrible prison? How is God working for good for Christians in El Salvador, who have endured torture, disappearances, and murder at the hands of thugs with guns? How was God working for good for those who have died in terrorist attacks?

I can argue that suffering yields benefits—revealing our sins, teaching us wisdom, making us better servants to others, even drawing us into greater communion with God. But if death is the last word, then all of that is ultimately useless. Without a conviction that there is more to our existence than this life we now see, God's promises for perfect restoration of joy amount to what the Hebrew Bible describes as *hevel*—vain, meaningless, evanescent as the morning mist. Unless there is some life beyond this life, where God truly does heal our diseases, free us from all sin, wipe away every tear from our eyes, then God's promises are empty betrayals.

In Romans 8:18 (RSV), Paul writes, "I consider that the sufferings of this present time are not worth comparing to the glory that is to be revealed to us." Paul, who wrote this from prison, who threw away a successful career in order to preach about Jesus all over the Roman world, who repeatedly suffered beatings and imprisonment as thanks for his faithfulness to Christ, who died a martyr—this Paul was convinced that all the suffering he experienced and witnessed was nothing compared to the glory to come in some other plane of existence. Otherwise, as he frankly writes in a different passage, "If only for this life we have hope in Christ, we are to be pitied more than all men" (1 Corinthians 15:19).

Should we place our hope in these promises? When I watch with horror and guilty shame news reports depicting desperate women in Africa with their dying, skeletal babies; young girls compelled into the sex trade in Asia; or children abused and neglected in my own country, I can only say to God in my anger: "Whatever you've got in store had better be really really good." Can it be so? Did Julian of Norwich hear correctly when she heard the Lord say to her in one of her visions of God's grace, that "All shall be well," and "all manner of things shall be well"?[12] Can there be some existence so saturated with joy that all the terrible things of this world will seem like nothing in comparison?

Because my older two children are now reading novels, I recently reread *A Wind in the Door,* by the children's author Madeleine L'Engle. In it a girl named Meg, her brother Charles Wallace, and their friend Calvin find themselves involved in a battle against evil forces called echthroi. The echthroi seek only to destroy, to erase creatures from existence. The children discover that their only defense against the echthroi is to be "Named." Some other character in the story has to know them, love them, and say out loud, "I Name you!" The idea is that once they are truly known and loved by another, nothing can destroy them. L'Engle is pointing to the way in which God's intimate knowledge of us is our assurance that death does not destroy us.[13]

I saw a news report about Rwanda, ten years after the ethnic genocide of 1994. The report showed a Rwandan man carefully writing down the names of all those who had been killed. He was still writing after ten years so that people might know what happened to their relatives. Then the camera turned to a woman whose husband and child had been murdered. She had been captured by the enemy army and gang-raped repeatedly for a month. She now suffers from AIDS. She showed the reporter a large photo album of people, many of them children, all dead. She herself is dying. She only hoped, she said, that she would not be forgotten. She wanted someone to remember her name. I wanted to tell her that God's eye has never turned away from her and that her life and her name, Anne-Marie Mukamara, are held in the palm of God's hand.

Nothing can separate us from the love of God in Christ. Because I have myself experienced God's care for me, God's comfort and guidance in my particular circumstances and troubles, I believe that God has named me and that God names anyone who seeks him. Nothing can *un*name me. Because of the resurrection, death is not the end. I believe that Eric Wolterstorff was not annihilated by that mountain fall but that he lives in God's presence. So does Leanne, so does Ed, so will Anne-Marie even when AIDS takes her life. Death is not the final word but the transition into a new life that can never be taken away.

The hope of this resurrection life floods into the present. God gives us signs of it, tokens that help us believe it is true. I've seen those

signs in my own life when periods of difficulty and struggle gave way
to seasons of joy and new beginnings. I've seen it in others' lives too—
the pain of divorce yields to the healing of a new, healthy marriage.
Addiction yields to recovery. Griefs heal and start to yield to new joys.
My friend Charlotte lost her father in a car accident when she was in
college. Within ten years she had lost her mother to cancer. Charlotte
knew loss and endings too well at an age when most people are enjoying their youth and the promise of their future. Nothing can make up
for what she lost; her wounds will always be a part of her. But within a few years after her mother's death, she reached a new horizon of
joy in giving birth to a baby girl. Charlotte and her husband named
the baby after the grandmother she would never know in this life.
Two years later, in what seemed like an extra helping of new life in
response to her extra helping of grief, Charlotte gave birth to healthy
triplets.

The beauty and power of Christian hope is that it endures even
when the healing doesn't come in this life. My colleague Terry, after
learning that he had cancer, read a book written by another man suffering from cancer. Terry wrote on his Web site that he admired this
author's "desire to be obedient, not give in to despair, remain engaged
and contributing and to honor God and point people to Christ
throughout the journey." Reading the book, Terry explained, made
him face the possibility that he might not survive this cancer. But
from within that realization, he felt God asking him, "Are you willing
to completely trust me in this?" Terry wrote, "The answer is yes, by
God's grace." Over Easter weekend one of his colleagues went to visit
him, bringing the family a meal. She told me that the atmosphere in
the house was not one of gloom and sadness but joy. Terry himself,
though very thin, spoke to her with sparkling eyes and told her of his
love for Jesus. As he neared death, Terry's joy came in his secure hope
that he could trust God through this: that God had conquered death
and that God had a life waiting for him beyond what he could now
imagine.[14]

When we consider the sufferings of the present time, where do
our sorrow, anger, and longing come from? They have to come from
somewhere. Why do we desire joy and life? Why do we sometimes
feel their power? Perhaps our sorrow, anger, and longing are drops of
God's own sorrow, anger, and longing. Perhaps our joy is the full truth

into which we are being called, not partially but fully and forever. This is the Christian good news: there is more than what we now see; and because of Christ, the truth of that more floods into the present.

The fundamental question for all of us is this: How big is our hope? Will we let our hope be small and feeble, invested only in the human spirit and the temporary endurance of our remarkable and terrible species? Or will we fling out our hope beyond the stars themselves toward the repair of all things? When we hear the promises of the Bible, when we see light in the love of others, in deeds of mercy, in gestures of hope amid despair, in the renewing seasons of creation, in new life, what will we take that light to be? Pinpricks in an enduring field of darkness? Or glimpses of a real light beyond that darkness, a light more true in the end than the darkness?

Paul wrote to the Colossians that he wished for them the "full riches of complete understanding, in order that [you] may know the mystery of God, namely Christ, in whom are hidden all the treasures of wisdom and knowledge" (2:2–3). The Greek here for "complete understanding" is more literally translated "underflowing"—the deep interconnection among all things. In the depths of God, all things are ordered and harmonized, even the jangling surfaces of our suffering. We cannot explain it; we can only begin to touch that underflowing by receiving the transforming hope offered us in the mysterious, suffering love of Christ.

LIVING
THE
CHRISTIAN LIFE

CHAPTER SIX

𝒞𝒵

SEEKING THE HEART OF GOD
Prayer

I SOUGHT THE LORD, AND HE ANSWERED ME.
—Psalm 34:4

𝒞𝒵 I received a request recently from a writer who wanted to put together an article on prayer for a Christian magazine, an article she was calling "Giving God the First Fruits." She explained enthusiastically how she herself had changed her daily prayer time from evening to morning and found that she suddenly started to grow spiritually and felt her life transformed. She was looking for similar stories to fill out this piece on putting prayer first in your day. I tried to reply to her request; but I could only observe that since I started managing a job, three young children, and a husband who works evenings, if anything my prayer life had gone downhill. I pray for a few moments in the morning; I pray when I first get to my desk at the office for a few minutes as I wait for the electric kettle to boil water for tea; I pray in snatches while driving or stirring supper on the stove or waiting for programs to load on the computer; and sometimes on a good day, I pray for a few brief moments before I crawl into bed. I finally gave up trying to put an inspirational twist on this tale. Reports on prayer struggles were not what this person was after. She wanted triumphs and turnarounds.

I am always a bit intimidated by prayer enthusiasts who are temperamentally suited to getting up at the crack of dawn for their daily business meeting with God, equipped with a written agenda. I am also intimidated by people of a mystical temperament, who spend long stretches in contemplation, repeating the same words over and over and achieving states of inexpressible divine communion. I wish I could better conform to either pattern. There was a time when I took long walks almost daily and spent that time in prayer; but during these middle years of my life, I find that my private prayer times are fidgety, irregular, fragmented, and characterized mostly by tiredness and ill attention.

Thankfully the private daily devotional time, although a marvelous practice I sincerely wish to cultivate again in my own life, is not the only way to survive spiritually. In fact, it's rather common to have trouble with it. John Chapman, an English Benedictine spiritual adviser and biblical scholar, offers reassuring words:

> It is right, I think, to feel perfectly satisfied with our prayer
> (after our prayer) that it *is* all right when it *feels* all wrong. . . . It
> is of the very essence of prayer that it does not depend on us.
> It depends on circumstances—our stomach, our preoccupations,
> much more than on our will—for the character it takes; and
> naturally, on God's special grace. But possibly the *best* kind is
> when we seem unable to do anything, if then we throw ourselves
> on God, and stay contentedly before Him: worried, anxious,
> tired, listless, but—above all and under it all—humbled and
> abandoned to His will, contented with our own discontent.
>   If we can get ourselves accustomed to this attitude of soul,
> which is always possible, we have learned how to pray.[1]

Mere openness to God, amid the turmoil of our thoughts and emotions, is all that is required for prayer to begin. And the rest, thankfully, does not depend solely on us. God enters into our steely discipline or pathetic flounderings and even works against our resistance. Christians of all times and places strongly recommend putting effort into various practices of prayer; but as with all spiritual practices, we must surely recognize from the start that our most determined efforts are laughably inadequate and that we depend on God for the will, the opportunity, and the ability to engage in the action at all. The first step, the one we must take over and over, is simply to lower the drawbridge, to open the fortress of our deepest selves to the presence of God.

I have prayed all my life in one way or another; so despite my current lack of discipline, the idea of sensing the presence and guidance of God in prayer feels natural to me. If I weren't used to it, it might seem incomparably odd to speak out loud or in the mind to an unseen person, let alone to imagine that this person's replies can be somehow discerned. But instead, a life devoid of such mysterious communion would seem terrifyingly empty to me, as if all but one dimension of the universe had suddenly dropped away. Those who have never or rarely tried it, and who may be unsure whether someone is in fact listening, naturally feel self-conscious and silly at prayer. For the skittish or the perennial doubter, a perfectly good beginning is: "God, if you are really there . . ." It's worth opening this door even if you're not entirely sure you've heard the doorbell.

WHAT'S THE POINT?

Prayer offers the same kinds of benefits as meditation. It promotes relaxation and focuses the mind on essentials for a time rather than on the usual trivialities that crowd our mental states. But the primary goal of religious prayer reaches beyond a self-defined well-being: prayer nurtures a relationship with God. Prayer is the breathing of the spirit. Until we begin prayer, our spiritual selves are not yet truly born. The Quaker writer on spiritual disciplines, Richard Foster, describes prayer as "the deepest and highest work of the human spirit,"[2] an essential practice with an expansive scope. I might argue that love is the deepest and highest work, but prayer is the whispering of the divine lover to the human beloved, to which the human murmurs in return.

The thirteenth-century German mystic Mechthild of Magdeburg represents a whole category of mystics who pictured their relationship with God like that of lovers. In one of her notebooks, she wrote:

> I call Thee with profound desire
> And piteous voice.
> I wait for Thee with a heavy heart,
> I cannot rest, I burn without respite
> In Thy flaming love.

As with any deep love, Mechthild also experienced the pain that such an intense relationship with a being so much greater than oneself can bring. She imagined the voice of God speaking to her, saying,

> However lightly I touch thee
> I cause thee bitter pain.[3]

There's a certain risk in an intimate relationship with God, and my own sense of that risk is the reason I often avoid prayer. I fear learning the ungainly truths about myself that God might reveal to me. I fear what God might demand of me. I fear that God might teach me to love someone when I would rather hold on to annoyance or avoidance. I fear whatever change might come about, good or ill, for myself or others. I suppose it's part of our nature to cling to what we know even when a small effort promises something better.

I know I sometimes avoid prayer exactly because I believe in its power. Others might avoid it because they remain unconvinced of its power. The more pragmatic want to know whether or not prayer *works.* Does it change things? Why should it, when God supposedly already knows everything and controls everything? Certainly prayer works in the sense that it changes *us.* Put yourself consciously and willingly in the presence of God, and God will begin to reshape you, probably in ways you cannot predict. In the spring of Ron's last year of seminary, our big question was: Where do we go next? Ron had an interview for a college chaplain job in Pella, Iowa—a town of ten thousand souls situated amid miles of cornfields. I was, to say the least, not enthusiastic about this. But I sat at my desk one day, praying through my worries about the decisions ahead, and I received a very clear sense that I ought to get over my prejudice and think kindly of Iowa. Weeks passed; we prayed more and talked to people we trusted; and eventually it became clearer that we were somehow being led to Iowa. That summer we packed up and moved to Pella, and I learned to love it immediately. We lived there for four rich, wonderful years.

That prayer changes *us* is the easy part. Most often what people really want to know is whether the operation works the other way, whether prayer changes God. Can praying for a particular outcome be predictably expected to bring about the outcome? When we pray that the prematurely born baby will live or that the tumor will disappear or that the marriage will improve, are we merely surrendering to the charming illusion that we have some say in the matter, an illusion God permits despite the fact that he's going to do what he pleases anyway?

Lately researchers have been attempting to demonstrate prayer's effectiveness with clinical trials. Results have been mixed, although a large 1999 study concluded that heart patients who were prayed for without their knowing did better than heart patients who were not prayed for.[4] Of course, both the researchers and their critics acknowledge that it's very difficult—perhaps impossible—to do a rigorously scientific study on prayer. How are you going to ensure controls? If you were a member of one of the secret prayer teams in this study, wouldn't you be tempted to add at the end of your prayers: "And please heal the people we're *not* supposed to be praying for too"? How does one take into account "background prayer" or the "noise," as researchers rather humorously call it, of people all over the world praying for the sick in general?

Moderately scientific attempts aside, we can observe that the Bible encourages us to believe that God responds to our requests. The Old Testament patriarch Abraham negotiates with God with savvy determination, and as a result God decides to let nephew Lot and his family escape the city of Sodom before it gets destroyed (Genesis 18). A woman named Hannah pleads for a son, and God gives her baby Samuel (1 Samuel 1). God responds again and again to Moses' and other prophets' pleading on behalf of Israel. Jesus calls out to the Father at one point to heal a blind man and at another point to raise Lazarus from the dead, and both events happen. And Jesus tells stories that encourage persistence in prayer, like the story of the widow who nags and nags an indifferent judge until he finally grants her request only in order to get her off his back (Luke 18). But sometimes even those most dear to God in the Bible do not get what they pray for. King David pleads for the life of his infant son, born to Bathsheba as the offspring of David's adultery with her. But the baby dies (2 Samuel 12).

We can also consider the question in light of mountains of anecdotal evidence. Any believer who has been at this for a while will report many specific prayers answered and many not. Sometimes the tumor disappears; sometimes it doesn't. Some babies beat the odds; some don't. Some marriages heal; some crash and burn. One classic summary is that God always answers specific requests; and the possible answers are yes, no, and later. These answers neatly account for the results but leave open the question of whether our requests figure into the calculations. The best strategy here is to avoid overstating the case either way.

On the one hand, we do not run the universe with our prayers. Some recent novels of spiritual warfare depict angels and devils hovering about human characters, responding to their prayers as if supernatural beings inhabit a cosmos that operates like a video game (with extremely high stakes) and we—we mighty ones who pray— hold the joystick. I object to this because we in fact know very little about supernatural beings; imagining, even in a fictional narrative, that we can control them as they duke it out over our fates risks underestimating their real power. It also arrogantly overestimates our role, turning us into prayer action heroes—or the idiots who fail the universe. Better to remain mostly agnostic about what angels and devils might be up to and focus instead solely on God. God is not so unmerciful as to rest our fate entirely on the competence and fervency of our prayers. All would be lost for sure!

Yet it cannot be that our prayers merely amuse God and do not move him. A recent theological movement called open theism is particularly concerned with the idea that our prayers change God. To explain how our prayers are able to alter God's plans, however, open theism qualifies the omnipotence and omniscience of God. God knows the big outcomes, these theologians argue, but decides the details as we go along through history. I see this as a fix for a problem that doesn't actually exist; it's a problem that only *seems* to need fixing because our understanding is limited by the linear nature of the space-time continuum. Any time you place God in a timeline, any time you start using the words *before* and *after* connected with God's knowledge, the foul whistle ought to blow. God is eternal; God's view of history is always complete and in what we would call the present. We are the ones whose understanding of events must run through the before-during-after sorter. However, just because we have limited perception, it does not follow that we are merely playing out the script God wrote before time. See? There's the foul whistle. History is in God's control, but God has *always already* shaped history with a generous condescension to our small and scattered wills. Yes, the baby lived and grew up, and that was always God's plan; but perhaps it was God's plan partly because so many people were praying for the baby.

The analogy of parents and children helps a little here. God sets the rules for the household of this world. But our presence in it does change things, just as children, as they grow up, bring their own characters, gifts, and desires to the overall family dynamic. And like a good parent, God honors our requests with an answer, depending on what is good for us and consonant with a larger design we can't always perceive. Yes, no, later. My friend Elizabeth taught me another shorthand way of describing how God answers prayer. After struggling with infertility for years, Elizabeth became the mother of four adopted children. She felt God answering her prayers with "not *that* but *this*." She describes what seems to be a common way God responds: graciously acknowledging our desires but guiding us toward outcomes we could not find on our own.

The bottom line is this: to embark on a life of prayer is to encounter a mystery. My pastor friend Mary encourages her parishioners not to try to sort out all the technicalities beforehand; instead, she says, "Go with what you know." The Bible urges prayer; people have practiced it for centuries. Give it a go. We should certainly not judge prayer by whether or not every specific request is granted. Prayer is not an invoice that God must pay—or else. C. S. Lewis wrote that although God is all knowing and all powerful, God invites our prayer so that we might "assume the high rank of persons before Him."[5] God will never refrain from saying yes to creating a relationship between himself and the praying human being. The parties involved are infinitely unequal, yet the weaker of the two is raised in dignity by God's love. The wisest advisers on the life of prayer agree that as our relationship with God deepens, our requests will be answered more often because we ourselves will become more attuned to the character and will of God. More and more we will ask those sorts of things that God is glad to grant.

Prayer is both so simple that any child can do it and so complex and inexplicable that it seems fathomless. I'm encouraged that even Thomas Merton, the twentieth-century mystic and beloved writer on the subject of prayer, wrote: "We do not want to be beginners. But let us be convinced of the fact that we will never be anything else but beginners, all our life!"[6] Praying is bound to feel awkward and difficult at times. To seek the presence of God is to resist the results of the fall. We are reaching across the breach. But when we do, we find over and over that God has already bridged that breach with love.

MANY KINDS OF PRAYER

As I struggled with feelings of failure in response to that magazine writer's request for inspiring prayer stories, I began to realize that I was holding up only one model of prayer as the ideal—a daily time of labor-intensive prayer characterized by a Protestant penchant for improvisation. There's nothing wrong with this model; it will indeed yield the fruit of spiritual growth. The problem for me is that it's very difficult to keep up. My friend Susan felt the same way, laboring dutifully over her prayer list every day, writing down in a notebook her requests and the answers received, secretly feeling that prayer was a big burden, another duty on her to-do checklist. After studying a book called *Space for God,* she finally felt liberated.[7] She told me, "I realized I could stop praying as if it were another thing to get done. It was perfectly all right to sit quietly and say *nothing* to God. Just listen instead. Why hadn't I figured this out before?"

We often get stuck in particular models or hold up as superior particular ideas about prayer—usually ones we can't achieve. So in deciding exactly how to go about this prayer business, we can relieve some of the confusion and performance anxiety by acknowledging that prayer can take many legitimate forms. I took an inventory of the different kinds of prayer I have experienced or at least heard of and came up with a list of formats that can be combined in all sorts of ways.

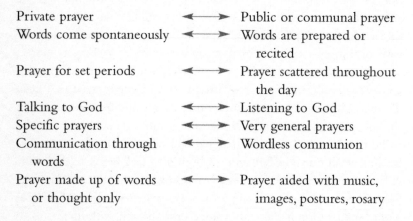

Private prayer	⟷	Public or communal prayer
Words come spontaneously	⟷	Words are prepared or recited
Prayer for set periods	⟷	Prayer scattered throughout the day
Talking to God	⟷	Listening to God
Specific prayers	⟷	Very general prayers
Communication through words	⟷	Wordless communion
Prayer made up of words or thought only	⟷	Prayer aided with music, images, postures, rosary

A public prayer might be offered from a prepared manuscript, offering specific requests and leaving periods for silent listening. Private prayers might be scattered throughout the day, offering spontaneous thoughts of praise or very general requests for peace. A set period of time each day might be spent repeating a simple phrase and listening to God's leading. Just about any combination of these formats can make up good prayer. As I run the combinations here, I realize that it might seem a bit odd if someone were to launch into spontaneous public prayers at random times throughout the day. That may fly just fine within some subcultures of the faith; among others it might prompt friends and family to suggest medication.

The only way I can think of to go about building a prayer life is to find several formats that fit one's temperament and situation. Probably the only indispensable elements run along two of the spectra listed: private and communal, talking and listening.

STEADYING WORDS

My personal prayer life would never survive at all without an ample supply of communal prayer to bolster it. The prayers I have heard in worship services, for example, have been excellent teachers; they continue to teach me how to confess sins and praise God and ask for help from God for myself and others. Good prayer in worship also helps us put our individual prayers in the larger context of God's work in the world and in history. But of course, communal prayer is more than a training program; it is a powerful phenomenon in its own right. I have found this to be especially true of the prayer of intercession or congregational prayer that figures regularly in a wide variety of worship services, from the staid and formal to the loose and spontaneous. This time of sustained prayer is meant to provide opportunity to bring the specific needs of congregants, community, church, and world before God.

While I was growing up, I referred to this time of prayer as the long prayer or the really long, boring prayer. It was ideal daydreaming time, what with the quiet breathing of people around me, the whir of the fans in summer or the blank darkness beyond the windows on winter evenings, and the rising and falling of my pastor's familiar baritone voice. I still think it's not a bad idea to have regular daydreaming time in one's life. Now, though, I understand better the strange energy that flows through communal prayer. People gathered in a room, leaning their thoughts and hearts into the leader's words, can invite a powerful sense of God's presence, as if God is palpably "bowing thine ear to our cry" as the psalmist might put it (Psalm 31:2, paraphrase). Ron, who is often called upon to lead such prayers, reports that when things are going well, when he is focused and the congregation is flowing its intention and attention through his words into one stream, he sometimes experiences a kind of out-of-body sensation, as if part of him is levitating. This is similar to the phenomenon psychologists call flow. I too have felt prayer energy in a group. What comes from us seems to have an upward surge, while the Spirit presses God's presence down on us in return, brooding, as poet Gerard Manley Hopkins wrote, with "warm breast and with ah! bright wings."[8]

Worship services are not the only place where communal prayer invites the Spirit's presence. When I was a young girl, I remember visiting some dear friends of the family around Christmastime. The father of the family had died suddenly of a heart attack only a year or two before, leaving his wife and four young children. Before we sat down to eat on this occasion, the mother of the family led us in prayer; and I remember how easily and beautifully she addressed the God she loved. Her words clearly arose out of constant communion with God, and I understood just a little where she found the strength to go on. I can think of many other occasions too when hearing someone else's voice in prayer seemed to quell anxiety, imparting a sense of peace and confidence. I remember praying with my dear friends Andrew and Dawn just before they returned home from a few days' visit with us. I was only a month away from giving birth to my third child. We had code-named the baby Jubilant, and Andrew prayed that he would be born safely and be a jubilant child. Hearing Andrew's voice say the words, I knew all would turn out as he prayed it would. The prayer became for me, in all my maternal anxiety, a means for God to grant me peace. And the prayer was answered. We often say that our son, whom we actually named Philip, has a "low joy threshold."

We all need inspiration to draw us into a life of prayer, and we all need to hear the voices of others praying on our behalf—in worship, in small groups, around a table. Communal prayer does have its dangers. It can become a routine recitation. The participants can pay little attention. The leader can become a performer and pray a little *too* eloquently or stumble and mumble and succeed only in annoying the participants. People who pray in public both authentically and with a little eloquence have a special gift. We need them. But done well or done clumsily, praying together is essential. In hearing others' voices, we learn from each other, join our energy together, and steady each other with our words.

Who's There?

Finding one's way in private prayer requires some experimentation. Fortunately we have many effective models, and what works at one stage of life may not work in another. Before getting into the wide range of what to say in prayer, it's important to acknowledge the wisdom, expressed across the Christian tradition, of saying nothing at all in prayer on a regular basis—only listening.

This is not how I was taught. Prayer was always a pretty wordy business as far as I could tell. Lately I've been encountering other traditions of prayer and have been learning the rather obvious truth that if one expects God to speak, it's a good idea to be quiet and listen. Nicky Gumbel, the English pastor featured in the popular Alpha Course videotapes for people exploring Christian faith, explains that prayer without deliberate listening is like going to the doctor, listing off all kinds of dire symptoms, and then walking out the door before hearing what the doctor has to say in response.[9] Ancient traditions of contemplative prayer encourage the practice of emptying oneself before God in silence and stillness of thought, so that one might be filled with God's presence.

Even when we are excessively chatty, however, God can get the message across. God can speak through the words of the Bible, through sermons, through hymns, through the words of others, through events and our reflections on them, through pop songs on the radio, and just about anything else you can think of. But there's no point in forcing God to interrupt all the time. Better to sit quietly once in a while and invite God to speak.

Recommended methods for promoting a posture of listening in prayer include deliberately emptying the mind (very difficult) or focusing the mind on a repeated prayer or single phrase of Scripture (not quite as difficult). How can we recognize God's voice when it comes to us in these times of listening? That's not a matter of technique but of trust and experience. Our minds are full of weird voices, but with practice it is possible to get a feel for which one is God's. One evening as I tucked my five-year-old, Philip, into bed, we were talking about prayer. I explained that when he got a little older, he would start learning to hear God talking to him in his heart. Apparently he liked that idea, because a few days later he said to Ron:

"Dad, I think I'm old enough now to hear God speaking to me in my heart."

Not having heard about my talk with Philip, Ron was absolutely astonished by this early sign of a tender, receptive soul. "Really?" he responded gently. "What do you hear God saying?"

"That he loves me."

Oh, how precious and profound is the innocence of children! thought Ron, with a tear in his eye. The next day, however, after Ron had refused to give Philip a snack before supper, Philip stormed out of the room, only to march back in after a few minutes and announce that God had told him he could have a candy bar immediately.

In my own experience, sorting out when we are hearing messages from God means waiting for words or inner thoughts that come with a feeling of settledness, a sense of rightness and peace. This does not mean that I've heard only what I expect or want to hear. On the contrary, I sometimes hear challenging or surprising things that I don't much like; but I still feel that they come to me from God. It's possible to test whether one is hearing God's voice by asking some important questions: Does what I think God might be telling me comport with the great currents of Scripture? Does it promote the love of God in oneself and others? When I tell what I think I'm hearing to wise people whom I trust, what do they say about the matter? What does my own gut tell me? And here's an important one too: Does the word, whatever it is, keep coming back to me? I've found that God is not at all above repeating something over and over. As any parent knows, distracted children often don't get the message the first time; and I'm sure from God's point of view we often resemble distracted children.

Praying with the Psalms

Listening is an excellent practice, but when it's time for words, how do we find them? For all kinds of prayer, communal and private, Scripture offers an abundance of models. The most ancient and still the most important for Christians are the Psalms. Jews and Christians for centuries have regarded the Psalms, a collection of 150 Hebrew poems, as *the* authoritative guidebook on prayer. The Psalms are a varied selection of prayers, many of them in what poets call the lyric mode. They present an individual voice engaged in intimate prayer, as, for example, "O Lord, you have searched me and you know me" (139:1). They cover a great deal of emotional terrain in their addresses to God, from the dark depths of Psalm 130 to the ecstatic heights of Psalm 150. Not all psalms are purely lyrical; many invite communal acts of worship (for example, 95, 96, 98, 100), present wisdom sayings (for example, 1), or meditate with varied attitudes on the states of nations or God's historical deeds (for example, 2, 78). They range in vision from the deep sorrows of a single heart to the cosmic dance of the universe—always constituting this vision through engagement with God.

Because of the Psalms' great depth and comprehensiveness, ancient Christian monastics developed schemes so that the community could pray through the entire collection every month, week, or day. The sixteenth-century Reformers praised the Psalms as a compendium of all scriptural types, a précis of all doctrine, a catalog of the believer's emotions. Forms that shape worship services and worship songs of all varieties and from all ages are full of texts from the Psalms. The beauty, honesty, and flexibility of the Psalms keep them always in the mouths and hearts of believers.

I first learned the Psalms by singing them in church. My Dutch ancestors, who followed the practices of the Protestant Reformation, were fervent psalm-singers. By the time I came along, the songbook in the church pew had become the *Psalter Hymnal,* incorporating both singable psalms and hymns, with the hymns beginning only at song number 311.[10] The first 310 songs were arrangements of the Psalms (an average of more than two versions per psalm). When I chose a dissertation topic in graduate school, I was naturally drawn to sixteenth-century English psalm translations. *After all,* I thought, *why start from scratch when I have a head start on these texts?* Amazingly, even after spending three years immersed in psalm translations, this ancient, eclectic collection of prayers never felt stale or flat to me but always fresh and alive (if sometimes a little weird).

Studying the influence of psalm translations on English poets has helped me appreciate even more the vivid language and rough emotional terrain of the Psalms. I have come to appreciate the power of the "I" in the Psalms, that flexible little pronoun with its layering of voices. It is the key to the enduring power of the Psalms as a model for prayer. When I read or pray a psalm, the "I" becomes my own. It gives me words for my struggles. When I read in Psalm 23, "He makes me lie down in green pastures," the "green pastures" become the pleasant, nourishing places where God leads in my own life. When I read "Even though I walk through the valley of the shadow of death, I will fear no evil, for you are with me," the "valley of the shadow of death" is a place filled with my own fears (verses 2, 4). Because I have been taught to pray the Psalms as my own words, even the weirder metaphors become porous, absorbing whatever meaning I can give them. For instance, when I read "Restore our fortunes, O Lord, like streams in the Negev" (126:4), I have a vague idea that the Negev is some desert in the ancient Near East, but I don't need to know exactly to pray those words. The Negev becomes a dry, barren place in my life. At the same time, because the Psalms are ancient, because Jews and Christians of all ages share these words, these prayers bring to bear a whole community of people, assuring me that I am not the first to feel doubt, terror, anxiety, fury, anger, gratitude, ecstasy—not the first to pass all these landmarks on the way to God. Even the "I" is a "we" in other words: thousands of thousands of voices, in many languages, have prayed like this before.

Because of this long and sacred history, the Psalms teach me to pray better than I would on my own. They show me that I need not hide anything from God. They express anger at God, even vengefulness and self-righteousness. They hand these uglier sentiments over to God and place them in the context of trust. The Psalms also lead me to spiritual wisdom I wouldn't find on my own: "Oh, how I love your law! I meditate on it all day long," cries the psalmist (119:97). Would it occur to me, without prompting, to meditate lovingly on God's law? Probably not. But I should, because it will be easier to stay on the right path when I learn from the psalmist that God's law is "sweeter than honey" (119:103). Finally the Psalms move me beyond my own troubles to those of others. I may not connect emotionally to a particular psalm on a particular day. "See how my enemies have increased and how fiercely they hate me!" (25:19) doesn't usually strike a chord with me. But somewhere a woman who lives among drug dealers and gangbangers faces very literal enemies. She is trying to protect her young children, and I can think of her and pray with her through those words.[11]

Ooo-Aah

The Psalms, along with other scriptural instruction about prayer such as, most famously, the Lord's Prayer, offer not only vivid words to memorize and adapt as our own prayer vocabulary but also a variety of modes that help us know what kinds of things to say when we pray. These modes are valid both for personal prayer and for prayer in public worship or other communal settings. Doing them well in communal settings helps us do them better in private and vice versa.

The most basic and natural acts of prayer are the same for beginners and for those who have lived long in the presence of God: gratitude and supplication. Or as writer Anne Lamott describes them: "Thank you, thank you, thank you" and "Help me, help me, help me."[12] Self-help gurus of all sorts recommend the practice of gratitude; Christian prayer aims it properly toward God as the source of all good things. In good times gratitude is easy; in extraordinary times it is irresistible. For a gorgeous sunset over the lake, for the birth of a healthy baby, for recovery from illness, for rescue from danger, for accomplishing some goal we've worked for, we naturally want to breathe or cry or sing or shout out our thanks. But the more one practices daily thanksgiving, the more one discovers reasons for gratitude in ordinary things such as sunshine and a comfortable bed—and the more one can find reasons for gladness even in adversity. I've heard the pastor of my home church, Jack, tell of the day his father died. Jack was away at college, far from home, and the college chaplain called him into his office to deliver the shocking news. They prayed together, and the first thing the chaplain said was, "Dear Lord, thank you for airplanes, so that Jack can go home and be near his family now." Airplanes were not the first thing on Jack's mind, but when led to think about it, he realized they were things to be grateful for even in his grief. Giving thanks in all circumstances as a habitual practice, as the author of the New Testament book of 1 Thessalonians recommends (5:16–18), gives God the credit that is rightly God's, but it has further benefits: it helps summon in us a strength to endure and cultivates a spirit of joy.

Branching off from "thank you, thank you" is the mode of prayer that we might call ooo-aah, or praise or adoration. This is slightly different from "thank you" in that thank-you prayer acknowledges what God has done *for me,* whereas adoration simply revels in who

God is—or in creation, apart from my particular enjoyment of it. God *is* gracious, whether or not I feel grace showering on me at the moment. The forests *are* magnificent, whether or not I use them to meet my own recreational needs. So adoration also helps get myself out of the picture for a bit and acknowledge that God is bigger than my particular wants or perceptions. As John Milton put it,

> God doth not need
> Either man's work or his own gifts.[13]

The Lord's Prayer, the primary model for prayer that Jesus offered to his disciples (Matthew 6:9–13; Luke 11:2–4), opens with a request that all people and all creation engage in adoration: "Hallowed be thy name." In the gospel texts, the prayer ends with "deliver us from evil"; but especially in the context of communal worship, Christians have long added a final flourish of adoration: "For thine is the kingdom, the power, and the glory forever" (or some variant on this). Adoration is important because it helps bring to mind the multifaceted nature of God, whereas we so easily emphasize some attributes of God and neglect others according to our prejudices and preoccupations. For instance, when I acknowledge in prayer that God is just, it reminds me that I must not blind myself to the grotesque disparity between my country's wealth and other nations' poverty.

Adoration is a natural act for public worship, where music can buoy the words and help arouse accompanying feelings of awe. In private prayer adoration can be done quite simply by opening a prayer with "God, you are . . ." and filling in the blank. Or by beginning a prayer with a form of address that expresses an attribute, such as "Holy One" or "Redeemer." In fact, beginning a prayer with adoration is an age-old practice in worship services as well as private devotions because it has a calibrating effect on what comes after. Getting straight to whom we are speaking is like addressing a letter properly.

HELP ME!

"Help me, help me, help me" prayer, otherwise known as supplication, comes naturally in a crisis. I've always been taught that no crisis is too small to bring to God in prayer. After all, as the hymn teaches,

What a friend we have in Jesus,
All our sins and griefs to bear!
What a privilege to carry
Everything to God in prayer!
O what peace we often forfeit,
O what needless pain we bear,
All because we do not carry
Everything to God in prayer![14]

I imagine the exclamation points are more than just a convention of the nineteenth century, when this text was composed. They may suggest an insistence aimed at people like me who wonder if God gets bored with my daily blathering about helping me do my job properly, be good to my husband and children, deal with financial worries, and think up some decent idea for my next research project.

I remember during the first several months of Philip's life, when he was waking up several times every night and my mind was utterly numb with exhaustion, I wondered whether it was all right to pray: "Dear God, please make this squalling child fall asleep right now and sleep for the next eight hours. I'd even settle for four hours. How about two?" Even though this method did not produce instant results, I finally took comfort in the understanding that God does not mind this sort of thing. Jesus' models of supplication in the Lord's Prayer— "Give us this day our daily bread" and "Lead us not into temptation, but deliver us from evil"—cover a lot of ground with two very general statements. At the same time, Jesus assured his disciples that the very hairs on their heads were numbered; so we are invited to come to God with all our anxieties, large and small. God is willing to keep track of details.

I have found that among whatever daily concerns I bring to God, I ought also to focus on one request that falls under the heading of spiritual growth. Jesus' recommended prayer "lead us not into temptation" fits into this category. But I might also pray, for example, for wisdom or compassion or courage or a stronger love for God or even to become a better pray-er. Prayed simply and repeatedly over months, one plain request like this can put all other needs in context and—who knows?—even change my soul.

Like "thank you, thank you," "help me, help me" branches out into other modes. In the darkest of circumstances, "help me, help me" can become "why, why, why?" While giving a lecture at the college where I teach, the Holocaust survivor and writer Elie Wiesel scolded his largely Christian audience for not sending our *whys* to God often enough. He pointed to the thread of protest in the Jewish tradition and wondered why Christians seem to mute this mode.[15] I think Wiesel was advocating protest as a way of arousing our sometimes somnolent sense of injustice and of encouraging lament in solidarity with those who suffer. Christians sometimes suspect that protest prayers represent a challenge to God's sovereignty over all things. We are not supposed to ask why but only to bow our heads and say, "God has a reason for this" and "Thy will be done." However appropriate that final submission, there is clearly room for anguished questioning on the way. The Psalms are full of *whys*: "Why do the nations rage?" (2:1); "Why, O Lord, do you stand far off?" (10:1); "How long, O Lord?" (13:1); "Why have you rejected us forever, O God? (74:1); and of course, "My God, my god, why have you forsaken me?" (22:1). At the extremes of our lives, we find in Scripture and tradition an invitation to bring our own anger and suffering, and the anger and suffering of the world, to God. What better thing to do with it? The Christian conviction is that God, in the person of Jesus, has already overcome it.

OOPS

Another branch of "help me, help me" could be described as "oops" or even "arrggh." This is confession—rather like taking out the garbage of the soul. In the Lord's Prayer, this mode is connected with our responsibility to forgive others also: "Forgive us our sins as we forgive those who sin against us." Roman Catholics advocate confessing out loud, to another person who is trained to oversee the process of repentance and forgiveness. This has the advantage of accountability to another person and an actual, audible voice assuring forgiveness. Protestants insist that we ought to go straight to God in the privacy of our rooms. This has the advantage of convenience and utter intimacy. Most branches of the church practice some version of confession in public worship.

These days any sort of confession is better than our natural tendency to avoid facing our own wrongdoing. In the hymns, sermons, poetry, and other literature that previous centuries of Christians left behind, I'm amazed at the preoccupation with sin and repentance. These people seem to have thoroughly explored every difficulty involved in examining one's soul, every feature of that elusive state of true repentance, every nuance of fully accepting forgiveness. It may be possible to obsess about confession; but in some domains of American Christianity these days, we may be emphasizing God's love and acceptance to the neglect of proper housecleaning.

Private confession ideally involves considering the sins of a particular day—how I have hurt others and found excuses to indulge in selfish actions or inactions. Even more important, confession is an ongoing search for where I hide my most cherished sins. It's a matter of facing the truth about ourselves, however uncomfortable or painful. It's impossible to be exhaustive in confession, of course. Fortunately God forgives us for the sins we do not name and haven't even noticed. Still, trying to notice specifics makes it easier for God to work changes in us. It's like teaching a young kid how to tidy up his room. You can't merely say, "Clean this place up!" because the average seven-year-old simply does not see a problem with books sprawling off the bookcase, an unmade bed, Legos spread across the floor like confetti, and dirty white socks strewn on the chair. It all looks perfectly fine to him—cozy and familiar. You have to go step-by-step: "Put the socks in the laundry hamper; put the Legos in the bucket and the bucket in the playroom; tuck the covers under the mattress." You might even introduce the concept of dusting and vacuuming. Eventually, if several miracles occur, he'll not only know how to tidy up, but he might even keep the room clean without your nagging; and he'll realize how much better it is to live in a clean room. That's the miracle that confessional prayer aims for: the possibilities for life that open up when the junk and dirt are out of the way. As the psalmist puts it (51:10, 12 RSV), the aim is for "a pure heart," "a steadfast spirit," "the joy of salvation."

HELP THEM!

Finally "help me, help me, help me" ought regularly to accompany "help her, help him, help them." Praying for others is called intercessory prayer. When doing intercessory prayer in private, one challenge that arises is that of managing a potentially infinite prayer list. I used to pray for my college roommates, but I've long since given up on that. When did they scroll off the list? And on what grounds? Presumably they all still need prayer. And just how dire or severe does the request have to be before it makes it onto my list? Do I pray for the woman who works across campus who was just diagnosed with breast cancer, even though I have never heard of her before? Do I pray for all the missionaries my church supports, or should I just pick one? However the list gets made up, there is another dilemma: how specific to make the request. Should I pray, "O God, please help Mary to find a good apartment this weekend"; or should I pray, "O God, I just lift Mary up. . . . I just lift her up to you"? After all, how do I know what's right for Mary in God's eyes?

I've struggled with both these dilemmas. When I had more opportunity for sustained prayer, I had a pretty long list that included a rotating assortment of family, friends, neighbors, nameless citizens of suffering countries, and so on. There are some pretty good strategies for managing lists like this. One strategy, which I learned as a teenager from a wise older woman who gave a talk on prayer at a youth conference, was a concentric circle plan: begin with yourself; move outward to your family and friends; then to your church, your city, the nation, the world. She also suggested trying it the other way around because, she said, once you've prayed for everyone else, you'll find that your own needs seem very small. For a while after college, when my friends were scattered all over the country, I prayed for them with a mental map of the United States in my mind, moving from one coast to another. Some people suggest alternating groupings throughout the week: pray Monday for family; pray Tuesday for friends; and so on. I know a woman who uses the alphabet to guide her prayer for others when she can't sleep in the middle of the night. With one niece named Amanda and another named Zoe, and with her propensity to fall asleep half way through the alphabet, she has to alternate beginning at one end of the alphabet or the other lest the two girls get unequal treatment.

I've always leaned toward specific requests, simply because they make me think more carefully about a person's needs, which in turn helps me love that person more. Often people ask for specific prayers when they ask you to pray for them. Always I pray with a spoken or understood, "But of course, we could all be very mistaken about this, so please do whatever is best for that person." In fact, Jesus suggested that we begin prayer with a kind of thesis request that puts all other, more specific ones under its sway: "Thy kingdom come, thy will be done, on earth as it is in heaven." That's the big outcome any of our little prayers ought to be promoting.

Lately, because my current prayer conditions necessitate that my prayer lists be short, I have been following the advice of those, like Richard Foster, who suggest that we simply ask God to guide us in who to pray for and how to pray for them. This advice has come as a relief to me because it makes so much more sense than trying to keep some enormous mental database. I find I can manage about six people outside my immediate family on the roster, with a specific request for each. I've also been experimenting with wordless imaging prayer, in which I simply picture that person having already benefited from the answer I'm seeking. So I picture Clara holding a new, healthy baby, just as she and Sam hope for. I like this method, as I don't have to repeat the same words over and over but can rely on the eloquence of a simple image.

I pray for my list more or less daily until I feel guided to move to someone else. For my husband and children too, I've learned to pray one simple thing for months at a time. Of course, I can always add in particular intercessions as they come to me for other people or situations. But by asking for God's guidance, I feel less like a systems administrator and more like a student who's simply been given my prayer homework assignment. All I have to do is fulfill it the best I can.

Some people are especially gifted as intercessors. Among these are older people who have been praying all their lives and people in religious communities like monasteries, many of whose daily routines are ordered precisely to intercede for the world. They are heeding the call to represent the world to God, through Christ. We are all sustained by their prayers, I have no doubt. But I wonder if each of us isn't particularly gifted to intercede for one or more people we know. Augustine's mother prayed for him for decades before his many philosophical quests and spiritual struggles finally culminated in his Christian conversion once and for all. I am sure that my mother's prayers for me have lifted me over many of the hurdles in my life. I'm a little awed by that level of responsibility. For whom might I accept such a burden?

CEASELESS PRAYER

The author of Thessalonians urges his readers to "pray continually" (1 Thessalonians 5:17), a seemingly impossible ideal. Augustine wondered if this means that we are to "ceaselessly bend our knees, to lie prostrate, or to lift up our hands." But he admitted, "I do not believe we can do so all the time." He then offers an alternative understanding of this instruction: "Yet there is another, interior kind of prayer without ceasing, namely, the desire of the heart. Whatever else you may be doing, if you but fix your desire on God's Sabbath rest, your prayer will be ceaseless. Therefore if you wish to pray without ceasing, do not cease to desire."[16] Could it be that my clamoring desire is somehow spiritually useful? What a relief. We do not always need to be chattering away at God or even every moment in a posture of attentive listening. We go about our daily business: we dress the children, make the coffee, teach, go to meetings, talk to customers, and do the grocery shopping. But beneath that daily business, if there remains a kind of musical bass line of desire, the pulse of longing for the peace of God's presence, then that becomes a ceaseless prayer. Above that we add, like harmonies and melodies, practices of mind and tongue and body that we more commonly label prayer. They respond to and are ordered by that pulse of desire, and more and more they help us to be conscious of the presence we hear in it.

I know from experience that there are places of grief and desperation when even that heartbeat of desire seems to go silent, when it is beyond our strength to form even a shadow of a prayer. At those times we depend on the prayers of others and on the knowledge that prayer "does not depend on us." Here I turn to that passage from Romans 8 so necessary whenever I think about prayer: "In the same way, the Spirit helps us in our weakness. We do not know what we ought to pray, but the Spirit himself intercedes for us with groans that words cannot express" (verse 26). When we pray, and also when we do not pray, we are surrounded by the prayers of others and sustained by the Spirit.

In fact, we are surrounded by the prayer of creation itself. That heartbeat of desire to be drawn into the heart of God rises wordlessly from the colors, sounds, and structures of creation. The psalmist writes that

the heavens declare the glory of God;
the skies proclaim the work of his hands. [19:1]

Paul adds that the creation "groans as in the pains of childbirth," awaiting freedom from its "bondage to decay" (Romans 8:22, 21). The pulse of that praise and longing sets our tempo.

Even when we cannot pray, the creation itself cries out to God. The wild irises bloom, the waves crash, the trees wave their branches, humpback whales set their tails toward the sky and sing.

CHAPTER SEVEN

WORDS OF LIFE
The Bible

I HAVE HIDDEN YOUR WORD IN MY HEART.
—Psalm 119:11

At my high school, seniors customarily spent Memorial Day weekend camping at a state park on a Lake Michigan beach. For a Christian high school, this was a carnivalesque occasion—a bunch of more or less decently behaved, churchgoing young people engaging in an unauthorized, illegal, surreptitiously alcohol-soaked bacchanalia. Of course, younger students, if they could possibly swing it, arranged to be there too to observe in amazement and maybe even participate. When I was but a tender tenth grader, my girlfriends and I, by swearing to be very good girls, which we sincerely intended to be, managed to convince our parents to let us take a pop-up camper out to the beach. Meanwhile, there was a certain fifteen-year-old, cello-playing boy who sat next to me in high school orchestra and who was handsome and funny and mischievous; it was pretty clear to both of us that we were starting to like each other. I mean, really *like* each other. So as I packed my duffel bag, the big question on my mind was: Would we see each other at the beach?

Are you kidding? Next thing I knew, there I was alone with him on a starry spring night, sitting beside him on his corduroy jacket beneath a giant beech tree. I don't remember exactly what happened, but somewhere in the maelstrom of my fifteen-year-old feelings, a thought occurred to me: *If I kiss him now, then he's my boyfriend. Is that going to be OK with God?* I remember somehow excusing myself from the situation, trotting back to the camper and—yes, it's true—opening my Bible. It's a mark of my youthful piety that I even took my Bible along that weekend. But just what kind of guidance for the occasion was I expecting to find by opening the Bible at random as if it were a Ouija board or something? I could have landed on "Do not be mismated with unbelievers" (2 Corinthians 6:14 RSV) and left the poor kid in the lurch that night on the premise that he was not religious enough for me. Or I might have landed on "I arose to open to my beloved, and my hands dripped with myrrh, my fingers with liquid myrrh, upon the handles of the bolt" (Song of Solomon 5:5 RSV), and then, well, God only knows what might have happened. If I had known the Bible better, I could have rigged it to get just the guidance I wanted. On this occasion, whatever passage I actually turned to was no help at all. I guess God, no doubt thoroughly amused, let me make up my own mind. I went back out there and kissed the boy.

Eventually I figured out that seeking God's will is more a matter of daily prayer than consulting an oracle in an emergency. But my teenage silliness demonstrates that when Christians say the Bible is a guide for life, they are making it sound a lot simpler than it really is. The Bible is not a rule book or a self-help manual or a crystal ball. Protestants especially like to think that we must simply obey the plain meaning of the Word of God, a sentiment that echoes good Reformation sensibilities. When Martin Luther launched his protests against the Roman Catholic church in 1517, he soon after translated the Bible from Latin into ordinary German and, with the help of the printing press, put it, for the first time, in the hands of anyone who could read. In response to a horrified Roman Catholic authority structure, who argued (with good reason) that the people had no idea how to understand the Bible, Luther countered by claiming that the Bible is quite clear enough for any reasonable person to figure out, provided the person follows a few basic rules. Frankly I think Luther was exaggerating. The avalanche of scholarly commentaries, marginal notes, devotional guides, and sermons that appeared in the first decades of the Reformation suggests that the Reformers didn't trust the laity quite as much as they sometimes claimed. They all knew that reading the Bible well requires plenty of expert guidance.

The description of the Bible as a guidebook for life also fails to convey the richness of experiencing the Bible as a living text. I was taught as a child that the Bible is part of God's special revelation. The beauties and patterns of the natural world, along with anything we can come up with by employing observation and reason—all that is general revelation. God is evident in these things, but such knowledge is not enough to understand sin and the ways that God rescues us from it. Jesus himself and the Bible that points to Jesus are God's special effort to reveal himself to us. Because the parents and teachers and pastors who raised me believed this saving knowledge to be so necessary and so wonderful, they made sure I and all my little peers knew the Bible well. As a small child, I sang Bible songs about building one's house on a rock and made little craft projects involving sheep or arks or a young boy with a slingshot. Through years of sermons and Bible classes, I learned that the Bible records God's glorious redemptive plan unfolding throughout history like an enormous tapestry. I memorized many psalms, countless single verses, and even at one point the names of the kings of ancient Judah and Israel. I heard the Bible read aloud at church, school, and home. I have read it privately for comfort and guidance since my teenage years. I studied the Bible as literature in college and graduate school. I overheard my husband studying Greek and Hebrew in seminary and still help him wrestle with passages as he prepares to preach. My whole life has been drenched with the words of this text.

Still I can't get enough. More important than anything I was ever taught *about* the Bible, I was taught to *love* the Bible. I think any attempt to respond to the Bible as a sacred text must begin there. The Bible can be a weapon, a wedge of division, a fetish, a great source of confusion. It will be a living word only if we read it with love.

Sinking In

Christians believe that the Bible is divine revelation. It is not merely produced by human beings but given to human beings by God. We express our reverence for this by weaving the Bible's words throughout our religious practices: in meditating privately on the Bible's words, reading or reciting them publicly, responding artistically to them, setting them to music, and so on. These practices reflect a belief that a foundational quality of this sacred text is that it generates meaning in ways other texts, however lovely, do not. This is the work, Christians say, of the third person of the Trinity, the Holy Spirit, who works in a mystical way to bring a message from God.

For me the Bible has certainly been the sourcebook of authoritative teaching about the Christian faith. That the Bible should instruct is to be expected. But more wonderful, in my experience, is its generative power. Considering all the biblical words I might run into in a given week, it's fascinating to me how certain ones will stick with me for a while, sink in, and speak. It's a little like how a song or an advertising jingle gets stuck in your head—only spiritually helpful rather than annoying. Or like putting up little sayings on a bulletin board or refrigerator so that your eye runs across them often—except that I'm not always doing the choosing. For instance, for some reason, Proverbs 16:9 stuck with me throughout my teenage years: "A man's mind plans his way, but the LORD directs his steps."[1] These words, which I transposed to "a young woman's mind" and "directs her steps," helped me understand that while I went about setting goals and making decisions, God was still directing the currents of my life. This was true even when I got around to wondering about God's approval only *after* figuring out what *I* wanted. This verse and others like it kept me humble about mapping out my future—reminding me that I may think I've weighed all the options and made smart choices, but I can't see the whole picture as God does. As the saying goes, "If you want to make God laugh, tell him your plans." Coming round and round again to me, these words assured me that even awkward moments with a boy at the beach wouldn't result in irreparable mistakes, and meanwhile it might be a good idea to get myself in tune with God's direction on a regular basis.

In late high school or college, I memorized Romans 8, that great meditation by the apostle Paul on salvation, suffering, and ultimate things. At a time when I was beginning to ask the big questions about the world, this passage settled into my mind several beautiful and concise phrases encapsulating the basics of the faith. As is apparent from my use of this passage in other chapters, I have carried the jewels of this treasure box with me ever since; and I take them out whenever I need them:

> There is now no condemnation for those who are in Christ Jesus. [8:1 RSV]

> I consider that the sufferings of this present time are not worth comparing with the glory that is to be revealed to us. [8:18 RSV]

> The Spirit intercedes for us with sighs too deep for words. [8:26 RSV]

Whenever I wonder about God's plan for my life, these words, loved by so many, place my little troubles in the perspective of the expansive hope of the Christian faith: "We know that in everything God works for good with those who love him, who are called according to his purpose" (8:28 RSV). All this in a single chapter—quite amazing. Although Paul's writings can sometimes be crabbed and convoluted, he will at other times build long, magnificent crescendos of utter beauty. Passages like these from throughout the Bible first awakened my love for words and my sense of their potential effect. God can use humble or beautiful words to reveal, but the beautiful ones seem to have a special deftness in sculpting the soul.

The story arcs, characters, and symbolic materials of biblical narratives have shaped my imagination from my preschool days; and they continue to yield new meanings. Only as an adult did I begin to connect deeply with the patriarch Jacob (Genesis 25–35), for instance. Here's a fellow who knows God has promised that his grandfather Abraham will become a "great nation" through his descendants. But Jacob is not content to sit around and wait for God to make this happen. He's even willing to use a little deception to get in on this plan, to make sure God delivers the goods. He conspires with his mother to fool his blind old father and gain the blessing that rightfully belongs to his older brother. After fleeing his angry brother, he goes to work for his uncle, a shifty fellow who is almost Jacob's match but not quite. Jacob practices clever animal husbandry so that the portion of the sheep and goats his Uncle Laban has promised him suddenly starts multiplying like crazy. Jacob is a go-getter: impatient, ambitious, not terribly trusting. He's the one who, in the famous story, wrestles with God through the night and comes out of it with a wound and a new name—Israel, which means "struggles with God." My husband, Ron, and I both see ourselves in this figure. We're not engaged in shady business deals or deceptions, but we do connect with Jacob's restlessness and his difficulty waiting for God's purposes to work themselves out. At the same time, we see how God loves Jacob, holds on to him even when Jacob seems resistant, and uses even Jacob's less lovely qualities to effect a larger purpose. This gives us assurance that God loves and gathers into his purposes people like ourselves.

Sometimes a particular text, in some new circumstance, will jump from dormancy into life. I had heard many sermons on Romans

12, for instance, a passage that always strikes me as an odd grab bag of advice. But the first verse, "Therefore, I urge you, . . . in view of God's mercy, to offer your bodies as living sacrifices, holy and pleasing to God" became a living text to me when I became a mother. Pregnancy, birth, and nursing—what was all this if not offering my body as a living sacrifice to my children, to the future of humanity, in the context of a life lived for God? That's not what Paul originally meant by this passage, I'm quite sure. But that too is part of the Bible's generativity. A text can have layers of meaning, some layers always in operation, some only alive for certain people in a particular circumstance.

The Bible also acts as a living text by pulling and straining against my present mood or situation. One of my most powerful experiences of this was when I was suffering from depression after the birth of my third child. One night, at a point when I felt most bewildered and helpless, I happened upon Psalm 30. I found exact descriptions of where I was, scrambling on a steep downward slope with a mix of anger and desperation and wondering why God wasn't helping me out:

> To you, O Lord, I called;
> to the Lord I cried for mercy:
> What gain is there in my destruction,
> in my going down into the pit? [verses 8–9]

But as so often happens in the Psalms, these words of despair are followed closely with confident praise:

> You turned my wailing into dancing;
> you removed my sackcloth and clothed me with joy,
> that my heart may sing to you and not be silent.
> O Lord my God, I will give you thanks forever. [verses 11–12]

As I traced the psalmist's move from despair to joy in this psalm, the words became a hand of rescue to me. Even though I did not get better that very minute, I remember that night as a turning point. The psalm said to me that I had not been forgotten, that God was present in this suffering. Those words began to pull me out.

Hundreds of texts have knit themselves to certain experiences in my life and left their mark forever. These words are, as the psalmist says, "hidden in my heart" (Psalm 119:11). It's difficult to describe how this works. Perhaps it's similar to any body of knowledge that one carries around in one's head. The difference is that, in some odd way, the right words come to me, apparently by the Spirit's prompting, when I need them. Studying the Bible is really a way of stocking up on those words, giving the Spirit a bigger repertoire to work with in speaking to you—more Post-its on the bulletin board.

INS AND OUTS

No one taught me the term *generative* as I was growing up, although the ways in which I saw people using the Bible certainly demonstrated that it had that quality. The word my Christian enclave usually used to describe the Bible was *authoritative*. Both words suggest that one ought to approach the Bible with trust and respect. Come to the Bible with a skeptical eye, and you may well be horrified, especially if you start on page one.

English writer and editor J. R. Ackerley wrote: "I am halfway through Genesis, and quite appalled by the disgraceful behavior of all the characters involved, including God."[2] The Old Testament presents page after page of stories about a wrathful God, as well as sordid tales of incest and rape, supposedly righteous heroes engaging in unsavory episodes of adultery or deceit, some frankly sexual poetry, and decidedly R-rated (for violence) prophetic visions of vengeance against God's enemies. And then in the New Testament, Jesus himself pronounces numerous enigmatically hard sayings; Paul makes blatantly sexist statements; and the book of Revelation—yikes. "Get the bandage of reverence from your eyes," said nineteenth-century politician and agnostic Robert G. Ingersoll, "then read the Holy Bible, and you will be amazed that you ever, for one moment, supposed a being of infinite wisdom, goodness and purity, to be the author of such ignorance and of such atrocity."[3] Even Augustine was dismayed when he first read the Bible. In comparison with the beauties of the classical Greek and Latin poetry and rhetoric in which he was educated, the Bible seemed plain and crude.[4]

Blistering scorn for the Bible is something of a minority opinion. Most people acknowledge that the Bible is fascinating, in places supremely beautiful; that it contains some excellent moral teaching and outstanding poetry; and that at the very least, it is the source of some unforgettably good stories. But the Word of God? The less savory passages and inner conflicts of the Bible make that a much more troubling idea. Christians throughout the centuries have had to reconcile their experiences of the Bible as a living text with the various problems they and others notice. Thus, different groups of Christians have developed terms to describe exactly how they believe the Bible is the Word of God. Different opinions on the matter are represented with the three *in*s: inspired, infallible, and inerrant.

The centrist view is that the Bible is inspired. Other religious faiths also claim that their special texts are inspired, but not everyone means the same thing by that word. Christians derive their views of inspiration from Jewish views, and both groups hold the books of the Hebrew Bible or Old Testament sacred. Christians apply views of inspiration to the New Testament as well. For Christians especially, inspiration is an idea with a great deal of tolerance for the messiness involved when the divine attempts to communicate in human forms. A general explanation might go like this: God specially inspired certain ancient authors to write some things down (word for word? Christians differ on that one), but these people were all deeply imbedded in their particular times and places, in their cultural understanding and their literary style. This shows. Nevertheless, God worked through this process to get some key messages across. Moreover, God worked through the layers of editing that occurred over centuries, through the process of sorting manuscripts and bringing various texts together into the canon of texts that became the Bible. Even today—and now things are getting very messy—the Holy Spirit works through the process of translation and interpretation. So the Bible is the Word of God in French and Swahili as well as Hebrew and Greek. The concept of inspiration for Christians, then, means that the Holy Spirit is active not just at the launch of the sacred text but at every step of a very human, culturally imbedded process, right down to the reading of Philippians 2 in your very own bedroom. The word *inspiration* means "God-breathed," not as a single, originating exhalation but as a pattern of respirations.

Some Christians further explain that the Bible is infallible or even inerrant. These are beliefs meant to assure readers of the Bible's authority despite the messiness of the inspiration process. *Infallible* means that the Bible is reliable and without error in all that it intends to teach. This idea runs defense for the Bible in a way by suggesting that if people get crazy ideas from the Bible, it's not the Bible's fault— they're reading it wrong. They may be attempting to derive information from the Bible on matters it does not intend to teach at all (the classic example is the precise process, scientifically speaking, by which God created the world). Or they may simply be misinterpreting a passage. Infallibility acknowledges that one can misuse the Bible; it retains the belief that some meanings are anchored in God's intentions for the text, whereas others are not.

Those who believe the Bible is inerrant are even more uncomfortable with the messiness. They claim that the Bible is completely without error in everything that it says, including numbers, measurements, and other matters of empirical observation. This idea has become very important for that subgroup of Christians termed fundamentalist, those who derive their beliefs and sensibilities from an early twentieth-century American movement founded to defend the faith against the challenges of the modern world, particularly the claims and methods of science. Inerrancy causes immediate trouble, in that ancient manuscripts of the Bible differ in many small ways, so that those who hold this view are compelled to claim that only the original manuscripts (which no longer exist, as far as anyone knows) are the only completely error-free documents. Another problem with inerrancy is that the Bible often reflects ancient-world views of what is factual and real, truthful and correct. Modern ideas about scientific fact and historical accuracy were not available to ancient writers, so it's awkward to apply those standards to ancient texts rather than understand them on their own terms.

Many people are attracted to Islam partly because the Koran's claim to authority is uncomplicated by any of the Bible's messiness. Muslims believe that the Koran was dictated directly by an angel of God to Mohammed, word for word. This makes the Koran the simplest sacred text to explain: it is holy in only one version, in the original language (Arabic); and its authority is absolutely direct from God in every word. Such views tend to give people confidence in a text's authority.

But I find that level of inerrancy neither necessary nor defensible. So although I sympathize with the need for a totally reliable holy text, I can't share the inerrantist view. My confidence in the Bible's authority does not depend on whether or not Noah actually lived precisely 950 years or whether Jesus fasted in the desert for precisely forty days. My confidence is not particularly shaken when archaeologists dig up Nineveh and discover that never in its history was it anywhere close to as large in circumference as the book of Jonah claims. (I'm quite happy to attribute this to literary exaggeration in the context of this book's frequent, subtle humor.) Inerrancy does not solve the problem of conflicting interpretations either, as demonstrated by debates about major issues among different branches of Islam. So I'll remain satisfied with the word *infallible* if I can take it to mean that the Bible is authoritative and trustworthy and that it offers everything we need to know *about God* if we read carefully and seek the Spirit's continued guidance. I hesitate to use the phrase "without error" at all when describing the Bible's qualities, most pointedly because people use the Bible erroneously all the time. So to my dynamic view of inspiration, I would add that the Spirit will repair or salvage our monstrous mistakes in reading the Bible—eventually. How long has the Bible been used to defend the oppression of women, with all the weight of church authority behind it? Too long. Yet the Spirit continues to work, through texts in the Bible that compel against oppression, through dissenting readers within the church, and even through pressures from the world. The Word of God is infallible, but we readers are certainly not.

I like to think of biblical inspiration as analogous to talent. When we say that a certain person has musical talent, it sounds as if we mean that the person carries around this mysterious commodity, talent, and she can dispense some of it whenever she gets near, say, a piano. But that's not how it works and certainly not how it feels to her. A pianist, for instance, is more likely to explain that music is something that flows through her when she plays. Whatever talent is, she does not "have" it. In fact, if she is a humble person who does not take her talent for granted, she may wonder every time she sits down at the keyboard what will happen next, especially if she is an improviser such as a jazz musician. No matter how many performances she has given, how many awards she has won, a little voice inside her may whisper, "Well, tonight could be the time nothing happens." What we call talent is more like a consistent, frequent phenomenon, a series of events in time rather than a commodity. Almost always, when our pianist sits down to practice or perform, something beautiful happens. Without taking her talent for granted, she may still learn to trust it, even to shape her whole life's work around it.

I think of the inspiration of Scripture in a similar way. The Bible does not contain some magical dust that makes people glow when they open it. It may fail to impress and may even offend. However, God has chosen to work through the Bible frequently and consistently across the centuries, to reveal, comfort, inspire, challenge, convict, and otherwise profoundly influence its readers.

It's a tool of God. We honor it and love it but only as a tool. Making it any more of a fetish would be turning the Bible into an idol. As we have already seen, in the opening of the Gospel of John, the gospel writer intentionally parallels the opening words of Genesis to begin his meditation on the life of Jesus:

In the beginning was the Word,
and the Word was with God,
and the Word was God. [1:1]

John is not talking about a text but a person. Jesus is the Word of God. The Bible is the main witness to that living Word, and a living text only as it testifies to him.

The Mess

If revealing God's plan of salvation for the world, most especially in the person of Jesus, is the main purpose of the Christian Bible, why does it include all the seemingly excess stuff about every last king of Judah, obscure prophets ranting about obscure political situations, and more details about the practice of circumcision in the early church than we really care to know? Doesn't this simply make matters more confusing? Sure. Bible readers have to love a challenge.

Actually the Bible's complexity and apparent excess offers some important advantages. For one thing it's always a good idea to face the present with plenty of knowledge about the past. The Bible records how people understood God working in the world over the course of about fifteen hundred years. It builds the history of God's interaction with humankind in layers, demonstrating how promises God makes way back in Genesis get fulfilled over and over again, how the story of ancient Israel serves as both historical preparation for and typological foreshadowing of God's rescue of all God's people in Jesus' life, death, and resurrection. (This is a Christian interpretation, obviously, and not how Jews regard the story of Israel.)

Along the way we get thick description. The books of Chronicles and Acts, for example, are steeped in the particularity of their time and place. From this we see that God works through particularities of time and place, and from that it may dawn on us that God is working in our own time and place. We can learn from how God acted in the lives of others and how they have understood that action. We can observe, for example, that God can be friends with some deeply flawed people. The Bible is full of disgraceful behavior because the writers of these ancient texts let the disgrace show, even in the big hero figures. Rebecca? Clever but deceptive. (Where do you think her son Jacob got it?) King David? Shrewd politician, lustful and proud. The disciple Peter? Hotheaded and often clueless. Paul? Smart but difficult to get along with. This is good news for us. It means that God can make friends with us too. If the Bible were a volume of saints' lives detailing nothing but exemplary behavior, I wouldn't trust it. It would be intimidating, not encouraging. The disgraces in the Bible drag us toward the realization that we need grace.

Even acknowledging that there is plenty of honesty about human wickedness recorded in the Bible, other passages are much harder to ignore or explain away. What on earth do we do with the book of Joshua, for instance, in which the people of God slash and burn their way through Canaan with God apparently looking on in approval, even commanding the slaughter of entire cities? Ron recalls many occasions on which his father, a down-to-earth man with very little patience for pretense or meanness, would read such passages and declare, right there at the dinner table, "That's a *mistake* in the Bible. Those Israelites thought they heard God telling them to do that, but they heard wrong!"

Not exactly an orthodox attitude, but we enlightened moderns are not the only ones to have been horrified by these old stories. Among the early church fathers, a strong current of biblical interpretation considered these texts spiritually useful when taken allegorically: they presented compelling pictures of how God leads us out of captivity to sin and how we must eradicate sin and allow Jesus to conquer our inner pagan lands.[5] Other interpreters estimate that what we read in those bloody Old Testament episodes is how people in that time understood God's direction. The ancient world was a rough place, and God had to work with the cultural material at hand. At any rate, Ron says that his father's evident love for God combined with those occasional out-bursts about the Bible prepared him to face life at Princeton Seminary. There the practice of historical criticism—an often skeptical study of the history of the biblical texts—had a way of deflating students' con-fidence in the Bible's authority and even shaking their faith. But Ron had already made peace with the fact that the Bible is a book colored by its authors' human limitations, and thanks to many good examples of its use, had kept his confidence that the Spirit uses the mess even so.

Augustine made his peace with the Bible's rougher spots, too, and eventually began to enjoy the challenge. He summed it up this way: "Accordingly the Holy Spirit has, with admirable wisdom and care for our welfare, so arranged the Holy Scriptures as by the plainer passages to satisfy our hunger, and by the more obscure to stimulate our appetite."[6]

PLAIN MEANING

The Bible is a fascinating window into cultural systems of the past and an account of how God's plan for salvation has unfolded through history. But that's only part of what makes it a living text. If the Spirit continues to breathe through this book, then it can mean something for us right now as believers in this age, even on an individual level. God speaks to *you* in this book.

Well, what is God saying? How does the Bible help us figure out how to live here and now? It would be nice if we could open the Bible, read the instructions there, and then simply obey them, like choosing from a stack of cards in a board game. But it's important to admit openly that deriving guidance from the Bible is not always a transparent process. For instance, let's say I turn to 1 Timothy (2:9–10) and read: "I also want women to dress modestly, with decency and propriety, not with braided hair or gold or pearls or expensive clothes but with good deeds, appropriate for women who profess to worship God." Dressing modestly sounds like the sort of good advice God might give through the ages; but how literally do I take the business about braids, gold, or pearls? Should I take off my gold wedding band? Would silver be OK? I don't wear expensive clothes (by American standards anyway), but it seems I had better turn in my bikini. And who is the "I" anyway? This is supposed to be a letter from Paul to Timothy, but do I transpose this into the voice of God? The next verses pose a much tougher problem: "A woman should learn in quietness and full submission. I do not permit a woman to teach or to have authority over a man; she must be silent." Some groups of Christians, for the sake of obeying this verse in the Word of God, do not permit women to teach Sunday school except to groups of other women. (Interestingly some of these same groups do permit gold jewelry and pearls.) But the college where I teach, which also officially claims the Bible as the Word of God, blithely employs female professors to teach both young men and women, even in the religion and theology department. And believe me, our young women students, many of them serious Bible readers, do not typically learn in quietness or full submission.

Obviously one problem with obeying God's Word is that people disagree very seriously on what parts of the Bible constitute direct commands, either to everyone or to particular groups. The other problem is that we are often faced with specific dilemmas about which the Bible says nothing. I read a story recently on a Web site for Christian mothers written by a woman who did not know what to think about birth control. She had heard that one ought to trust God and let him be in control of one's fertility. She and her husband asked pastors and a Christian doctor what the Bible said about this, and each of these authority figures, without quoting the Bible, assured the woman and her husband that it was permissible for a married couple to use birth control. The couple remained unsure, however. After three children, difficult births, and several health problems (including postpartum depression), she and her husband overcame their misgivings and he had a vasectomy. Later, their persistent guilt led them to a book that claimed the Bible has plenty to say about the sinfulness of conception control, and after reading this book they decided to have the vasectomy reversed. Three more children came along and the woman, now a happy mother of six, believes God rewarded her for her obedience. Is she right in her conviction that she and her husband had sinned by using birth control? If I think using birth control within marriage is acceptable as a way of being a good steward of my fertility (not to mention my other gifts), have I simply not read my Bible well enough? Speaking of control, what does the Bible say about insurance? If I buy auto or home insurance, am I not allowing God to be in control?

Deriving guidance from the Bible needs to be done with a broad view. As I try to explain to my literature students, we all have a literary theory. Whether we are conscious of our methods or simply assume that our way is the only possible way, we all come to any text with notions of how properly to interpret it. This is especially true of the Bible, and the stakes are especially high. It's a matter of simple honesty to acknowledge that we who claim to live by the Word of God are always weighing some passages against others and considering whether a particular word of instruction has eternal relevance or was meant only for a particular time and place. Even the most strident advocate of biblical obedience, for instance, will admit that if his skin breaks out in boils, he ought to go to a dermatologist to be examined and not, as the book of Leviticus commands in chapter 13, to the high priest. The passage from Timothy about women's silence is more controversial. Some hold to it as an eternal principle, but many of the major Christian denominations have decided that it was an instruction meant only for a particular situation. They weigh other texts against it, noting the countercultural honor with which Jesus treated women, accounts in other New Testament texts of women leading house churches with Paul's evident approval, and Paul's statement elsewhere that among Christians old divisions and hierarchies ought to dissolve: "For all of you who were baptized into Christ have clothed yourselves with Christ. There is neither Jew nor Greek, slave nor free, male nor female, for you are all one in Christ Jesus" (Galatians 3:28). Besides bringing one text to bear on another, we also have to bring our own reason and observations to a text. In the case of the Timothy text, we might observe that women frequently exhibit splendid gifts of teaching and preaching. Does it seem right to shut them down on the basis of two verses? What about long passages in Corinthians encouraging all Christians to encourage one another in using their spiritual gifts faithfully?

Perhaps you have seen the worst kind of biblical authority-wielding, a little game Ron likes to call "proof-text poker." Let's say two fellows are discussing what constitutes proper Sunday observance. Is it all right to mow the lawn on Sunday, or is that work and therefore forbidden?

Player 1:	I've got two verses from Deuteronomy that say anyone who fails to observe the Sabbath ought to be killed.
Player 2:	Yeah? Well, I'll see your verses from Deuteronomy and raise you a verse from Jesus himself that says the Sabbath was made for man, not man for the Sabbath.
Player 3:	Yeah? Well, I've got one of the Ten Commandments that clearly says "Honor the Sabbath day to keep it holy."
Player 4 (wife of Player 1):	Fine, but you all like to eat a nice dinner on Sundays and you don't object when your wives do all *that* work. How about if *you* make the gravy and *I'll* mow the lawn?

In this game the words of Jesus himself are always an ace and quotations from Paul the face cards. However, three of a kind from the Old Testament can beat a pair from Revelation. Yes, we weigh some parts of the Bible more heavily than others. But proof-text poker becomes a parody of this, taking single verses out of context and cleverly maneuvering to prove as God's holy word anything you please to prove.

Judaism openly espouses a kind of concentric-circle view of authority: the Ten Commandments at the very center, then the mitzvoth (the rest of the ancient code of Jewish law), then the whole Torah (all of Genesis through Deuteronomy), then the books of the prophets, then the Writings (Chronicles, Psalms, Proverbs, and so on), then the Talmud (commentary from early centuries), then Midrash (more commentary) on the Talmud. The authority of any text is weighed by its proximity to the center. The orthodox Christian view makes no official distinctions: the entire Bible is inspired, period. But in practice some texts do operate more centrally. The repeated refrain, for instance, "The Lord is compassionate and gracious, slow to anger, abounding in love" (Psalm 103:8 for example), occurs so often throughout the

Bible that it outweighs any conclusion about God's nature one might derive from reading three grim chapters about the Israelites' conquest of Canaan as described in Joshua. The Bible interprets itself, even dissents from itself. Ecclesiastes, the classic text of dissent, challenges all the earnest proclamations of truth elsewhere with the refrain "All is vanity" (1:2) and a poetic resignation about the futility of trying to find meaning in life. The Gospels are another example: rather than a single account of Jesus' life and death, there are four accounts, each with different preoccupations, purposes, and points of view.

Those who first gathered the canonical books were wise not to winnow out too much for the sake of a perfectly unified presentation. As a result the Bible has the depth and complexity to keep serving as a conduit of God's guidance, as long as we don't expect to read it as if it were a copy of *Life for Dummies* or a technical manual. It's fine to admit that we cannot go to the index and look up direct, made-to-order answers about abortion, genetic engineering, war, homosexuality, or other of the most trying questions of our age. God expects us to exercise some responsibility and figure it out. To that end a long and distinguished tradition of study and interpretation offers broad principles to which we can continue to return: the sanctity of life, the justice and mercy of God, the saving grace of Jesus, the healing peace of the coming kingdom.

I do believe we have to keep putting the whole Bible in front of us as a Christian community. We might keep certain texts in the high-access file cabinet and others in the storage room or odds-and-ends drawer, but it is important not to throw any out. If we believe the Spirit was working in the process of gathering these texts together and continues to inspire Scripture, we have to trust that even something in the book of Judges, with its bloodshed and impiety, could have a word for us (perhaps how *not* to approach interethnic relations?). And we should have the generosity to allow that a text that seems offensive or simply dead to us may speak a powerful word to some other group of Christians. The book of Revelation, for example, may make you want to run and hide. But what about people in the midst of a modern-day apocalypse, amid ethnic cleansing in the Balkans, for example? The instructions to the first-century churches that begin the book of Revelation, picturing for them a Christ who sees their suffering as well as their shortcomings and who encourages them to endure humbly in the faith despite the collapse of the sky itself—this may be exactly the word of hope needed for some Christians today.

READING IN COMMUNITY

When different groups among the larger body of Christians argue with one another, outsiders may mock and insiders may nearly go mad with frustration. But such disputes actually prove the importance of reading in community with others. In considering how to apply the broad themes and specific passages of the Bible to the great questions of our day, different groups put pressure on one another and challenge one another's blind spots. The liberation theologians of Latin America, for instance, put pressure on the establishment churches of North America, highlighting Jesus' radical words of liberation for the poor—sharp words that comfortable rich folk have always tended to soften. In the variety of interpretations applied to a given question, we know there are bound to be mistakes, ranging from the small to the outrageous, so at least we're on the lookout. The lively cacophony of dissent keeps everyone on their toes, from the most prestigious scholar to the most ordinary pew-sitter.

Christians may have major arguments, but a sacred text does give us something we agree on as a common ground, something from which to argue. We return and return to the text, testing and considering, looking for how Christians before us have interpreted and seeking how it speaks to us today. One thing postmodern literary criticism has forced us to face, kicking and screaming, is that multiple interpretations are inevitable. In the end that's a strength. Anything existing in the medium of language has a certain flexibility by virtue of its medium. As a collection of writings in numerous genres produced over the course of fifteen hundred years, the Bible is an especially complicated, intricate fabric of symbol and story. We should expect it, then, to yield a plenitude of meaning; that's what keeps it fresh and relevant over the centuries. Certainly there are wrong interpretations. It's not as if anything goes. But we can trust that when we read it faithfully and well, always seeking the Spirit's guidance, God will not only help us find the right way (or *ways*) but also have mercy on our errors.

READING US

Making a space for faithful reading to happen, both privately and within larger subgroups of the church, mostly depends on ample exposure to the text combined with the right intentions. Any text will yield different results depending on a reader's intention. Go to a text looking for support for a particular political agenda, and you will probably find it. This kind of interested reading is all the rage in literary studies: the rule is that the critic must be conscious of his or her agenda, announce it, and then go ahead and whittle away at *Moby Dick* or *The Taming of the Shrew*. As long as you plainly announce that you are on the hunt for how gender is phallologocentrically constructed in the text—or whatever—you can proceed. This consciousness is certainly healthy, but the best literary critics still understand that the whole enterprise is rather pointless unless you leave some room for the text to resist your agenda, unless you are willing to admit that the text might contradict rather than support the framework you bring to it.

When reading the Bible, this kind of readerly yielding is crucial. When we insist on having power over this text, it will become opaque. If we go to the text looking to prove that Christians should not drink alcohol, for instance, we will see only certain verses and ignore others. We will perceive a surface facet we wish to see, while other dimensions will become hidden to us. On the other hand, when we come to the Bible with openness, allowing the Bible to have power over us, to read *us,* then it can be transparent to the presence of God. So we must expect to meet the living God in the text and signal that expectation through prayer, approaching the text with the agenda of love for God and neighbor.

The psalmists often praise the Word of God as a lamp, a light, a food sweeter than honey, a treasure more precious than gold. Christians take these images to refer appropriately to the whole of Scriptures, and they aptly describe how the Bible's words can bring peace, comfort, and guidance. But the Word of God can sometimes be a sword. Paul writes that Christians ought to carry with them the "sword of the Spirit, which is the word of God," and the author of the New Testament book of Hebrews writes: "The word of God is living and active. Sharper than any double-edged sword, it penetrates even to dividing soul and spirit, joints and marrow; it judges the thoughts and attitudes of the heart" (Hebrews 4:12). The Bible can point and cut as well as feed. Jesus' warning, "Do not judge, or you too will be judged" (Matthew 7:1), for instance, can stop one's mouth in the middle of a sentence. Or how about "There is a way that seems right to a man, but in the end it leads to death" (Proverbs 16:25)? That tends to put the damper on little rationalizing thoughts such as "But it feels so right!"

I experience the Bible as a disruptive presence most often when helping Ron prepare to preach. During the week before he preaches, it seems as if his text moves right into the house and takes over. I wrote a poem once to describe this phenomenon, personifying the text as a somewhat self-satisfied intruder.

LECTIONARY TEXT
Once you invite me in, beware:
I toss you from your favorite chair,
I snip the daily news to shreds
And interrupt you in your bed.

By week's end you wish me away—
I drag around your thoughts all day.
You wrestle me down, chop and twist,
But I, with ancient art, resist.

Come Sunday, sweet as Spirit's dew
I gentle fall on folks, through you.
A maddening mystery? Thus your part
To sink a word into a heart.

After Ron has preached the sermon, we manage to tidy up the household, as it were; but whenever I meet that text again, I tend to greet it like an old friend with whom I've recently had a few arguments.

STUDYING AND CHEWING

Christian practice has always encouraged encountering the text in both communal and private settings. I recently had the opportunity, with a group of students, to have a conversation with N. T. Wright, formerly a theologian in residence at Westminster Abbey in London,

now bishop of Durham. In registering his love for the Anglican practice of daily matins and evensong, the morning and evening services
of prayer and Scripture reading, he explained the benefits of reading
the Scripture according to the lectionary, a predetermined cycle of
reading. In the Anglican church, the lectionary is a plan for reading
the Bible aloud at daily public services so that the congregation gets
through virtually the entire Old Testament and New Testament in a
two-year cycle, with the Psalms getting read or sung aloud in their
entirety every month. Wright said that reading the Bible like this is
"like looking through a window on the whole story. You summon
that broader story up in your mind's eye in order to praise God for
the divine sweep of history." The lesson for each day, he continued,
helps us "reorient ourselves and pray in the light of" God's whole
redemptive plan.[7] In other words, public reading helps listeners place
a given text in the broader context of the whole Bible and the whole
world. A lectionary cycle also, not incidentally, prevents our avoiding
uncomfortable passages. They come up in the cycle whether we welcome them or not, and we have to listen again for what they might
reveal to us.

Wright argued that the primary purpose of public reading is not
instruction but rather this invitation to view the whole story and
praise God for it. However, I think instruction in community is also
indispensable. I say this out of deep appreciation for the almost forty
years of good preaching that has shaped my understanding of the Bible
and the direction of my life. Luther and the Reformers, for all their
bluster about the clarity of Scripture, were also strenuous advocates for
frequent, well-informed preaching. They knew that people needed
winsome explanation, rooted in expert study, in order to get the proper ideas about the nature, work, and will of God out of the Bible. Today
the popularity and explosive growth of churches whose services feature lengthy, Bible-study-style sermons suggest that many people long
for this kind of good preaching. The best kind, in my opinion, begins
by digging carefully into a particular passage, studying what it meant
in its historical context and to its original audience as best we can discern. Then the preacher makes the leap to his or her particular congregation, asking what the passage could mean for us today.

Somewhere on the spectrum between public reading and preaching and private devotional reading is the Bible study group, another

way people learn passages well, chew on their texture, and store them up in the heart. In many American churches, one can hardly turn around without elbowing a Bible study group. Churches of all varieties sponsor Bible studies, usually led by nonexperts and eagerly supplied with materials by the Christian publishing industry. These groups operate in all sorts of different ways; they range from coffee-and-conversation groups to highly disciplined courses with homework assignments and strict patterns of group interaction. Some churches have a weeknight system in which everyone shows up at church on Wednesday evening for a meal before splitting up into groups for Bible study, including the children. My neighbor, an African American gentleman who goes to a Pentecostal church, stopped over one Wednesday evening to drop off some of my mail mistakenly delivered to his house. He was dressed in a fabulously fashionable suit, so I asked him where on earth he was going. "Bible study," he replied, as if it ought to have been obvious. Apparently Bible study is quite the event at his church. I admired the way that his church, by making Bible study into a dress-up occasion, showed respect for the practice. Many people swear by the Bible study group as the best way to learn about the Bible and keep oneself spiritually challenged. As with anything, such studies are only as good as the people in them and the supplementary materials used.

I have found Bible studies less helpful than the quiet waters of private Bible reading. Because I have a solid Bible background, I can usually manage on my own without getting distracted by nagging questions such as "What *is* an apocalypse anyway?" I can simply open the book and read. I'm not very systematic about my private reading. Thankfully I no longer open the Bible at random hoping for a word in a crisis—although we should never completely discredit a practice that worked at least once for Augustine. Usually I work through the Psalms, one per session, or set myself to reading through a gospel or a Pauline letter over the course of a season. Many people use devotional books or daily lectionaries, some of which are now available on the Internet.

Some people, particularly those new to the Bible, try to read the Bible straight through. This is like when Europeans come to visit relatives in New Jersey and cheerfully announce they would like to drive out to San Francisco for the weekend: they just have no idea how immense is the crossing. Often new readers of the Bible who start on page one get rather bogged down in Leviticus, lose heart, and give up. The more intrepid make it past Deuteronomy, cringe their way through Joshua and Judges, and then sigh with relief when they get to the good stories in 1 Samuel. Then it's smooth sailing for a while until they reach the ecstatic highs and very low lows of the prophets. When I was growing up, my family practiced a devotion time after supper consisting of reading a section of the Bible every day, one verse per person going around the table, then concluding with prayer. We plowed through the whole Bible, and I can assure you certain sections make for very peculiar conclusions to a meal. We'd often close our Bibles, look at each other, and go: "Hunh."

It's all right, especially for newer readers, to be selective in private reading and focus on the books and passages that are more amenable. Whatever you read, the most important thing for private reading is to expect and pray for the living God to speak through the text. This is a rather mystical process, no doubt about it. Since ancient times, Christians have practiced and advocated a method called *lectio divina,* which is Latin for "divine reading." *Lectio* involves four steps. First, the reader begins reading a passage very slowly, consciously listening for God's guidance and waiting for a sense that a particular verse or phrase is meant for deep, personal consideration in that moment. Once a particular verse or phrase seems relevant, the reader simply repeats it in her mind, considering how it interacts with her own thoughts, feelings, memories, and worries. After a time of meditation, the reading turns to prayers of response to the word or whatever seems appropriate. Then follows a time of contemplation in which nothing is accomplished, just resting in silence.

Since ancient times Mary, Jesus' mother, has been held up as the perfect model of Scripture reading because she was a person who, as the Gospel of Luke says "pondered all these things in her heart" (2:19). Even more, because she was the person who, out of obedience to God, allowed Jesus to become human in her—she allowed *the* Word to become flesh. Thus Mary's pregnancy wonderfully becomes a metaphor for the ideal reading method. Another equally ancient and even more earthy way of describing *lectio*-style reading is with the metaphor of chewing. Just as food dissolves within us and gives us energy, so the words of Scripture, chewed thoroughly and taken into ourselves, change our thoughts, feeling, and action. Through the mystery of the Spirit, words sink in and become enfleshed in our daily lives.

Even though it's my job to chew on literature every day and encourage students to do so, I find contemplative Bible reading difficult. It resists my tendency to buzz through texts, get the job done, accomplish something. Unfortunately the Bible gets little opportunity to be a living word under such rushed conditions. The fact that I can barely do *lectio* because I am too crunched for time and fidgety strikes me as a serious problem with my life, our culture, and our typical practices of reading. I have better success when I set myself the task of memorizing passages. That appeals to my habit of seeing everything as a task to be accomplished, but it also allows that repetition and chewing to happen along the way.

BREAD FOR THE JOURNEY

Reading and interpreting the Bible well depends on good technique and proper authority structures and shelves of scholarly study helps. But underlying all of the more technical matters and rules of good practice must be a love for the Bible as living word. To picture this love, I let all the scholarly models and tendencies and complications recede and instead place in the foreground the image of my Grandma Minnaar.

I never knew her well. She was already in her eighties when I was born; and hardening of the arteries had made her confused, though generally cheerful. She had lived an immigrant's life, coming from the Netherlands as a teenage orphan, working for many years, marrying, giving birth to seven children, going to church, growing old. I used to visit her with my mother when I was a small girl, and I remember that her pastor would come over and write out Bible verses for her in very large, block letters. She would sit in her chair and sift through the pages, smiling. Little of her mind was left as she approached her last days on earth, but whatever was there she set upon the Word of God. It was bread for her journey in life and bread for her journey home.

CHAPTER EIGHT

❦

SHAPING OUR SOULS TOGETHER

Worship

MY SOUL YEARNS, EVEN FAINTS
FOR THE COURTS OF THE LORD;
MY HEART AND MY FLESH CRY OUT
FOR THE LIVING GOD.
—Psalm 84:2

❦ E very few months or so, I have a dream that returns me to the church of my childhood. Not to a worship service necessarily but to the interior of that building. I haven't actually been there for more than a decade, and the congregation among whom I grew up merged with another and now meets somewhere else. But my memories of the rooms and passageways of my growing-up church, and especially of the high-ceilinged sanctuary where we gathered for worship, still form one of the main stages of my imagination. I see the curved platform spanning a corner of the sanctuary and the padded, theater-style seats fanning out from it. I see the warm wood panels with their repeated cross pattern behind the pulpit, the grass-green carpeting on the steps and down the aisles, the gold and green stained-glass windows. I see the balcony sweeping around, part of it behind and above me, for my perspective is predictably based where my family always sat: on the right, back a dozen rows from the front.

No matter how long I live, no matter how many other churches I belong to or visit, I suppose I will continue to have dreams of being a little girl at Alpine Avenue Church, running around the balcony after the service, pounding down the steps to the basement before catechism class on Wednesdays, counting the ceiling panels during the service, wondering how the giant burnished metal chandeliers and the balcony itself could remain securely stationed above.

My growing-up church enters my dreamscape, I suspect, as a symbol of a more important architecture. Church is about shaping the soul so that we might bear the presence of God. Everything else about going to church—and there is plenty—flows into that purpose.

Showing Up

By some accounts Americans—particularly young adults—are now going to church in droves. Whether there was a decline in church attendance over the last fifty years in this country is a matter of disagreement, but some observers are using the words *revival* and *movement* to describe the crowds filling not only shining, massive, theater-style worship spaces but also small, well-worn parish church sanctuaries.[1] People return to church or show up for the first time for many different reasons. A young, single woman is drawn in by her need for a social group other than her coworkers. A man in his forties has reached a dead end with a difficult marriage or an addiction or some other trauma; and despite whatever resistance he's had to the kind of life preservers churches toss out, he now figures he may as well grasp at anything that floats. A lawyer is searching for something in life beyond his own career success—or failure—and he cannot find in our pragmatic, often debased culture answers to the big questions. A college student, fearful about her own future and sensitive to the world's uncertainty and pain, is searching for something genuine and enduring, something that touches the eternal.

Revival or not, those who join the ranks of regular churchgoers do something brave, because their nonchurchy friends and family are likely to regard this as an odd or even disastrous turn of events. For many people, telling your friends that you have been going to church lately is not likely to get the kind of congratulatory response you would receive if you announced you were joining a health club and starting a new fitness regimen. Wanting a fitter body is a culturally certified desire, but to admit that you need to work on your soul might raise eyebrows. And to join up with such a shabby enterprise to do it? The church, with all its contentions, all its public embarrassments, all its day-to-day mediocrity? How can that be good for a person? And supposing this church business, against all odds, does end up changing your soul? Will it be a change for the better?

I hear from my pastor friend Mary that many of the new people showing up in her pews these days have the opposite problem: their thoroughly churchy family members are all too thrilled to have them back in the fold. How embarrassing, in your thirties, to please your parents!

Whether your family and friends respond with unbearable delight, puzzlement, or hostility, dealing with those responses requires courage, as it is only the beginning of the many humiliations and forbearances churchgoers must endure as part of joining a community. Then again courage, humility, and patience are among the most important lessons our souls need to learn.

STAYING HOME

Plenty of people still find ample reasons to stay away from their community's houses of worship. The classic objection, so well worn by now that it's fraying around the edges, is this: "The church is full of hypocrites." On the surface this one always works quite well because it's always true. There are snappy, traditional replies, such as, "Of course. You'll fit right in. Come join us!" Or "Yes, but we would be even worse if we didn't go to church!" That is essentially C. S. Lewis's reply to this objection: The question is not whether Christians are perfect but whether they are any better than they would be without Christ.[2]

This is an adequate defense of your garden-variety hypocrites; but some of the people who cite this reason for staying away from church are not talking about the everyday failures, confusions, pettiness, and stubbornness of Christians. They are talking about betrayal and abuse—clergy and laity who use the power, authority, or beliefs of the church to cloak their lust for the pleasures of power and exploitation. Jesus himself recognized long ago that such people keep others away from God. He had harsh words not for those who were kept away by such abuses but for the abuser: "It would be better for him to be thrown into the sea with a millstone tied around his neck than for him to cause one of these little ones to sin" (Luke 17:2).

Wounds that the church itself has inflicted are the most serious reasons people stay away. Or if not specific wounds, then serious failures. I heard a woman describe her childhood in the Roman Catholic church as consisting of going to Latin mass weekly with her father and her sister. None of the adults involved had ill intentions, but neither her father nor the priests or lay leaders in the church managed to explain to her what the mass could mean and why it was important. As a result, the whole operation was an exercise in missed opportunities.

It's only fair to recognize that you can't judge the music by the less skillful players. Even so, people find other reasons to stay home on Sunday morning. Showing up at church takes discipline, and once you start showing up at a church, sooner or later you're going to wind up on a committee or in a program or part of a Bible study, and there goes more of the time you might otherwise spend reading the newspaper with a latte. Of course, these days, some churches serve lattes.

Another common objection is that the church is full not so much of hypocrites but of entirely too sincere varieties of weirdos. They raise their hands and close their eyes when they sing; they chatter incessantly in a jargon only insiders understand ("born again" or "repentance" or "anointing of the Spirit"); they teach their children dippy little ditties about Jesus. This is another objection based on truth. But the range of weirdness in the Christian church is quite impressive. Anyone can get started in church life by finding a particular little knot of weirdos whose quirks fit comfortably with his own.

Probably the most common reason people give for staying away is that they don't think they need church. "I believe in God and everything," a resister might explain, "but I'm not going to do the whole church thing. I don't care for institutional religion." In any human endeavor, the theory is always more beautiful than the praxis. But saying that one appreciates Christian ideas while avoiding actual Christians is like saying that one enjoys baseball statistics but does not care for the actual game. One can indeed pray and study and read the Bible and be of service to the world without being part of a congregation. But there's a tinge of arrogance about this. A person who believes she can homeschool her own soul has a rather high view of her own ability. Our individual distortions so easily become full-blown preoccupations that we all need accountability to others. And we need the example of others who are farther along than we are. Moreover, the risk of becoming too inward looking is rather high. Praying and reading are vital practices, but so are service and supporting one another. Belonging to a church, ideally, keeps a constant pressure on our selfishness, keeps pointing our attention not only to God but to others and to the world.

Christianity is definitely a team sport. The apostle Paul used the analogy of the body to counter this age-old tendency to disdain or be shy of one another. Followers of Jesus become part of the body of Christ. Together they act as his physical presence in the world. And every part needs every other in order to be whole and function well. "The eye cannot say to the hand, 'I don't need you!' The head cannot say to the feet, 'I don't need you!' " (1 Corinthians 12:21, paraphrase). The arrogance inverts itself and becomes misplaced humility. To say you do not need the church also resists the recognition that the church needs *you*.

You can always turn up anecdotal evidence to prove that church is a terrible thing—some story like the one about awful Aunt Trudy who convinced her ladies' mission society to lobby for banning certain books at the local school. At some point, the fair thing to do is stop letting the Aunt Trudys of the world be an excuse or spoil the whole idea. I heard of a woman who, when asked what she thought about religion, replied that her father was a pastor who preached in favor of racial segregation in the 1950s, and even as a child she knew he was using his position of authority to perpetuate an injustice. Since escaping her parents' supervision, she has never gone back to a church. What puzzles me is how effectively people can hold on to bad examples and why they are not more inspired by good ones. Why do I never hear someone say, "I have been impressed with Jimmy Carter's integrity since I was a girl, and as a result I have never left the church"? I think people sometimes carry bad examples around like a "Get out of church free" card, pulling them out whenever an occasion arises to consider the church again.

Extraordinary people—the great souls of the world—can inspire us to lives of commitment and faith. But ordinary people can too, if you let them. It's worth finding some good ones and placing yourself among them. The woman I mentioned who attended Latin mass as a child is now passing through the doors of a church again as a way of seeking God. She is wary, but she is encountering many good people who, although keenly aware of the institution's failures, have themselves found a decent church life. They can offer her the gifts of encouragement and healing, and they are eager to help her give it another go.

The church people in my life have given me a wonderful gift simply by hanging on, as best they could, to something great and real. Mine is not one of those marvelous stories of a failed religious upbringing later repaired by a chance encounter with a charismatic person or a midnight reading of the Gospel of Mark. My path has been more of a steady plod, living on the basic rations of worship and church life and learning to perceive how God works through ordinary things to seek and find us.

No doubt the church is a sprawling, bawling, crazy enterprise. To join up even with a good church is to throw in your lot with something unlikely. Amid the unlikeliness of it, God's work becomes clear; and that's what makes it wonderful.

The Ordinary Wonders of Worship

Every part of life can be directed toward seeking God, giving honor to God, and responding to God—and so could be described as worship. But engaging with others regularly in acts of worship like singing, prayer, and Bible reading combines the formative powers of community with the formative powers of worship. Thus churchgoing, when it's working properly, is like the central workshop where God engages in his soul-shaping work.

It's difficult to discuss worship and community separately because their effectiveness emerges when their energies combine. I will begin with attention to basic elements of worship services and questions of style because these issues may create the most immediate confusion for those unfamiliar with worship conventions. The sacraments deserve special attention here because they are the most mysterious element of worship.

The weekly hours spent in communal worship are the heart of any church's life. Worship is what pumps the blood through all of a church's other activities—the small group meetings, the service projects, the youth groups, the classes and outreach programs, and each member's private devotional life. Worship services reveal a church's most important secrets. Not because you find out the latest news about people during prayer-request time but because worship structures and styles reveal what a congregation really believes church is all about—whatever they might say.

In my own little corner of the world, among the Dutch immigrant-founded congregations of West Michigan, the worship services used to be very clearly built around the sermon. We sang hymns and prayed, but it all led up to and away from the thirty- to forty-minute sermon. This revealed an overriding concern with getting the people in the pews to know the Bible well and get their theology straight. Do that and everything else would follow—I believe that was the idea. Before Vatican II in the 1960s, Roman Catholic churches followed a pattern for the mass in Latin that went back centuries. This suggested that the church's job is to get the sacraments—those rituals believed to be special means of grace—performed the right way, according to authority and tradition. Everything else would follow from that. In Pentecostal churches, whose services have their own formula of exuberant singing and sweaty preachers and dancing and swaying and falling, the church's main job is to operate as a conduit where the supernatural shakes up the everyday. And God only knows what will follow from that out in the world, and that's the point.

The variety of Christian churches can be entirely confusing, and sometimes the official denominational labels mean very little to an outsider—or even an insider. Evangelical Lutheran versus Missouri Synod Lutheran, Southern Baptists versus American Baptists, Reformed Church in America versus Christian Reformed Church in North America, Presbyterian Church-USA versus Presbyterian Church of America. These divisions have to do with fine theological distinctions, matters of church government, and each group's history. I've heard much talk lately about the church entering a postdenominational age. And in fact, it's almost more helpful now to categorize churches not by the sign on their front lawn or cornerstone or by their denominational letterhead but by their ecclesiology—their idea of what the church is about, as reflected in their worship and overall ethos. If churches could take personality test, here is what the results page might look like:

If you believe church is about . . .	*you are probably . . .*
• being a sign of God's kingdom in the world, especially through the sacraments	• Catholic, Episcopal, or Anglican, grouped as high liturgical
• saving souls	• evangelical
• equipping us to make the world a better place	• mainline
• defending the truth	• fundamentalist
• getting us filled with the Holy Spirit	• pentecostal or charismatic
• pulling back the veil on the eternal	• Russian Orthodox, Greek Orthodox, or another variety of Orthodox[3]

If you were to propose to an actual person attending a particular service that his church seems to have a certain overriding view of what church is for, he would probably say, "Yes, but there's more to it." A Catholic may adore the Eucharist so that receiving the wafer is the high point of worship for her, but she might also view serving the poor as a direct response to that sacrament. An evangelical may advocate for a seeker-sensitive service, but he may also long for an experience of transcendent mystery in worship. We all want it all at some point.

The trouble is that there's so much going on in worship that it's difficult to do it all at once. Everything does *not* always follow from a given way of worshiping, and week to week we all put up with some lack. When sooner or later someone, or a group of someones, sees a major pattern of lack in worship, that's when reforms happen. When John and Charles Wesley, in eighteenth-century England, saw fewer and fewer people attending Anglican services and saw the services themselves becoming dry as sawdust, they started something new—a movement now known as Methodism. John began holding preaching services on weekdays, and Charles started writing new hymns that emphasized intimacy with God and emotional engagement with the faith. In the last century, Roman Catholic leaders at Vatican II observed that the Latin mass, whatever other important things it accomplished, did not effectively engage the people's active participation. So Catholic leadership, for this and other complex reasons, decided to encourage the use of vernacular language in the mass so that laypeople would understand better what was happening and be able to participate more fully.

Current upheavals in worship style among North American churches are another prevalent example of this reform phenomenon. The worship style I grew up with—a solemn male pastor leading the whole service, hymns from a hymnbook accompanied by organ, a long theological sermon—did some things rather well. It created an atmosphere of reverence and supported theological teaching. I learned quite a bit of theology from sermons and even more from hymns. But large numbers of people from many denominational backgrounds began to complain in the 1970s and 1980s that this style of worship did not evoke much joy or exuberance, engage with contemporary culture, or draw outsiders into the church. Hence the dawn of contemporary worship, with praise songs, drum sets, and PowerPoint slides projected on screens.

Many congregations from a wide variety of denominations have gone over completely to contemporary worship by now. In fact, contemporary worship is so well established that for some it has become the old news they wish to move beyond. The newest worship trends, sometimes called emerging worship, seek to adapt very ancient forms— such as chant, icons, and ritual acts like hand washing—into services that also feature video technology and ambient music. Meanwhile, other churches, resisting fads as a matter of integrity, proudly maintain their well-rehearsed choirs and highly trained organists. Some bigger churches struggle somewhere in the middle of all this by pulling off a traditional and a contemporary service every Sunday morning, by allowing the seventeen-year-old drummer to tap along with the organ, or by maintaining a determined group smile despite visible strain between the on-beat and off-beat clappers. This can be rather baffling to someone who enters the sanctuary of the tall-steeple church in town expecting an organ fanfare, only to find four singers with cordless microphones and a guy on a drum kit.

TAKING A DIP

Experts who watch this sort of thing from denominational levels have been grappling with the crosscurrents in the American church these last twenty years. That's putting it nicely, as in some churches the crosscurrents have been bitter enough to merit the term *worship wars*. The bitterness comes because, although people are not always able to explain exactly what worship ought to do, they like and need what feels familiar to them; and they have a sense that worship is a complicated business that must serve a number of important functions. Worship is supposed to get certain things done, but people also want to get something out of it. The two impulses are interrelated.

What is worship supposed to get done? We worship, I've heard it said, in order to declare the worth-ship of God. This involves praise and generally getting straight who God is and who we are. Along the same lines, we worship to get ourselves right with God, knowing that during the week we inevitably get distracted and stray off. Others say we worship in order to have an encounter with God or to receive grace and be reassured of God's love for us. Some emphasize the teaching function of worship: worship is where we learn about God and learn properly to practice things like prayer and Bible reading. Another view, one that I favor, is that worship is covenant renewal—a ritual reenactment of God's loving promises and our grateful response, a dialogue between God and people that over time changes the kind of people we are. These are just a few examples, and they're all right. Worship ought to do all these things.

Making all this happen at once is quite a challenge. It's as if we face a huge panel of meters, and they all have to read within the "effective" range. There's the Awe-o-meter, the Participate-o-meter, the Truth-o-meter, the Transcend-o-meter. People who plan and lead worship are supposed to calibrate them all.

I recently traveled around England and Scotland with fifteen "worship wonks"—college students and church professionals eager to discuss worship day and night for three weeks straight. To give contemporary relevance to our historical study of worship reform, we met with some of the people on the cutting edge of reform in the United Kingdom. Matt Redman, a singer-songwriter-worship leader active in Britain's contemporary worship movement, talked with us about balancing the old and new in worship. His view of the matter was that having only brand-new music and words in worship would not be compassionate; it would not respect how people are nourished by what they have learned to love over many years. On the other hand, using only old forms would not be prophetic: it would not challenge us to see the world in new ways. Alison Adam, a founder of a Scottish worship renewal group called the Wild Goose Resource Group, explained that worship ought to both "bless and disturb" us. All through our discussions about worship, we talked about these kinds of balances: between form and freedom, old and new, comforting and challenging.[4]

I know of churches that will not budge from the way they did things fifty years ago. On the other end of the scale, I know of a church in my town whose musicians never use the same song more than three weeks in a row. They write new music every week to keep things fresh. One of the perspectives my fellow travelers and I gained from our historical study is that neither of these extremes is the wisest approach. Fifty years ago was not the apex of perfection in the church's worship. And reinventing the wheel every week will quickly exhaust everyone (funny how all those new songs start to sound remarkably alike).

Worship points to a reality that transcends history as well as our current place and time; training our souls to perceive this requires a flexible tension between the particular expressions of this age and the wisdom of the church's history, all of it aimed at returning again and again to the heart of things. Worship ought to be bilingual in the sense of speaking our vernacular but also teaching us the basic grammar of a shared language of Christians everywhere in every time. We can expect to need to learn new words, different kinds of music, different ways to organize space and time. N. T. Wright explained to my group that when we worship, "we are dipping into the stream of the church's worship in all times and places."[5] If the worship of God is a stream we dip into, it is always the same stream but also always shifting and moving, with different qualities of light playing on its surface.

Because worship is a complex enterprise, no one type of church can do everything perfectly well. Although Christians should and do repent the divisions among us, we can be glad for a huge diversity of worship styles. When worship committees eye the church across the street or across the country or across the world with envious admiration, this is not an altogether bad thing. I am a thoroughgoing child of the Reformation when I give three cheers for the notion of *semper reformada* (always reforming). We learn from each other and challenge each other. We balance out one another's prejudices and overemphases. We keep trying to calibrate all the meters. We trust that God is worshiped well only by the whole church together.

BAD WORSHIP, GOOD WORSHIP

My friend Dawn, who is pastor of a church in South Dakota, is one of the most cheerful people I know. I have rarely heard her rant. But she recently worked herself into quite a lather over a funeral she had attended at another church. "Sometimes services are just *so bad!*" she fumed. She described how the pastor mumbled and the organist blundered and how the trumpet of hope that ought to sound at a funeral, metaphorically speaking, gave only a pathetic little bleat. She vowed, in her own church, to start giving her leaders the straight truth when a service falls short. "In the Midwest we always try to put a good face on things," she explained, "but we have to be able to say to each other, 'That didn't work very well, did it?' "

Bad worship is bad news. Style matters, but so does the proficiency with which any given style is executed, to use an unfortunate but sometimes fitting term. It certainly makes a difference in whether people show up at all, whether they keep coming, and whether they feel touched or spoken to. Any style can be done well or badly. I've suffered through deadly dull organ-led dirges as well as the smarmiest, most manipulative contemporary songs. But I've also experienced joyfully reverent traditional Protestant worship as well as breathtakingly beautiful cathedral worship, and I now go to a church that does a consistently good job at what I would call eclectic folk-liturgical. I've seen great worship-band-driven worship too, at my college's cutting-edge (I can't say "contemporary" because that is "*so* 1980s") Sunday evening student worship service, complete with projected song lyrics, guitars, amps, African drums, and spaghetti tangles of electrical cords.

It's safe to say that we talk about what makes good and bad worship a lot at my house, and I confess to a tendency to analyze the Sunday service in the car on the way home. But I know that far more important than the proficiency of any style are the underlying rhythms of worship and of the church life that flows from it.

It all comes down to the evident fact that we are obtuse, forgetful, stubborn, often hurting creatures who need and desire frequent reminders of what is good and real. Worship should present certain big truths, such as the faithfulness of God, and support those with more specific knowledge, such as the cultural background of the New Testament book of Acts. But shaping the soul in worship is more a matter of running oneself through certain rhythms and postures repeatedly over a long period of time. These rhythms and postures can be well dressed in many different styles, and they can manage to show through even threadbare worship.

TREASURES

After almost forty years of going to worship, I find it difficult to estimate how profoundly this practice has shaped me. But I can think of several treasures I carry with me thanks to a lifetime of churchgoing, treasures I wish everyone could share. They also make pretty good criteria when considering where to go for soul-shaping work. Whatever band of weirdos seems welcoming, whatever the style of music or speaking or praying, whether it's "smells and bells" or "bring your own snake," if your church is doing these things, your soul can get an education.

First, years of going to worship have taught me a language for joy. This may be particularly important in a postmodern (or post-postmodern if that's where we are) world that gives plenty of practice in cynicism, irony, critique, and complaint—the dominant modes in American entertainment and public discourse. The Declaration of Independence validates the pursuit of happiness, which advertisers seem to interpret as fun vacations, tasty restaurant meals, and well-toned and provocatively dressed companions. But where do we learn to perceive and respond to the fundamental wonders of our world, our lives, existence itself? In a culture that favors irony and complaint, do we lose our capacity for joy? What a terrible poverty.

In church I learned to express joy mostly by singing. Although we say and pray joyful things in worship too, particularly when reading certain psalms, nothing matches music for expanding our joy capacity. I've heard people scold that one should always pay full attention to the words when singing in church. I don't think that's true. Sometimes I simply enjoy singing the harmony, feeling the pleasure of the sounds; and that's all right. The language of joy doesn't always need to be in words. We can speak it through music, dance, architecture, and other arts too.

It's possible to learn to perceive beauty and feel awe and joy in places other than church. A mountaintop or a symphony hall, for example. I know musicians who do fairly well getting through life with music as their geography of transcendence. But worship, ideally, maps the experience of awe to its genuine source, the Creator, and gives people a means of response. I am beginning to understand that the Bible commands us to worship and praise, not because God is an egoist who loves flattery but so that we may not be left without a language for joy.

My mother-in-law, who has traveled all over the world, tells me she has witnessed the greatest joy in worship among those who suffered serious difficulty: at a leper settlement in Nigeria, among Chinese Christians afforded only reluctant government permission to worship, among Russian Christians before glasnost. Worshiping together meant mutual encouragement and comfort to them, but even more so it meant communing deeply with the God whose power and grace far exceed their daily troubles and pain. All of us need to find that deep communion with the source of all joy, especially in those seasons of life when joy does not come easily. I know from many years of experience that even when I go to worship feeling scarcely any joy but mostly sadness, frustration, or helplessness, the act of praising God in itself gives me comfort.

The second treasure I have received from worship is practice in encountering the Bible as an authoritative text that reads *us*. Familiarity with the Bible and frequent opportunities to hear the familiar words repeated help us experience the living Word. Much of that good work can get done through public reading and preaching. Since becoming an adult, I've attended churches that arrange their Bible reading according to the lectionary, which places all the right passages on the right occasions—prophetic texts about the Messiah leading up to Christmas, the nativity narratives near Christmas Day, narratives of Jesus' suffering leading up to Easter, and so on. This practice helps us interpret our own lives in light of Scripture by inviting us to fit our stories into an ancient and enduring story much bigger than ourselves. Good preaching, meanwhile, models careful study of the Bible and practices applying what the Bible meant then and there to what it might mean here and now.[6] Preaching helps us learn to listen for what the Word of God might be for us, whether it's judgment, comfort, challenge, delight, or all of the above.

Third, worship has taught me how to say "I'm sorry." It's taught me the posture of getting down on my knees: we don't do that literally in my particular worship tradition, unfortunately, but we do it in spirit. In worship we should be able to face the truth of our failures, both as individuals and as congregations, denominations, nations, racial groups, and so on. We ought to learn to recognize what we have done wrong, to speak the "I'm sorry" and taste the forgiveness that enables us to move on. In doing this we begin to trace a kind of penitential parabola—down and up, dying and rising, that fundamental rhythm of the Christian life. "I'm sorry" can also be about compassion. We can learn to say "I'm sorry" as a lament emerging from our own suffering and to kneel down in solidarity with the suffering of others.

Fourth, I'll gather all kinds of experiences together and say that church has given me the treasure of grace, that gift of blessing from the living God that comes in so many forms. People who complain that worship is dry or boring or shallow are not necessarily selfish consumers who care only for spectacle and novelty. They may simply be thirsty for grace. I find grace sometimes in a particular word or image or idea from a sermon that speaks directly to me. Sometimes grace is in good music that expresses the gratitude or grief that I currently feel. Sometimes grace is several minutes of silence in the middle of a prayer, the only silence I'll encounter in a frantic week of work and family activities. Grace can come through great church or boring church or mediocre church because it's not an automatic by-product of human skill—it comes from God. I've gotten used to demanding from worship services only what not-so-great golfers demand from an afternoon on the course: one good hole or even one good shot. That's enough to keep me coming back.

Still, it helps when worship is done thoughtfully and well. Beauty and skill are appropriate in worship because they reflect the nature of God and naturally awaken an appropriate sense of awe and delight. So I appreciate it when people put their best efforts into music and good preaching and thoughtful prayer. On the other hand, I've encountered worship leaders who seem to believe they can engineer grace. Anyone who has felt rather soured by a superslick performance, or who has curled back in resistance from those who keep insisting that he should be feeling God's presence now, knows that an encounter with God cannot be forced or manipulated. It's not technique or even an expectant attitude that brings grace to us. We do our best and pray for the Spirit.

Sacramental Grace

Since its earliest days, the church has understood that Jesus himself instituted two ritual practices that his followers were directed to perform regularly. These were meant to distill and signify the nature and power of God's grace and the means by which God pours grace on us: baptism and the Eucharist (also sometimes called the Lord's Supper or Communion). Protestant, Orthodox, and Roman Catholic Christians agree that these ritual practices were given to the church and that practicing them faithfully is a mark and responsibility of the church. Roman Catholics and Orthodox Christians have an expanded repertoire of sacraments, to which my explanation will not do justice, but here I'm trying only to give a broad overview and a sense of my own experience.

Not every part of the church is keen on making a big fuss over baptism and frequent celebration of the Eucharist. Some make a fuss over baptism but not over the Eucharist and others just the opposite. Some do them both but with very little fuss. A small minority of Christians, including Quakers, don't do them at all. Such groups have their reasons for this, but I have become increasingly convinced that we should not have to do without the sacraments—these reliable and mystical means of grace.

In the church where I grew up, we practiced both the sacraments, but they were done with a kind of solemn discretion, very decent and orderly. Infants were delicately sprinkled at their baptisms, and four times a year we passed around silver trays, some with tiny white-bread cubes and others with tiny cups of juice. I now think that the way we practiced these sacraments gave the subtle impression that God was stingy with grace. More frequency and drama in our practice would have offered a fuller picture of God's ways with us.

Alison Adam, who talked with us during that U.K. study trip, explained well why the sacraments are important, all the more so in the wordier worship traditions. "We worry too much about words, words, words in worship and not enough about heart and body!" she declared. She pointed out that the sacraments engage head, heart, and body. They communicate in ways beyond the intellectual and therefore can be means of grace especially powerful to children, the developmentally disabled, and people for whom words are difficult. Even more than that, the sacraments are the most tangible way we can be "in Christ" (2 Corinthians 5:17) or be "clothed . . . with Christ" (Galatians 3:27). They are the most obvious answer to the puzzling question: How exactly is Christ's saving work applied to us? In baptism we are buried with Christ—in the water—that we may also be raised with Christ (see Romans 6:4). It's a physical enactment of being cleansed from sin, reborn to new life, given a new identity, and named by God fully and forever. In the Eucharist we commemorate Christ's sacrifice on the cross with physical reminders of his broken body and shed blood; we take this body and blood into ourselves so that we can commune with him and each other, and we anticipate the banquet feast of the coming kingdom.

There are many good ways to do the sacraments. I come from an infant-baptizing tradition, but both infant and adult baptism have excellent biblical warrant. One of the problems with baptism is that you can't do it over and over to the same person. Once is all you get with this one, so that raises the question of how to do this sacrament more. The current approach to this problem at my church seems to be a constant supply of new babies, but that's not the only way. We can remind each other of our baptism even on weeks when we have no eligible babies or adults. For instance, we keep the vessel that holds the water, the baptismal font, right up front; and every week someone pours water very noisily and visibly into it just after we confess our sins and receive an assurance of forgiveness. We watch the water pour and hear its sound; and we remember that God's grace, like water, is life-giving and supple. It washes us, quenches our thirst, and ensures our survival.

The primary reason I have become a sacrament enthusiast is that I have learned to depend on weekly Communion. (My pastor is glad for this practice as well: "If my sermon is lousy, at least people have Communion," he says.) I've seen communion done in all kinds of good ways. I've knelt at a rail in Episcopal churches and received a wafer and a share of the cup from a deacon or priest. I like the humility of this method and the way the priest or deacon represents the church's authority and care. I no longer like the sippy-cup-in-the-pew method with which I grew up, but you could say it has the virtue of signifying that God comes to us where we are with grace; we don't have to get up and earn it. My favorite method is the circle method, in which people go up in large groups and encircle the Communion table; elders pass the bread and wine into the circle, and then the people in the circle pass these elements to each other. We use this method at my current church; and as the circles form and disperse, the rest of the congregation sings. I like the circle method because it emphasizes how the sacrament seals our communion with one another as well as with Christ. As I look around the circle at the faces of people whose sorrows I know as well as people I have never met, more than at any other time I understand what it means to see the face of Christ in one another. As we pass the bread and wine to each other and say, "The body of Christ given for you" and "The blood of Christ shed for your sins," we touch a mystery: the suffering Christ becomes the hospitable Christ. The one who welcomes us to the table is himself the nourishment we serve each other and receive into ourselves.

Splashing babies and dunking adults and passing around little pieces of bread and cups of wine or juice may seem silly. It's so simple. It has nothing of the razzle-dazzle our culture trains us to believe we need to have in order to experience anything profound. That is exactly the point. The sacraments take their authority from events recorded in the gospel accounts of Jesus' life. They resonate beautifully with ancient archetypes of cleansing through immersion in water and of bonding, commitment, or renewal through some kind of sacrifice. But even more basically they remind us that the most ordinary things participate in the eternal. God has chosen the simplest of things to become special means of grace so that we might see grace in the simplest of things. Over the centuries the church has fussed and argued over exactly how Jesus is present in the bread and wine and whether or not a baptism has to be done a certain way in order to take. I don't think propositional understanding is the main point with the sacraments, though. They speak to us in ways beyond words. They are, by definition, forgiving. The sacraments enact the sacred mystery of dying and rising with Christ; and as we participate in them over and over, we learn the contours of that mystery and conform to its shape.

Church Ladies

The over and over part is critical. Soul shaping takes time. Some people go to church a few times hoping for a dramatic encounter with God and an entirely new life—in six weeks! That does happen occasionally. As Jesus said, "The wind blows wherever it pleases," a metaphor he immediately applied to the Spirit (John 3:8). But instant transformation is not the typical pattern. What with our own obtuseness and tendency to suffer from bad worship and all, most of us require years of churchgoing before showing improvements. This is what is meant by *spiritual formation,* a term sometimes used to describe people's growth in the faith. People don't get stamped into spiritual shape on an assembly line. They're all handmade.

With that in mind, I must add a fifth treasure to my list: faithfulness. Faithfulness is a quality of soul our culture does not readily cultivate. Our typical approach to consumption, professions, relationships, and even philosophies is best symbolized by the television remote control. If you're bored or there's a problem, press a button and change channels. Faithfulness is everything we think we don't want: it's difficult, self-denying, countercultural, and limits our choices.

In my memories of growing up in that row on the right-hand side of my church, I can see the couple who sat in the balcony opposite. He was a short, silver-haired man with a broad face. She had a sharp nose, thin glasses, and silver hair smoothed back into a elaborate bun that looked something like an overabundant waffle. They both wore very neat, conservative clothes and crisply tailored overcoats. I don't remember any conversations with these people, and they were not leaders in the church. They simply showed up every week, like many of the other faces around me. But I am grateful to them because without even knowing it, they demonstrated that there is something redemptive merely about long-term commitment to a good and important practice. I recently found out that these people were watching me too. My mother took my son to the mall one day, and there they ran into the lady of the couple. She took one look at my son and, having not seen me in years, she still said, "I can tell he's Debra's. He looks exactly like she did as a child." There is evidently a close relationship between faithfulness and community.

People who criticize faithful pew-sitters as purveyors of empty ritual have a rather naive view of the religious life. Anyone who has been at this soul education process for a while will admit to having dry spells. Partly it's our own failures of will and attentiveness, and partly it's a result of dealing with a God who does not perform on cue, at the press of a prayer button. As with anything worthwhile that takes a long time, you must keep at it. You learn faster, and you get through the dry spells eventually if you don't give up.

In the religious life, this is called piety. Though I am not terribly disciplined myself right now, I aspire to piety, in the sense of going through the practices routinely whether I feel like it or not: Bible reading, prayer, and churchgoing. Piety can become empty and an end in itself, but that's not much of an indictment. Anything can become an empty end in itself. I think of piety as simply a matter of keeping one's sails up and hoping for wind. Or of practicing an instrument every day (or almost), whether the music sounds good or not. Freedom and ease arise over time, as any musician or athlete knows, from the discipline of constant, sometimes jaw-clenching practice.

I grew up among pious people, and I live and work among them now. Piety filled with love and devotion is a beautiful thing. Out of its fertile soil, hope grows. Mostly I have noticed that piety gives strength, holding people up when they're weak. In a crisis words and practices that normally seem routine suddenly feel like a blessed life raft. You've heard Psalm 23 a thousand times, but when you and your brothers hear that your sister has terminal cancer, you go to church numbly, expecting nothing. Then someone reads aloud those familiar words, "Though I walk through the valley of the shadow of death," and they seem written for you, for this moment. And they bring you into company with thousands of others who have also known pain and fear. Amid those words, your grief falls to rest on the cushion of God's faithful love.

My one ambition for my old age is to be a church lady. Not the kind who has turned bitter, complaining, and judgmental but the kind who has grown nearer to wisdom and peace. I will be the lady in the same pew (or whatever we sit on by then) every Sunday, and I'll know all the little kids' names. I'll show up at the potlucks and volunteer to tutor the neighborhood kids. I'll sing loudly even though the people standing around me will secretly wish I had retired my voice years ago. Mostly I will pray, pray for people even when they haven't asked for prayer.

I need more work on my soul yet before I'll be ready for that life. I need to become more patient, more silent, more disciplined in prayer, less restless and ambitious and fearful. But I know where to go to have that work done. Sometimes it feels like work; sometimes it's boring; but more often it feels like getting my balance again, like finding my orientation with everything around and also above me, knowing where I am and where home is. Or it feels like drinking deep at a well—at once satisfying and arousing my thirst for the living God.

CHAPTER NINE

𝒞𝓏

COMPANIONS ON THE JOURNEY

The Challenge of Christian Community

HOW GOOD AND PLEASANT IT IS
WHEN KINDRED LIVE TOGETHER IN UNITY.
—Psalm 133:1

𝒞𝓏 L ast fall during the Thanksgiving service at my church, we committed an act of utter liturgical recklessness: we invited people to come up front for an open-mike time. This was a risky thing to do in a congregation where people expect the service to move along decently and in order. After all, when you invite people up to a microphone, you never know who might take the opportunity to satisfy a long-neglected need for attention and stand up there for twenty minutes recounting every detail of the miraculous healing of cousin Freddie's bunions. Despite these dangers, people were duly invited to stand at the microphone and share with the congregation something they were especially thankful for. And it turned out fine. In fact, as I'm sure the service planners hoped, it turned out to be a time of great encouragement for us as a community because several people took the opportunity to express their gratitude for ways they have found help and healing through one another.

Among those who spoke was a woman named Linda. Linda has dealt with special challenges all her life, and she has a very unhappy past about which I don't know the whole story. These days she's an especially joyful Christian, one who has a pretty clear sense of what salvation has meant for her. She also has a tendency to take her time at the microphone; but once the congregation catches her genuineness and her self-deprecating humor, we can't help but be pleased to listen. On this occasion Linda spoke of her gratitude for the way the parents of small children in our congregation share their children's attentions with her. She said that she used to think she was a failure as a woman because she never married or had children, but she has come to realize that God has given her the children of our congregation to love. And she really does. She holds the babies and knows their names and engages the little tots in conversation after the service. She offers her own childlike qualities in friendship to our kids. She probably has annoying qualities I don't know about; we all do. But somehow our congregation has managed to create a place where she feels free to discover and exercise her gifts—which include, as I know from this and other occasions, the gift of encouragement.

If every one of us had been compelled to stand at the microphone that day and say truthfully whether or not our congregation exemplified Christian community, I fear we would not all have shared Linda's enthusiasm. I know some people feel that creating community is the dimension of church life in which our congregation is most lacking.

Community is difficult to define: Is it a feeling? A set of practices? Both? Of all the dimensions of the Christian life, community may be the most elusive of all.

THE IDEALS OF CHRISTIAN COMMUNITY

The church, both worldwide and locally, is supposed to be a place where people can practice a new model of human community, a model liberated from the usual features of division, whether petty or terrible. In Christian community people should no longer create barriers based on family, race, social class, nation, or gender. In Christian community people should no longer cause one another suffering through violence, injustice, scorn, exclusion, or even chronic nastiness but instead support one another, enduring and even defying whatever the rest of the world dishes out. In one of the most radical statements in the Bible, the apostle Paul writes to the confused and bickering church in Galatia that "all of you who were baptized into Christ have clothed yourselves with Christ. There is neither Jew nor Greek, slave nor free, male nor female, for you are all one in Christ Jesus" (Galatians 3:28). When people join up with the Christian church and are baptized, Paul is saying, all the former ways we enforce division should fall away. We have entered an alternative universe where all that matters is the fundamental condition we all share: our need for God and God's answer to that need in Jesus.

That's the way it's supposed to be.

Start hanging around any particular church, and you might wonder where this needful, noble vision sometimes disappears to. The ordinary displays of church community can be so lovely: women laughing together, men with cups of coffee talking after worship services, children running around among the legs of adults, the clink of dishes in the church kitchen, an elderly man handing a cookie to a child. But then comes a budget meeting, and tempers flare, and people go round and round about a lousy five-hundred-dollar expenditure for copy machine repair, then head for the parking lot in a snit.

What can happen at the local level is writ large in the major divisions in the Christian church among Roman Catholics, Protestant, and Eastern Orthodox, as well as among hundreds of subdivisions. These did not typically come about, you can imagine, somewhere back in history when different groups of Christians shook hands, wished each other well, and moved peaceably across the street just to give everyone more seating space.

Since ancient times, one of the most abiding symbols for the church is Noah's ark, that enormous bulk of a boat that, according to the book of Genesis, carried a few faithful people and a great many bewildered zoo specimens through history's most famous flood. The ark has long been taken as a symbol for the church as a God-given means of rescue from the perils of a broken world. I've heard church people joke that the ark also works as a symbol because, although floating along in the church may beat floundering in the flood, being inside sure can feel stinky and cramped. Sometimes churches manage to get so stinky and cramped that the floods of the world start to look pretty refreshing, and people run screaming across the deck and leap right off the bow.

Americans in particular, with individualism like granite in our cultural bedrock, may be tempted to wonder whether staying on the big boat is worth it. Why not take a chance paddling our own little craft? In recent generations our basic social structures have shifted from small, stable communities to a society more mobile and social groups more fluid than at any other time or place in history. Having grown accustomed to this flux, we tend to regard the spiritual life as a solo quest. We have learned to regard everything as a matter of consumer preference, so that we seek to make every aspect of life, including spirituality, suit our idiosyncratic desires. It is possible even to go to worship services regularly but still remain an individual on a quest for a private experience of God. We have learned not to trust what other people might offer us by way of companionship or help. After all, people fail in all kinds of ways, so isn't it rather dangerous and counterproductive to learn from failed examples? And even if you can find people to trust and learn from, chances are good you'll be moving away or they will or your little support system will break up somehow. You might as well face that you're on your own.

Despite our own and others' failures and the impermanence of even the best human communities, Christianity assumes that other people are more than occasional companions on an ultimately solo journey: they are part of the path. Worshiping in proximity to each other is not enough. In order to bear the presence of God, our souls also need the shaping forces of community. Christians have been given the gift and burden of a new vision for human community; and this vision declares that whatever it is God wishes for us to become, we have to become it together. Although we certainly have a difficult time living into this becoming, our failures do not invalidate the vision. The vision remains the antidote for division. So we have to keep at it, because in those not infrequent moments when we do live together as we are supposed to, when we glimpse what it means to have true fellowship with one another, we begin to understand something central about the character of God.

TROUBLE AND PLENITUDE

Ever since Paul and other early church leaders began mapping out what it might mean to follow Jesus' instructions to "Love each other as I have loved you" (John 15:12), Christians have struggled to rescue divinely inspired unity out of wearisomely familiar human conflict. Some Christians hold up the first-century church as the model to which all church groups should aspire, but this has always puzzled me.

A quick read through the last half of the New Testament immediate-ly reveals plenty of conflict among those who were first trying to sort out what following this Jesus might mean. By the fourth century, the new faith had weathered Roman persecution and established a struc-ture of local and regional leaders, called elders and bishops, including the chief bishop at Rome. In that period, major councils of church leaders managed to agree on statements of orthodox belief, but of course this required silencing voices of dissent, sometimes quite force-fully. Still, under the statements and governance structures confirmed at early councils of leaders, the Christian church remained unified—in the sense of acknowledging a central authority—for one thousand years, until the first major division into the Eastern and Roman churches was formalized in 1054. That division, like almost every other, involved a concatenation of troubles: differences in culture, lan-guage, worship practices; issues of authority; and of course, theologi-cal disagreement. Five hundred years later, the Reformation resulted in another major split, this time when the Protestant church estab-lished camp apart from the Roman church.

Ever since, Protestants especially seem to have become more and more expert at thinking up reasons to divide from one another. My own denomination, the Christian Reformed Church in North America, began as a splinter group in the nineteenth century from the state church of the Netherlands. A group of devout Dutch folk emi-grated to America and there joined up with other Dutch immigrants who had arrived earlier. The latecomers soon split from their Dutch-American brothers and sisters as well, though. Today both denomina-tions still exist, the issues over which they split having long since become irrelevant; and they now enjoy friendly, cooperative relations. However, for all its virtues, my denomination still seems to have schism in the blood. Another small group recently split off—upset over what they consider liberal views on, among other things, whether women should become pastors—and called themselves the United Reformed Churches in North America. Does the irony not sting?[1]

Although all these divisions are a source of shame and embar-rassment to insiders and either amusing or revolting (or both) to out-siders, they need not be entirely disillusioning. Despite all the divisions, there is still an identifiable center of agreement among Christians. The stories of the Bible, especially Jesus' crucifixion and resurrection, shape the thinking and practice of Christians everywhere and in every age, though these are understood in various ways and with various practical results. Christians everywhere share devotional practices such as communal worship, Bible reading, and prayer. Some branches of the faith are wary of formulations of belief, but most major branches affirm one or both of the summaries of Christian belief that date from the early centuries of the faith: the Nicene Creed (which dates from the fourth-century councils) and the Apostles' Creed (versions of which date to the first century). Individuals in any given denomination might find one or more of the statements in these creeds difficult to believe wholeheartedly every minute of every day, but it's still fair to say that official disputes among Christian groups are not usually over major points but over subpoints attached to the main points, matters of religious practice, or ethics.

The church's historical and continuing divisions are no one's idea of the way things ought to be. Wherever Christians have shown hatred for and practiced violence against one another, they have betrayed the words and deeds of the one they claim as Lord. Even when not violent, the church's divisions have always resulted from some kind of failure. Usually the failure comes on the part of Christians themselves—some of them failing culpably by succumbing to greed, lust for power, or bigotry and some of them merely failing to understand matters that are indeed difficult. Sometimes divisions have resulted from deceit on the part of people who cleverly distort Christianity just enough to retain its authority while promoting a deeply un-Christian agenda. No one said this unity business was going to come easily and naturally. Every day many millions of Christians pray for it, asking the Holy Spirit to repair our failures and bring unity among Christians and peace in the world. And they work for it too, forming umbrella organizations and planning cooperative grass-roots activities like community development projects and conferences.

Even if Christians had always treated one another with kindness and respect, we would still have amicable divisions. Any enormous group needs subdivisions simply in order to have some kind of human scale. We can hardly expect to *feel* unified with two billion other Christians. A sense of unity can be experienced only in concentric circles beginning with a group of Christians we actually know and expanding outward from there. Moreover, our differences have resulted in a Christian plenitude. The foundational beliefs and practices of the faith are lived out in a huge variety of ways, and each group has some emphasis or practice or habit from which we can learn.

For instance, the Mennonites, a group that dates from the Reformation and emphasizes the importance of baptizing adults rather than infants, have become champion volunteers. They are experts at arranging their lives for service to others all over the world. Roman Catholics have an ancient and enduring tradition of monastic vocation, believing that God calls some Christians to live apart in intentional communities whose days are structured around prayer and worship. In our spiritually hungry age, visitors are flocking to these communities to glimpse a peace and hospitality they have never experienced elsewhere. African American churches, as sometimes happens among those who suffer, have transformed their suffering and marginalization into something more valuable than diamonds: the most exuberant, original praise music in the church. Russian Orthodox Christians, with their expertise in creating gorgeous works of religious art, instruct us all in seeing through beautiful objects to the beauty of God.

I don't mean to ignore what our disagreements have cost Christians, but I can't help enjoying the resulting variety. C. S. Lewis suggested that the church is like a big house with many rooms. This is a particularly apt metaphor because the word used to describe cooperation among different branches of the faith, *ecumenism,* comes from the Greek word *oikos,* which means "household." Lewis suggests that if you find yourself standing in the hallway of this household, you should simply decide on a door and walk through it. He wisely adds that you should choose based on "which door is the true one, not which pleases you best by its paint and panelling."[2] However, there's more to finding a room than an analysis of doctrine. Temperament, style, and history are valid reasons too. I could find a home in many different denominations whose beliefs I could happily affirm, but I remain in the Christian Reformed Church because I have a family history here. My husband's uncle, on the other hand, just as Dutch as the rest of the family, began attending a Russian Orthodox church while studying Russian literature in college, and he has since made his home there. The Russian Orthodox room in the house of faith fits his temperament and dovetails with his life's work (as a professor of Russian literature).

The variety of Christian practice suggests that the truth of God is wide enough to allow—even require—expression in organ cantatas and the blues, in plain wooden pews and cathedrals, in living-room Bible studies and incense-scented pageantry. We can see clearly enough from nature that God loves variety and plenitude. Although I'm sure God grieves over our rancor, I'm also convinced that this plenitude was always part of the plan.

I hope and pray with others that the church as a whole is at last learning to reject violence and bigotry, both among Christians and between Christians and others. We will not, I am sure, stop disagreeing altogether. In fact, the growth of the Christian church in the southern hemisphere raises new challenges as Christianity spreads into a greater number of more disparate cultures. The usual human routine is to try to dissociate ourselves from those with whom we disagree because . . . well, because it's easier that way. It's more comfortable. The church often couches the official reasons for divisions in the language of purity: "We're the true church, and they're not." "If they think that, they can't really be Christians." But I suspect such statements are gestures of defeat more than anything else, gestures that say, "We can no longer be bothered with people who disagree." Or they are simply a sad capitulation to the pleasures of spiritual pride. Or both. One great challenge of the next century will be to figure out what unity might look like, assuming we will never achieve uniformity. How can we allow one another to have different convictions and yet remain in conversation? How can we acknowledge our differences and yet act and speak, at least sometimes, as united?

A couple of months ago, a student at my college named Katie sought some consolation from my pastor friend Greg. While Katie was away on a trip, her fiancé had made a surprise decision to join the army. She had no objection as a Christian to military service, only to the shock of this decision and the changes it meant for her and her fiancé's plans together. Greg, however, is an outspoken pacifist, so Katie told him her news with some trepidation. What would he say to her? After he offered her some words of comfort about dealing with change, she asked point-blank whether he thought her fiancé was still a Christian if he served in the military. Expressing his reassurance and acceptance as only a Kentuckian can, he drawled: "Shucks, it's all right. You can be a Christian and be stupid."

He may have hit on a workable step forward for Christian unity. If we can finish off all our arguments with this exchange: "It's all right. You can be stupid about [issue X] and still be a Christian." And "Sure, you can be stupid [about issue X] too. Here, let's share some bread." Then we might be able to move past the disagreement. Of course, it would be better yet if we could stop calling each other stupid. But one step at a time.

The more I understand about the different branches of the faith, the more I realize that even with issues about which I have strongly held convictions, the other side is hardly stupid. Both sides have valid and persuasive reasons for doing things the way they do. For example, Roman Catholics emphasize the importance of a central authority who can interpret Scripture for the whole church; Protestants emphasize the importance of every individual's ability to interpret Scripture even to the point of questioning authoritative structures. Neither side completely ignores the other way of doing things. Catholic laypeople read their Bibles, and Protestants rely plenty on interpretive authorities. It's a matter of where the weight of emphasis falls. Baptism is a similar case. Those who baptize infants emphasize that God's grace reaches out to us first, before we can even respond. Those who baptize only adults emphasize the importance of our responding to that grace with a decision. Both sides claim solid biblical warrant for their position. And both sides acknowledge both elements in the equation but emphasize a different part of it.

This is not to say that it doesn't matter which side you might take on a particular argument. Every choice has implications, some minor, some very serious. God could have provided a daily newswire from heaven with precise instructions on every issue, fully indexed and cross-referenced. Instead, apparently, God expects us to take some responsibility for figuring things out. So the arguments are painful but necessary. Christians may have some basic doctrinal issues officially settled (such as the Trinity), and we may have several decently functioning options on some other matters (such as infant versus adult baptism). But every age has new issues about which people are desperate for guidance, and so the debates continue. Abortion, homosexuality, gender roles, the ethics of armed conflict in an age of weapons of mass destruction, the relationship of government to religious faith— we grapple with these matters today, as ever, in a shadowy place. The

Bible's words, history, reason, and God's mysterious guidance give light; but our human finitude and our sin leave us in some shadow. Perhaps God allows us to live here so that we learn to seek divine light and so that we learn, even in our confusion and mutual frustration, to hold hands.

MEMBERS OF THE BODY OF CHRIST

One of the most important blueprints for what Christian community looks like when it's working well is in Paul's letter to the first-century church at Corinth. Paul is hardly naive about the difficulties of getting along. He offers the Christians at Corinth the helpful metaphor of the body and instructs them to let that metaphor turn their focus away from their disagreements and onto their tasks as Christians. This model for Christian community applies to the whole church, but Paul was aiming it where it must first be lived out: at the local level. Paul writes:

> Now the body is not made up of one part but of many. If the foot should say, "Because I am not a hand, I do not belong to the body," it would not for that reason cease to be part of the body. And if the ear should say, "Because I am not an eye, I do not belong to the body," it would not for that reason cease to be part of the body. If the whole body were an eye, where would the sense of hearing be? If the whole body were an ear, where would the sense of smell be? But in fact God has arranged the parts in the body, every one of them, just as he wanted them to be. [1 Corinthians 12:14–18]

This passage is embedded in a larger disquisition on the different gifts that people bring to the work of the church—preaching, teaching, healing, administration, and so on. Paul is asking, essentially, that members of the church celebrate diversity when it comes to people's abilities, for the obvious reason that any group needs people performing a variety of tasks in order to function.

Of course, it's easy to value people who are capable, attractive, and useful. Paul goes on to explain that the Christian faith requires much more than that: "On the contrary, those parts of the body that seem to be weaker are indispensable, and the parts that we think are less honorable we treat with special honor. And the parts that are unpresentable are treated with special modesty, while our presentable parts need no special treatment" (12:22–24a). Paul recognizes that our tendency is always to rank one another in importance, to make constant calculations about status; but he insists the Christian community should operate differently. Not only should every member be valued, but those who are weaker or even embarrassing by the world's standards ought to receive greater honor. Communities of Christians, in other words, should be the place where people can go to shed all the world's status rankings. Children, women, racial minorities, homosexual men and women, poor people, unpopular people, people with awkward body shapes, people whose families have imploded, anyone who experiences the scorn of others—once they enter the church, they become an indispensable part of the body. The radical equality of all people before God—equal in our need for God, equal in our dependence on Jesus to enter that need and heal it—means that our value depends not on whatever strength or beauty we bring but on what God freely gives to us: himself.

Moreover, Paul writes, not only must Christians get along with one another at some discreet and comfortable distance; instead, they must invest in one another by suffering and rejoicing together: "But God has combined the members of the body and has given greater honor to the parts that lacked it, so that there should be no division in the body, but that its parts should have equal concern for each other. If one part suffers, every part suffers with it; if one part is honored, every part rejoices with it. Now you are the body of Christ, and each one of you is a part of it" (12:24–26). In a Christian community, members should be interconnected, sensitive to one another, wired together just as the parts of our bodies are connected by a nerve system that immediately communicates the pain or pleasure of the smallest part to the whole body.

This all sounds like an impossible ideal, and it is. I've seen the painful results of Christian communities that are stumbling on the way to this ideal. I know of congregations that, like other groups, succumb to a terrible pride, believing they have found the only way, focusing their energies not on showing the love of God to others but on drawing lines to keep out the riffraff. I know of groups that find ways to shame women for trying to exercise their gifts for preaching, accusing them of sinful pride and assuring them they must be mistaken if they believe God has given them such a gift. I've seen a congregation divide into rival cohorts—some loyal to the pastor, some eager for his ouster—until a large percentage of the membership left in disgust and the pastor, chewed up by bitterness and conflict, finally retired. We all like to form comfortable, insular groups made up of people who are just like us. And as with any group, when conflicts arise, the smaller the stakes, the fiercer the battles. It's possible for a church to die of pettiness, like a person getting stung to death by bees.

Churches get it wrong a lot, but they also have the resources to put things right. As Jesus said, "What is impossible with people is possible with God" (Luke 18:27, paraphrased). The standard Christian practices of examining one's conscience, admitting wrongs, and seeking forgiveness and reconciliation exert constant pressure against petty arguments, grudges, and insularity. Of course, it's possible to ignore these pressures. The woman who complains about how little the pastor works for his paycheck is probably busy enjoying her sense of superiority, keeping that part of her conscience insulated from examination. And it's possible to use the practices as weapons too, as when one person involved in a conflict insists that if the other person were *really* a Christian, he would come and seek forgiveness from him *first*. Still, regular churchgoers are bound to hear words of challenge from the Bible, from the pulpit, and even from one another with some regularity. Occasionally it does sink in.

I know even in my own soul, when I've wanted very badly to keep hold of a grudge and refuse to forgive or even see the good in someone I don't like, something has happened, through prayer and over time, to drain the anger and pride away. Christians say that reconciliation and peace are the work of the Holy Spirit, the person of the Trinity who creates movement and change in individual hearts and among groups. The Spirit brings our attention to where we are wrong, gives us the ability to admit it, and helps us change. The Spirit, like the forces of nature that transform a week of freezing rainstorms overnight into a warm sunny day, brings about reconciliation between warring parties, whether these are the pastor and the organist or the branches of the worldwide Anglican communion. If the church is a body made up of many parts, the Spirit is the life that breathes in it, animates it, and keeps it alive.

A DEEPER BELONGING

When deciding on which door in the great mansion of Christianity they wish to walk through, few people would take C. S. Lewis's advice and begin with a doctrinal analysis. Most people would listen around at the nearby doors for the group that seems to be having the best time together. Especially in a culture in which relationships are so often shallow or short-lived or both, people are thirsty for a deeper belonging.

The most obvious place to seek Christian community is in a worshiping congregation. But a congregation attached to a local church is not the only place where Christian community happens. I've experienced Christian community, for instance, among my family, my colleagues, many friends, and by now several congregations. Jesus once promised his disciples that "Where two or three come together in my name, there am I with them" (Matthew 18:20). In some ways I wish I had been able to live all my life in the same congregation, but on the other hand I value all these forms of community. Having moved around a little, I have a sense that God's people are everywhere, sort of like knowing that you have relatives in every city on earth. It's wonderful to sit in the parish church at St. James Picadilly, London, knowing not even one person's name yet participating in the baptism of a little girl and welcoming her into the whole church.

Christian community has come to feel for me like a great hall full of people doing some kind of complicated square dance. I know some other dancers well and others less well and others not at all, but we're constantly skipping around to the music we can all hear, linking arms and touching hands, weaving in and out of the groupings that form and dissolve and reform, smiling at one another and trying to keep the dance going. Christians call this connection among Christians of all times and places the communion of saints, which I suppose sounds better than "the great square dance of the saints."

The communion of saints is a mystical perception of that unity toward which we are striving; it's the way we all hear the same music. Maybe it's when we perceive that mystical connection that we know we have achieved Christian community. It can happen around a dinner table among friends. It can happen among a congregation as they sing with passion and attention. It can happen when a few people pray together or when strangers meet or in many other moments. When it happens, it is something more than mere pleasant human camaraderie or a diffuse feeling of spirituality. Real Christian community comes through a mystical perception always rooted in the ordinary stuff of life, when particular situations and particular people become transparent to a presence beyond them. The communion of saints occurs when our meals, our voices, our buildings, our humble bodies in proximity to one another are infused—at once inspirited and fused together—with some measure of the radiant peace of God.

ALTERNATIVE UNIVERSE

In order to find one's place in the house of faith, the most reliable method is to join up with a stable, located community—one that seems to be working diligently at the fundamentals of teaching, spiritual friendship, service, suffering and rejoicing, breaking down barriers, and—central to all else—worship.

Good Christian communities operate as more or less organized academies of the Christian faith. They thoughtfully enculturate children and adult newcomers by introducing them to basic matters of knowledge and practice. They also recognize that learning the faith is a lifelong pursuit and that everyone ought to stay in school together. So Bible stories and poems and other passages get read and preached about over and over in worship services; people continue to study the Bible in small groups; and everyone is reminded of the basics through music and other arts. People learn how to pray by listening to others do it. Preachers sort out matters of doctrine from the pulpit. And ideally members of the groups model for one another those qualities of love, joy, peace, patience, and so on that our salvation grows in us— what Paul called the fruits of the Spirit.

The teaching component, in order to succeed, must be embedded in an atmosphere of what we might call spiritual friendship. Christian communities provide a social group, and that's one fine reason to take up with one. But good Christian communities consciously cultivate friendship with a purpose, that of encouraging one another to keep on with the journey toward God. Spiritual friendships are what make large churches feel small: they provide individually tailored comfort as well as accountability. They help people figure out how to apply the general principles—like "Love the Lord your God with all your heart and with all your soul and with all your mind"—to your particular daily life. Networks of relationships with other Christians—some very close, some more distant, some official, some unofficial—give us contexts in which to ask not only "How are you?" but "How are you in your spirit?"

Some Christian groups create spiritual friendship instinctively, without a lot of programming and formality. I spent one summer a few years ago attending a small church in Holland, Michigan, that seemed to have mutual encouragement pretty well figured out. I could see this in the way church members gathered after Sunday morning worship in their fellowship hall, a large room comfortably trimmed out with bright lighting, carpeting, squashy sofas, and—unlike the worship space—air conditioning. They clearly designed the room with the intention to spend a lot of time there, and they did. Everyone lingered after worship and mixed together: married people, single people, old people, children, and most amazingly, teenagers. In my opinion teenagers are the canaries in the coal mine of community, and I've never seen a church with a more cheerful, involved crew of them. If, as in this church, teenagers are obviously known, loved, and (not incidentally) needed, if they are integrated into the daily tasks of the community with roles to play and work to do, something is going right. In this church teenagers were considered regular citizens, working in the nursery, playing instruments in worship, and running the sound board. They responded to this integration by accepting the mentoring of older people and also by providing their own capable mentoring of the tiniest members of the church. This cross-generational modeling was the primary active ingredient in the bonding compound that held this church together.

Other Christian groups, particularly very large churches, program spiritual friendship more deliberately. They figure out ways to get people into smaller groups, often appealing to them on the basis of some demographic feature like age, gender, or life situation. Some churches create Bible study or book discussion or service groups for singles, recently divorced people, just marrieds, college students, high schoolers with an interest in theater, and so on. Many churches offer accountability groups for people recovering from various addictions. Another recent trend is to take this business of encouraging spiritual growth, sometimes called discipleship, seriously enough to hire staff whose job is to make it happen. On the Web site for one famous megachurch—the kind whose membership count runs to five figures—I discovered an infrastructure of staff and fellowship groups so extensive and categorized in such detail that they even had a group specifically for hairdressers.[3]

Such full-service congregations are centers of church growth in the United States, suggesting that this model of carefully calibrated community has wide appeal. Having much in common with one's spiritual friends forms a shortcut to mutual understanding and in that sense makes encouragement and accountability that much easier. On the other hand, getting thrown together with an odd assortment of people with whom you have fewer things in common—other than journeying toward the same God—also has advantages. It tends to shift the focus directly onto that destination, for one thing. And if things go well, you can learn a great deal from people who are older, younger, darker-skinned, lighter-skinned, richer, poorer, more or less attached, or more or less educated than you are. All of us need spiritual friendships of both kinds, those with people much like us and those with people much different.

A network of spiritual friendships is the only context, moreover, in which most of us can find the strength to become the kind of people God wishes us to be. The ethical practices that the Christian faith demands we strive for—such as humility, truthfulness, sexual purity, an attitude of stewardship about money, and so on—are nearly impossible if we attempt them alone against the many counterpressures we feel from people and institutions that would have us act otherwise. Only among people whom we have learned to trust can we reveal our weaknesses and ask for help, and only in such a context can we call one another to account when we stray. Only in community can we hope to change our own hearts and practices and remain changed.

However, it's a matter not only of resisting bad behavior but also of finding new roles and actions. Paul's metaphor of the body is primarily directed toward finding and exercising what are commonly called spiritual gifts. I've said already that our value as individuals in the body depends not on whatever strength or beauty we bring but on what God freely gives to us: himself. God gives us himself in the form of gifts that serve others, and in community we can discover what those gifts might be. Some of the gifts Paul mentions in his discussions of spiritual gifts are wisdom, knowledge, faith, healing, miraculous powers, the ability to distinguish between spirits (we could call this discernment), teaching, preaching, helping, administration, encouraging, serving, contributing to the needs of others, leadership, showing mercy, speaking in tongues, and interpreting. We can explain or interpret or translate these gifts in different ways. For instance, speaking in tongues in some Christian traditions means coming under the influence of the Spirit so that one utters a strange babbling that sounds meaningless unless interpreted. That's not a gift many people have in my own tradition. But many Christians I know speak and write eloquently in their own language or have fluency in several languages. Both are also ways of speaking in tongues; both are gifts that can be used to serve God by serving others.

However you want to list or categorize the gifts that God gives people, the point is that when we live out good Christian community, we can find our gifts and use them to love one another according to the Bible's blueprint. When that happens, then the body of Christ becomes more than a metaphor. We, as a group of people, become more than the sum of our parts; we become something entirely new: the embodiment of Christ to one another and to the world.

God gathers us together because together we can create a critical mass of evidence to the world that God is real and loving and active. Together we are big enough to be noticed and weighty enough to shift the balance toward grace. Christian people together serve up platters of food to the elderly; they clean up the trash in the park; they hug small children; they found shelters for victims of domestic violence; they speak truth to power; they place themselves at the center of dangerous peacemaking efforts; they provide livestock for poor villagers; they found mission hospitals; they see suffering and weep and work for change. They teach the world why and how to praise the Creator and Savior of all things. All of this is service, but service can flourish only when rooted in community. We find ways to serve through the help of community, and serving together helps forms community too.

Suffering and Rejoicing

My parents have been part of a large circle of friends in their church congregation for over forty years, and these people have modeled for me the strength of Christian community over the long haul. Especially they have modeled for me the power of suffering and rejoicing with one another. Most of the time, the suffering and rejoicing have happened in small ways: they've met each other for coffee at restaurants, called each other on the phone, sent each other birthday cards, thrown parties and gone camping and attended each other's children's weddings. But terrible times came too, and that's when being together, although it did not stop the suffering, kept it from becoming defeat. The bitter funerals of children who died young, money troubles, illnesses, alcoholism, the loss of spouses—they've seen just about everything over the years. None of these people are professional counselors or clergy or doctors. They have no special training for supporting one another except faithfulness to God and to each other. They're not perfect either, and in a way it's the imperfection of their friendships that tells me something is binding them together beyond social parity or inertia. They know each other's faults very very well, and they get on each other's nerves sometimes. They occasionally bicker with each other over petty things and indulge in gossip that goes beyond mutual concern and borders on nosiness. Nevertheless, most of the time they accept each other, help each other, and enjoy each other, modeling the kind of long-term faithfulness that has helped me glimpse the faithfulness of God.

Many church congregations are pretty good at suffering together. They list prayer requests in the bulletin and organize meals for families in crisis and keep discretionary funds for people who find themselves in need of emergency money. One of my students once wrote a short memoir about how she, as a teenager, had been responsible for getting herself and her mother into a car accident from which she herself walked away but that left her mother's pelvis shattered. My student wrote about how people in her church provided meals for her family and helped with transporting the kids to school and lessons and practices for many months while her mom suffered and healed. This does not happen only in church congregations either. At the Christian college where I work, just about every week someone is writing in to the Listserv thanking everyone for the cards and phone calls that supported them through the loss of their parent or their cancer treatment or their child's recovery from a serious illness.

Weeping with those who weep has the flip side of rejoicing with those who rejoice, though in some circles this seems the less natural task. The pious Dutch among whom I grew up are not exactly known as the partying hedonists of the Christian faith—although I must say my parents' friends, for example, include some very funny people who know how to have a good time together. Still, I know from my own tradition's mild handicap in this area that rejoicing is a skill, like suffering together, that requires time, energy, and thought. I've seen churches with a knack for it. For instance, on the day my pastor friend Andrew announced during the worship service at his church that he had successfully completed his Ph.D., the congregation sent up such a spontaneous whoop of joy it brought tears to my eyes. One church I know out in the Michigan countryside throws a great party after worship services in the summer, complete with a homegrown band and barbecue. My brother- and sister-in-law held their wedding reception at a Greek Orthodox church campus whose banquet facility rivaled anything I've seen in an upscale hotel. When I first saw this place, I thought, *These people take celebration seriously.* Major facilities are not a requirement, though. When I moved to Iowa in 1992, I arrived newly pregnant; and even though people in my new church hardly knew me yet, a group of women decided to throw me a baby shower. We gathered in someone's basement recreation room and ate homemade food and a bakery cake and cooed over baby clothes. It was hardly a wild affair, but I was so grateful for their gentle celebration. They understood how important it is not only to enfold newcomers but to mark the great passages of life, both sorrowful and joyful, with one another.

BREAKING DOWN BARRIERS

Suffering and rejoicing with members of our own group is fairly nat-ural, but Paul's metaphor emphasizes extending that commitment to other parts of the body that feel different and distant. In other words, another fundamental feature of good Christian community is the evi-dent effort to break down barriers. My parents' group of church friends, who seemed to me as a child very different in personality and occupation, are all white, middle-class, and mostly the offspring of Dutch immigrants. There are certain kinds of barriers they have never had to cross in order to be Christians together. A number of years ago they faced a dilemma as they watched the neighborhood around their church building slowly change to a multiethnic, economically more uncertain neighborhood. They had to decide whether they could adjust their worship and their way of doing things in order to welcome people who were different. In the end they faced the truth that they simply could not make that big an adjustment. The point of crisis came when their pastor of over twenty-five years died of bone cancer, and they had to decide, as all congregations do at such a time, what kind of church they were now going to be. They decided to sell the build-ing to a Baptist church that *did* know how to connect with people in that neighborhood, and my parents' congregation merged with another church in a more suburban setting.

You could see that move as a kind of failure. In a way I think it was better to admit that they had neither the skills nor the commit-ment to make connections with the new neighborhood residents who obviously needed reaching and to step out of the way for someone who did. To give this congregation credit, it did manage a remarkably amicable merger with a sister congregation, avoiding petty power struggles that might well have ensued, particularly over finding a pas-tor for their newly merged church. And in the years following the merger, the congregation weathered a worship war by choosing the two-service solution, one traditional and one contemporary service every Sunday morning. I was impressed that the people of my parents' generation graciously recognized that younger people found hymns with the organ less comforting and expressive than newer styles of music and that the more traditional style did not represent the solemn dictates of God that everyone must follow. (A few exceptions left the church in a huff at the first whiff of contemporary worship.) Today this congregation lives with a certain generational segregation on Sunday morning—a lot of gray hair and suits at the early service, a lot of jeans and diaper bags at the late service—but in other ways it remains a unified body. So this congregation has put its energies into resisting the formation of internal barriers, and they have risen to that considerable challenge rather well.

My current church has more gifts for breaking down the kinds of demographic barriers that are so much a part of American public conversation. Our membership includes, for example, a number of people with physical and mental disabilities. We also seem to be a place where foreign nationals can find a church home; on a given Sunday you are likely to find among the white Americans numerous people from Nigeria, China, Sri Lanka, and Romania, some of them dressed in the style of their home country. Probably we have taken on this international flavor because, since our founding in the 1970s, we have had among us people with a heart for refugees. Recently we have undertaken an English-language tutoring program in order to offer assistance to the many immigrants now coming to our city. The demand for this service has become so great that we are constantly asking for more volunteers. In fact, overall we have done better in welcoming the world than we have in welcoming American racial and ethnic minorities. But we have recently been trying to work on that as well by partnering with an economically struggling African American congregation in town, trying to worship together once a month, provide support, listen, and build relationships among our memberships. We are now in the early stages of founding a deliberately interracial daughter church.

I discuss my own church not to hold it up as a model. We fumble and struggle every day and deal with apathy and resistance like any congregation. Many churches are breaking down barriers in ways far more extraordinary. I'm simply pointing out that ordinary Christian groups can contribute to the effort in numerous ways, based on whatever gifts and desires they have and the needs they discern around them. This is not a matter of sweeping along with some trendy multiculturalism but of responding to an ancient mandate based both on our creation and our destination. God created the world in variety and plenitude, and the variety of human qualities and human cultures is part of that blessed plenitude. Moreover, God's destination for that plenitude is to gather it to himself, and the church's job is to be a mechanism of that gathering. Both the Hebrew prophets of the Old Testament and the book of Revelation that concludes the New Testament posit a vision in which all nations come to God. The author of Revelation describes a holy city, a new creation (21:23–26), in which there is no temple because "the glory of God gives it light, and the Lamb [Jesus] is its lamp. The nations will walk by its light, and the kings of the earth will bring their splendor into it. . . . The glory and honor of the nations will be brought into it." Yes, there is a purifying process. Not every aspect of every culture is good. But all varieties of people have their splendors and honors, and all are needed to fulfill that final vision. Breaking down barriers is the foundation work for that new culture God is building. So Christian community at its best will always look countercultural; it is a new culture in the making.

WORSHIP AT THE CENTER

The final fundamental for a healthy Christian community is worship. In worship we become attuned to the Spirit's presence, and through that presence we receive the grace we need for all the other functions of community. Worship is central to Christian community because all the functions of community are enacted, in a concentrated way, in worship. Teaching happens in Bible reading, preaching, and praying. Gathering for worship gives people at least one opportunity per week to meet face-to-face, the foundational act in spiritual friendship. During worship services announcements can be made concerning who needs community in their suffering and who in their rejoicing, and worship itself gives us words and actions for doing both. The gathering of God's people in worship symbolically enacts the gathering of all God's people everywhere as we practice breaking down barriers by getting our bodies together in a room. And worship ideally motivates us for service and directs us toward means of serving. In fact, worship is itself service in one sense. The word *liturgy*, which describes the ordering of words and actions in worship, literally means "work." Worship is the main work of God's people.

We are physical creatures, and Christianity is not only about spirituality but about embodiment. Worship brings us together physically, reminding us that Christian community must be enacted in space and time. An Internet chat room—"click here to download sermon" and "click here to share prayer requests"—will never do on its own. Only perhaps as an opening gambit or a tool, a way to build trust or enhance communication. Christians have to get their bodies in a room together in order to remind ourselves of the physical nature of what we are and what we must do.

When we worship we get an emblematic picture of community. We see one another in the various stages of life: infancy, childhood, young adulthood, middle age, old age; working, prospering, struggling, suffering, wondering, lamenting. And we map each of these stages and phases to the God who is present in each one. In that way worship reorients community, pointing us together toward the one in whom we are united.

COMMUNITY AS THE NATURE OF GOD

I admit that I am sometimes ambivalent about community. Sometimes when a church I visit or the one I attend starts talking about the importance of friendliness and welcoming visitors, I feel as if Christians all have to be extroverts and community is primarily about shaking hands and smiling. These are pleasant actions, of course, but they don't take us very deep into the work of real community. On the other hand, I sometimes feel threatened by the depth of that work. I was once part of a group that met regularly in the hope of founding a new church, and one of the things this group wanted was more intimate community with each other. On one occasion, in describing her desire to share one another's burdens more intimately, one woman said, "I don't want just church *colleagues.*" Others nodded in agreement, but I was thinking, *That's exactly what I want. I like church colleagues!* As an introvert who is usually starved for silence and alone time, I felt threatened by her desire for greater intimacy and knowledge of each other. I had all I could do to bear the daily moods and events of my own family and workplace, and I wasn't looking to expand that circle. I liked a little distance.

I'm not saying I was in the right on this occasion. I was resisting, probably in a cowardly way, the idea of suffering and rejoicing with other members of the body. But this incident raises the question of closeness and distance in Christian community and just how much community business we are obliged to find time and energy for. Do I have to go to worship every week? Do I have to go to every Wednesday-night church supper? Must I be in a Bible study or a small group? Do I have to suffer and rejoice with everyone, or can I do so most intensely with only a few? And how do I build trust enough to be vulnerable with those few? In this too the eye must not say to the hand, "I do not need you" or "You ought to look more like an eye." We have different styles and gifts even for how we behave in community. I would hope that the heavily involved extroverts would not say to me, as a more retiring introvert: "You're selfish and arrogant." Nor that I would say to those who are especially gifted at intimate community, "You are a bunch of needy busybodies." We can help stretch each other without expecting everyone to be alike. Even our individual temperaments and gifts can change in different stages of life, influencing how many communal activities we can handle. At some stages in my life, I've been involved in church choir, Sunday school teaching, and several committees all at once. These days, when work and family require most of my energy, I do much less. The minimum for almost everyone is regular worship because faithfulness to that goes a long way toward creating the structures of community. Beyond that it's a matter of parceling out one's gifts and seeking guidance through prayer for doing so.

God put us together and gave us different roles in the body to prepare us "for works of service, so that the body of Christ may be built up until we all reach unity in the faith and in the knowledge of the Son of God and become mature, attaining to the whole measure of the fullness of Christ" (Ephesians 4:12–13). We need community because it helps us mature in the faith and because through community we find our gifts and our roles in works of service. But those things move us toward an even greater goal: perceiving and experiencing the fullness of God. God is not an autonomous singularity. As Father, Son, and Holy Spirit, God is communal by nature, existing in that eternal, dynamic dance. When we experience community, we come to a better understanding of God's character. More than that, by creating us and desiring relationship with us, God opens this communal self to welcome us. As individuals, yes, but as individuals who are being formed and molded into a community worthy and able to bear the presence of God.

God is all sufficient, as the theologians say. But God is also like the mother who is never entirely happy at the holidays until all her children and grandchildren are in the same room, eating and laughing together. Because God has spread open his own nature by creating and loving us, in a sense God is no longer complete without us. We are invited to the feast; we are invited into the dance. Only when we gather at the table he prepares for us, having forgotten all our quarrels in the joy of communion, are the purposes of God fulfilled.

CHAPTER TEN

℘

THE WORK OF OUR HANDS

Serving God and Others

ESTABLISH THE WORK OF OUR HANDS FOR US—
YES, ESTABLISH THE WORK OF OUR HANDS.
—Psalm 90:17

℘ **K**aren Ward, the Lutheran missionary who spends much of her time in the coffeehouses and clubs of Seattle, explains that the young adults with whom she frequently discusses the big questions of life are less interested in how religious people think than in what they do. These young people seek not so much a philosophy but a way of life; they are impressed not by systems of thought but by deeds of mercy. Karen's observations are supported by research on the generation of students now entering college, sometimes called the millennials. Community service is the norm among these young people, and selfishness is the cause they most frequently cite when asked what causes our nation's problems.[1]

The importance of service among younger people may be a response to their own hurts and fears, which have awakened them to the hurts and fears of others. The millennials have grown up among unstable, fractured families. They have heard round-the-clock news reports placing upon them the overwhelming weight of the world's brokenness. They live in a society in which everything, even human relationship, is commodified and marketed, and in which truth succumbs to spin. In such a world, we all have a choice: to become cynical and jaded or to do something. To give in or to counter pain with merciful action.

Psalm 90, one of the Bible's most melancholy poems, meditates on the brevity and fragility of our lives:

The length of our days is seventy years—
or eighty if we have the strength;
yet their span is but trouble and sorrow,
for they quickly pass, and we fly away.

The poem ends with a prayer that "the favor of the Lord" will rest upon us and that God will "establish the work of our hands" (verses 10, 17). In those moments when we take a longer perspective on our lives, we can see the wisdom the psalmist offers here. We are creatures who seek meaning, yet death threatens to evaporate whatever meaning we find or create. In the face of life's brevity and sorrow, what might God's favor look like? Like service, like something God gives us to *do*.

Many wisdom traditions propose that we defy our mortality by becoming useful to others, by leaving the world slightly better for our having been here. Compassionate people from all ages and parts of the world agree on this. They also agree that although people often seek fame and greatness as a way to defy their own mortality, this is not necessarily the best path. The quest for fame is fraught with temptations to vanity and corruption. And not everyone is cut out to accomplish deeds of renown on the big stage of history. Instead, certainly in the great religious traditions and most especially in Christianity, the recommended way, open to everyone, is humble service.

SERVICE AS GRATEFUL OBEDIENCE

For Christians, service arises out of obedience to God's will, and obedience arises out of love for God. Unfortunately Christians sometimes confirm the mistaken popular impression that religion mostly amounts to a set of thou-shalt-nots designed to spoil people's fun and make them rigid, conventional, and boring, not to mention self-righteous. I can see how people get this impression. We need guidelines for living, but some people adore rules too much and take inappropriate pleasure in condemning rule breakers. This is not the way Jesus described the proper motivation for right action, however. Jesus showed how obedience, to be genuine, must be transformed by the power of love.

Jesus often tried to help his Jewish listeners see their ancient laws as full-color portraits of the blessed life rather than black-and-white outlines of obedience. He, like all the prophets of Israel before him, urged his listeners to do God's will, not only with their law-abiding actions but also in their hearts, their inward being. The gospels of Matthew and Mark both record a particularly heated debate between Jesus and the Jewish teachers of the law (Matthew 22; Mark 12). When one fellow asked Jesus which of all the commandments was the greatest, Jesus reached deep into his people's Scriptures and touched the center of God's design for human life: "Love the Lord your God with all your heart and with all your mind and with all your strength" and "Love your neighbor as yourself" (Mark 12:30–31). Mark's gospel records that the questioner was entirely satisfied, and "no one dared ask him any more questions" (verse 34).

Jesus announced, in response to his critics, that he honored the ancient Jewish law and did not come to abolish it but to fulfill it (Matthew 5:17). Paul, in his later reflections on Jesus' teachings, continually insisted that Jesus did perfectly fulfill the law—he perfectly loved God and neighbor—and because he did so we can be saved by grace through faith and not by fulfilling the law. This means that we do not have to earn God's favor by following rules perfectly. If that were the only way to earn God's favor, we would be in trouble. We can never follow rules perfectly, let alone transform our inward beings so that we can perfectly love. God, by grace, has already given his favor through Christ. Our task now is to respond to that grace by following Jesus and learning to love God and neighbor through Jesus' example and power.

It turns out that the ancient laws, particularly the Ten Commandments, are excellent guidelines in helping us learn this love and set it into action for others. We do please God and gain blessing when we follow God's commandments. But a Christian understanding of obeying commandments must place obedience in the context of grace and service. We are sinners; we are saved by grace; and then we go do something about it. As I was taught to sum it up: guilt, grace, gratitude; or sin, salvation, service. This is one way in which the Christian view of service is distinct from other religions' and philsophies': Christians believe that we can show love for others only because God loves us first. Our service to others flows not out of our own inner goodness or loyalty to humanity—for those can be terribly fragile and intermittent—but out of God's fierce loyalty to humanity. We serve out of obedience, but obedience is gratitude at work.

FOLLOWING JESUS' SIGNPOSTS

The Ten Commandments form a basic Christian guide for action, as do many of the broader principles of ancient Jewish law, such as communal care for the vulnerable and the outsider. But the primary Christian model for grateful service is Jesus. Christians seek to imitate what Jesus did: heal all kinds of physical and mental distress, touch emotional pain with gentleness and truth, forgive and encourage people, and—not incidentally—call things by their proper names. Jesus was a savvy enemy of spin, particularly among religious people. He called to account the religious leaders who criticized others for small violations of the Jewish law and set themselves up as superior in their obedience to the law. He unmasked people's pride, asking them, for example, why they were looking at the "speck of sawdust" in others' eyes while paying no attention to the "planks" in their own (Luke 6:41).

Jesus accompanied his acts of healing with words about the coming kingdom. His disciples wanted him to bring the kingdom of God to Israel right then and there, the whole thing, now. But instead Jesus provided signposts of what the kingdom will look like: people who are blind will be able to see; people who have diseases will be cured; people who are poor will hear good news (Matthew 11:15). All the most unlikely people will be invited to the best parties (Luke 14:15–24). Jesus showed his followers a vision of something much greater even than the prosperity and liberation from Roman authority that Israel desired. He reminded them of the inclusive vision of wholeness and flourishing that the Hebrew prophets had imagined; he reminded them about shalom. He did it through signs and words and then left the rest to his followers: "I've pointed you in the right direction—now it's your turn." Christians say that Jesus ascended into heaven, which is to say that Jesus' physical presence is no longer in this world. However, we are; and Jesus' Spirit empowers our actions in the world. We are the hands and feet of Jesus now, and we have to keep pointing to the kingdom. Jesus instructed his disciples to pray to the Father, "Your kingdom come, your will be done, on earth as it is in heaven." We serve others as a response to that prayer.

NOT-SO-SECRET AGENTS OF SHALOM

The idea that Christians have work to do in this world is bred in the bone for me. My whole sense of the faith was formed in a kind of work-ethic epicenter. Multiply the famed Protestant work ethic by the Dutch work ethic by the immigrant work ethic and you have where I live. It has always amused me that in this tradition where we remind each other at frequent intervals that we can do nothing to earn our own salvation, we all seem to work so hard.

In some branches of the faith, tradition holds some ways of life as more dedicated to God than others. In the Roman Catholic tradition, for example, joining a religious order or becoming a priest are ways to give your life more fully to God than, say, being a plumber or selling insurance. In some American evangelical circles, serious Christians signal their dedication by entering full-time Christian service, as a pastor or missionary or director of a Christian agency. But the Reformers, particularly Luther, insisted that everyone in every station of life can serve God equally well. Working as a plumber, a missionary, a teacher, a builder, a lawyer are all equally valid paths for the service of God. Everything we are, everything we have, everything we do, whatever it is: give it to God. Any task, done with integrity and gratitude to God, is service. Sietze Buning, a poet who wrote about Dutch immigrant life on the farms of Iowa, described how his father used to feed the animals extra food on Sundays so that even that part of his work reflected God's Sabbath rest. Buning acknowledges in the poem that overfeeding is a bad idea, even in God's name, but also affirms his father's commitment of all his work to God, as if "Holiness to the Lord" were inscribed on every milk pail, sledge, and hay rake.[2] The apostle Paul wrote to the Colossian church: "And whatever you do, whether in word or in deed, do it all in the name of the Lord Jesus, giving thanks to God the Father through him" (3:17). There's a particularly strong emphasis on this in the Reformed view, but all kinds of Christians would agree.

I do think some people give themselves to God more fully than others; most of us have corners of our hearts and areas of our lives that we hold to ourselves, afraid of what might happen if we surrender them to God. But I also believe it's quite correct that service is a matter of the heart and not of one's particular profession. After all, if we are praying that the kingdom will come, well, there's plenty of work to do and we need all kinds of workers. The gospel accounts tell us that Jesus could heal people with a touch and a word; he didn't have to build hospitals. But people who follow Jesus most often have to bring about healing and hope in the usual, slow, difficult way. They have to study medicine, learn to do psychological counseling, grow food and help other people grow it better. They have to teach and care for children, build useful things, write music, challenge injustice, paint murals, call things by their right names, and try to change bad systems against all odds.

I have found over the years, however, that a work-centered view of the Christian life requires living with paradox. One paradox involves the importance of what goes on in this world, in this life, now. Does it matter? If God is planning a new creation, why bother to fix this one? After all, if someone is building you a brand-new house, why would you bother to put new kitchen cabinets in the old one? Why not relax and wait around till the new place is ready? That analogy doesn't hold, however. *This* is the creation that awaits liberation. God in the person of Jesus entered *this* world, so we know that this world matters to God. *This* is the old house God has begun to renovate. We can either keep making the place worse, stand around and do nothing, or pick up a hammer.

Another paradox involves the value of our help. On the one hand, nothing we do, no matter how noble and self-sacrificial, earns us points with God. There are no points. Salvation comes by grace through faith, "not by works, so that no one can boast" (Ephesians 2:9). However, another strong current in the Bible suggests that our behavior has enduring consequences. The author of the New Testament book of James writes, "faith by itself, if it is not accompanied by action, is dead" (2:17). Jesus told a story of the "Son of Man" (a title he used for himself) sitting in judgment and separating people like sheep from goats. The sheep are the ones who have acted in mercy and helped those who were hungry, thirsty, strangers, naked, sick, or imprisoned. The Son of Man welcomes them to receive their "inheritance, the kingdom prepared for you since the creation of the world." The goats are the ones who lacked these deeds, and they wind up going "to eternal punishment" (Matthew 25:31–46). Sermons on this passage predictably make people squirm. Is it all about grace or not? Do our deeds matter or not?

This is another example of a useful tension in Scripture, and different branches of Christianity tend to lean toward one side or the other of it. Roman Catholics traditionally emphasize the importance of works and Protestants generally emphasize faith, but both acknowledge the necessity of both. I was taught to resolve the tension by declaring that good works do not *earn* salvation but are a *sign* of salvation. Good works grow naturally when God replants us by grace, like sick little trees, in the soil of himself. That's true; people do experience that kind of natural result when they surrender their lives to God. Roman Catholics would wisely add that good works can serve as restitution for our sins and help us along that path of salvation. At any rate, we have to retain the tension and live with it. The "works count, so watch out" passages in the Bible do not express the final truth about salvation; but they remind us that God cares about what happens here and now, and they can keep us, shall we say, highly motivated.

When we manage to do good works, the question remains whether our service accomplishes anything. If we all work very very hard, do we actually bring in the kingdom? After all, good hospitals and schools and just governors and well-motivated scientific advances do make a difference in the world. At the college where I teach, we expend a great deal of effort urging students to find their gifts and use them to build the kingdom; to go out there and infiltrate every field of knowledge and every profession, from accounting to filmmaking to civil engineering; and to infuse a Christian perspective into everything they do. We often sound like cheerleaders: "Engage the world! Redeem culture! We're hard-working Protestants and we can do it! Yes!" I believe with all my heart that God uses people's efforts to heal and bring hope; I see it every day. But the danger is that we might get all triumphant and think that *we're* doing it and not God. Humanity is evolving; we're contributing to progress; and if we keep at it, someday angels will descend on clouds to thank us.

This kind of self-congratulation amounts to self-flattery. We would all love to be worthy of God's favor; we would love our work to earn points with the Almighty. Probably that's why the staunchest saved-by-grace people work so hard: deep down, we would rather earn it. We like to think of ourselves as competent and deserving, so that grace is harder to accept than fair wages. This is, at heart, the sin of pride. A tendency to work too hard, even for God, can participate in the idolization of work in the culture around us. We might put a label of Christian service on it, but hard work without rest can be a mask for a sense of our own indispensable importance and a desire to look good and earn God's favor. If we're honest when we look under the surface of even our best efforts, we see them tainted by vanity, ignorance, arrogance, hypocrisy, foolishness, and any number of other flaws large and small. Better to rest from our work regularly and remember that whatever good comes of our service is God's doing.

What a great relief, because no matter what you choose as your contribution to the world, you will have many moments of failure, frustration, discouragement, and even despair. My sister-in-law Rachel spent years lavishing good attention on an at-risk young girl I'll call Lisa through the Big Sister program, hoping to help steer her away from the trouble and poverty for which she seemed destined. All went fine for a time, but when Lisa hit adolescence, she failed in school, hung out with the wrong people, and got pregnant. Rachel could not steer her away from all mistakes and could not protect her from all sorrows. Rachel might well wonder what good her friendship did. Well, there's no formula for such a calculation, and it would be deadly to invent one. No matter how many surgeries you perform on children in Guatemala with cleft palates, many more will still need help. No matter how many homeless alcoholics you shelter and help, many more will die on the streets. The world's pain is far too big for you or your government or your organization to solve completely. We have to credit our successes to God so that our failures also can rest in God's open hand.

Leaving the outcome to God frees us from the need to succeed. We're not planning the entire kingdom operation, and we're not responsible for its ultimate success. We're just the agents. We have to do our own part the best we can, with God's help, and let the Spirit of God move freely in fire and wind. At my college we like to talk about Christians' role in the world as agents of shalom. We use the word *agent* in the sense of *one who acts in the interest of,* but it always make me think of us more like secret agents, sitting at our desk jobs wearing black suits and dark glasses. It all seems very sneaky and exciting.

The truth is that most of the time, we ought to concentrate our efforts on staying out of God's way. We are probably less like secret agents and more like the little kid who wants to "help" bake cookies. He spills flour and measures things inexactly and eats a lot of the chocolate chips. Mom has to intervene to clean up the messes if any of the cookies are going to turn out. It's a terribly inefficient operation. Yet it has value other than efficiency, in teaching the child and in the loving companionship built by a shared task. I imagine God sometimes would like to shoo us out of the way and get down to business without our help. But like a wise mother, God generously welcomes us back again and again into the kitchen.

OF SACRIFICES AND TINY LIGHTS

I recently read a hip, funny Christian novel in which a young, single man moves to South Carolina and starts going to church in order to meet women. His strategy succeeds: he meets an attractive woman who turns out to be a missionary to Ecuador home for a short visit. She returns the protagonist's romantic interest but only with coy little hints that keep him at arm's length. In the course of pursuing this woman, our hero winds up falling from a fishing yacht, knocking his head on the boat's edge, and surrendering himself to God in his hospital bed. After this he begins to lose interest in his job as a stock broker. He gives up a promotion to a high-powered position at a brokerage in Manhattan and instead joins the beautiful missionary at her orphanage in the Amazon. The novel ends with him at peace in the jungle, even though—much to my disappointment anyway—he never persuades the woman to so much as kiss him.[3]

Despite the novel's many clever lines and funny moments, I ended up peeved at the protagonist. I don't mind so much that he never got it together with Miss Missionary. But why stay in the Amazon trotting around behind her like a spaniel? Once he surrendered to God, he wanted his life to change somehow, to look different. But he never seriously asked what he already had that God might want to use, such as his head for numbers. Fascination with this woman got him onto the plane to Ecuador, and he stayed there vaguely imagining that life is always more spiritual and closer to God in a jungle.

Maybe he did what was true for his character at his stage of understanding, but I thought the novel would have concluded much more
interestingly if our hero had gone back to New York and started figuring out how to be a Christian stockbroker.

People often put well-meaning but mistaken limits on how God
might use them. They have narrow ideas about what it means to serve
God, and God has to invite them to expand their imaginations. Those
of us who are converted and ever converting rightly expect that the
little boats of our lives travel differently than they would without God
at the helm. The word *conversion*, after all, literally means "turn." But
how big is the turn, in terms of what we do every day? Twenty degrees?
One-eighty? Three-sixty?

Yes. Any of the above. Just pick one.

Through years of asking in prayer what God wants me to do at
this or that point of decision, I have been repeatedly surprised by how
uninterested God seems in making me fit any self-constructed mold of
the ideal Christian life. Some people do go to seminary and become
pastors or priests; some head off to the Amazon or the Congo; some
preach on the streets. But those paths have not become my path, and
I don't think that means I have missed the exit to the great heaven-
ward highway of my life. Through all the twists and turns on the back
roads, it seems that God has guided me to teach college and write and
raise a family and try to be a friend. None of it quite fits any mold or
even all fits together neatly. So what? Why should my story be simple?

It seems that God guides people toward service in all kinds of
individually tailored ways. Some people carve out time after their regular jobs to help immigrants learn English or to serve on boards of
nonprofit organizations. Some people manage to get jobs that allow
them to spend their income-producing hours directly helping those
in need, like teaching in an at-risk school or doing social work. Some
people spend enormous time, energy, and skill doing the behind-the-
scenes volunteer work that keeps a church or school in operation. I
especially admire the people who have the vision, political savvy, and
administrative skill to start big things, like the fellow at my church
who thirty years ago began a Habitat-for-Humanity-style housing
ministry committed to rebuilding our city's deteriorating neighborhoods and providing safe, affordable housing for low-income families.
Today anyone can drive down streets in the middle of town and see

what he and the people he has gathered into this effort have accomplished: lovely, well-kept homes where there used to be trashy vacant lots and collapsing, rat-infested hovels. He can quantify his service in terms of families helped, grant monies won, homes built. I sometimes wish my little forms of service had such obvious results.

Still, I find it comforting that Jesus described service in much simpler terms. He told his followers that they were like salt in the world, like a light on a hill, or like the yeast in a lump of dough—all small, barely noticeable things that nevertheless make a big difference (Matthew 5:13–16; 13:33). So I can be salt and light without founding a nonprofit. I can be salt and light with only a kind word to someone every day. In that famous sheep-and-goats passage mentioned earlier, the deeds Jesus names as winning the sheep their inheritance are simple and local: giving food to the hungry, a drink to the thirsty, a visit to the prisoner. The sheep don't seem to run refugee ministries or lobby Congress to fund world hunger initiatives—although that is exactly the sort of thing this passage has inspired some people to do. I take the passage to mean that God also and perhaps especially cherishes those who, like my own mother, perform the simple, unnoticed deeds of mercy without which this world would quickly turn dark and flat. When I think of all the cards my mother has sent to senior citizens living in the nursing home, all the cakes she has baked for people to comfort them as they grieved and planned a funeral, all the little goody bags of practical supplies she has dropped off on the doorsteps of struggling families, I see a string of tiny lights stretching across her life, so many that together they give off a dazzling brightness. I recently attended two funerals of my mother's good friends. On both occasions, when I greeted the deceased person's grown children, all they could say to me, through their tears, was how grateful they were for all my mother had done for their families. They're not talking about anything spectacular; Mom never loaned them large sums of money or anything. But she showed up again and again even at the most unattractive moments, often joining her friend Shirley, for example, when she went to the Alzheimer's care unit to help feed her husband his supper. Such deeds seem precious to those who receive them. What have I ever done that would mean so much to someone? It's a question, if we dare, we all could ask ourselves.

Give What You Have

Curiously the sheep-and-goats passage follows directly in Matthew's gospel on the heels of the parable of the talents. Perhaps in trying to be sheep, the best way to begin is to take inventory of our talents, which we can understand to mean abilities, experiences, desires, opportunities, and levels of courage. We should consider even our faults potentially useful. I know God has often used my ambition and pride to prod me into following through on worthwhile things even when I get discouraged.

Deciding how to take one's own basketful of resources and spend them in God's service is a little bit like emergency first aid: unless you are in immediate moral or mortal peril, the best strategy is to stay where you are and take inventory. What can you do right now with what you have right now? For some people this is obvious. Lawyers can do pro bono work, and doctors can volunteer time in inner-city clinics, for example.

Some of us have to hunt harder in our baskets to find a creative way to serve. I know a woman named Barb whose children were all grown and her garden flourishing and her house perfectly clean. She thought, *Now what? What do I know how to do?* She considered using her sewing skills but was not quite ready to "turn that over to God." Still, after some struggle she asked God to help her find a way to use sewing as service. Two days later she got a call from a community center in an economically struggling neighborhood asking if she would help teach a workshop on starting a business by making items from donated fabric. Since then she has taught neighborhood kids and adults how to sew, helping them gain skills and a sense of pride and accomplishment and building a small community of friendships. "What's amazing to me," she told me, "is the way everything we need gets laid at our feet—if we need machines or fabric, it always comes to us somehow. That's what happens when you give what you have to God."

Probably we all have more in our baskets than we think we do. In one of the more famous gospel stories, Jesus feeds a crowd of people beginning only with some loaves of bread and a few fish, multiplying the resources until everyone is fed and there are baskets of leftovers. (Luke 9:10–17 is one of several accounts.) Through the ages this story has been received as a picture of the way God often takes a small gesture offered in trust and grows it into something miraculous.

YOUR DEEP PASSION AND THE WORLD'S GREAT NEED

In the course of discussing how to make service more than an extracurricular activity in one's life, Christians often use the word *vocation*. To live your whole life in service to God, the standard wisdom goes, you must discover your vocation or calling in life. Writer Frederick Buechner has famously defined *vocation* as "the place where your deep gladness and the world's deep hunger meet."[4] This line gets slightly misquoted in interesting ways. I've seen it as "the place where your *greatest gifts* and the world's deep hunger meet" or "the place where your *deepest pain* and the world's deep hunger meet." What's at stake, of course, is whether you seek ways to serve out of your strengths or your weaknesses. You can look around and see people operating effectively either way. I know a woman who turned her gifts for science into a degree in botany. She now works for an organization called ECHO that serves as a research institute, seed bank, and information clearing house for development workers trying, quite literally, to ease the world's deep hunger. She is serving out of her strengths. A couple in my church, on the other hand, found in their deepest pain—infertility— the inspiration to become foster parents and then adoptive parents. I know they think of caring for their new son not as service but as a joyful privilege. Often there's little distinction when service is done right.

Curiously many people find that their greatest gift comes precisely from their deepest pain. This is why so many charitable organizations are founded by parents who have lost a child. Their terrible grief gives them the energy to lobby for stricter drunk driving laws or to raise money for leukemia. So I think the best misquotation of Buechner's definition is this: vocation is "the place where your *deep passion* and the world's deep hunger meet." Passion refers both to deep joy and deep pain; both can release enormous energy.

Although I certainly agree that we should all seek those places where our passion and the world's hungers meet, I'm actually skeptical of the word *vocation*. I have seen how my college students tend to equate vocation or calling with career and then agonize over finding the perfect job. They want God to lead them into an income-producing activity that uses all their gifts, serves others, and supports the family. Getting these requirements lined up nicely usually works all right for nursing majors, but many other students get completely stymied. The problem is that the term *vocation* appears singular. It implies that there is one thing we each must do, from now to eternity, and we simply have to find out what it is and avoid doing anything else. Meanwhile God, of all the annoying things, typically does not send telegrams with the correct answer. Besides, for most of us, the path we travel is not that straight. We try one job, move on to another, retool for another, quit or cut back to care for children, deal with surprising opportunities, face bitter disappointments, and all in all struggle at every stage in life to take a sensible next step with, let's face it, no knowledge of the future.

I've given up on the word *vocation* altogether. When my college students come in for advising before graduation, I tell them to seek guidance through prayer and through talking with wise people who love them and then take a step—any step. I assure them that they can base their decision only on what they know right now. They can't know now what they will know in ten years, so don't bother to try. They need to take a step whether or not it launches them on the most direct trajectory toward some true destiny. I try to be gentle and encouraging about this, but the subtext is: "Just do something! The fate of the universe does not hang on this one step! Life is full of twists and turns! Get used to it!" This is advice I've had to learn to dispense to myself over and over again.

Some people's passions are obvious, and God leads them through those passions into a single path of service. Mother Teresa, for example, or the lifelong kindergarten teacher, or the musician who offers his skillful playing every day for God's glory and other people's joy. Others, like me, have less obvious passions: what gives them energy develops over time or remains partially hidden or blooms suddenly in response to new situations. As a result such people offer an assortment of odds and ends as service: a regular job done with integrity, some volunteer work, a career decision that seeks service over money and prestige, kindness to neighbors, maybe a late-life passion for going on mission trips or teaching teenagers appliance repair. Their lives may not have the clean simplicity of vocation, but at the center of everything they do is a deep love for God—and *that* is everyone's true vocation.

I've learned that God treasures the lives made of a single piece of cloth, cut in the shape of service. But God also values the lives that look more like a bag of fabric scraps, some big pieces, some tiny pieces, different colors and weaves. At each stage in my life, with each piece of it, I try to ask God, "How can I offer this to you?" I have to trust that if I offer all the odds and ends of my life, God will stitch together the pieces in some lovely pattern and receive it as my gift.

Will It Hurt?

Despite years of brainwashing into the Reformed tradition, with its genius for turning everything from organ playing to lawn mowing into Christian service, I sometimes still think that if I really loved God I would be a missionary, preferably in some remote village where people spend most of their time skewering poisonous snakes and whapping insects the size of fists. Not that I have any practical skills, experience, or even an ounce of desire for such a life. In fact, that's exactly why this thought teases me sometimes, because some weird little voice still whispers occasionally that one is not truly serving God unless one is miserable. In many Christian circles, unspoken point values get assigned to various forms of service. The less appealing the recipients of your care, the more points you get. The further away from home you travel to serve, the more points you get. The more dangers and discomforts involved, the more points you get.

But wait: it's not about points.

Nevertheless, we generally do, in any endeavor, measure the degree of someone's commitment by the sacrifices they are willing to make in order to accomplish something important. Christian history is filled with people who gave up wealth, health, or homeland to perform some service in the name of Jesus. Christian history is filled with martyrs. After all, Jesus warned that anyone wishing to follow him must "deny himself and take up his cross and follow me" (Matthew 16:24). Jesus himself became the ultimate model of willingness to suffer and die for others. On the other hand, Jesus also said, "My yoke is

easy and my burden is light" (11:30) and promised that any grief paid
in his name would be reimbursed with interest: "Everyone who has
left houses or brothers or sisters or father or mother or children or
fields for my sake will receive a hundred times as much and will inher-
it eternal life" (19:29). No wonder people get confused about whether
or not service ought to hurt.

This question may be a little like wondering whether raising
children ought to hurt. It's not so much that it *ought* to hurt, and so
you go into it precisely because you think labor pain and sleepless
nights and the grief of letting go are good for you. No, you go into
it hoping for love and delight; and you accept the pain involved simply as part of the package, the part that you try to handle for the sake
of the greater wonder. So with service. It's a mistake to choose some
line of service *because* you expect it to make you suffer. This is the kind
of false notion that Buechner's line about "deep gladness" is designed
to correct. Not that God can't use even an odd desire to feel pain.
Certain Christian mystics, including the English mystic Julian of
Norwich, displayed a strange fondness for suffering because they
believed it enabled them to love the suffering Christ more dearly. But
precisely because any kind of service will inevitably involve frustrations and perhaps even pain, only passion is the right beginning, the
source that will continue to flow through that pain.

The pain involved in service may not be as obvious as a snakebite
or a close call with a knife-wielding drunk. Sometimes service can
bring about pain as subtle as a growing sense of one's own need to shift
priorities, a kind of integrity discomfort. The suffering that comes
with service also sometimes comes from the realization that the supposedly most noble endeavors tend to lose their romantic sheen.
Missionaries have petty turf battles and get paralyzed by church
bureaucracies. My friends Trevor and Linda admit that the stress of
their work with kids and teenagers in Jersey City has sometimes been
hard on their marriage. I used to think my husband's grandmother,
who married a missionary doctor and spent twenty-five years in
Pakistan and Nigeria, was one of the most peaceful, noble servants of
God I knew. I still think she is, but I also know now that when the
suffering came, she felt it. She made her first trip from the United
States to India by boat across the Pacific, during World War II, while
pregnant. She gave birth prematurely in Rangoon, Burma, under the

care of ignorant nurses and an unsympathetic doctor; and she avoided puerperal infection only by walking defiantly out of the hospital
with her new infant. Shortly afterward the Japanese attacked Pearl
Harbor, and then she got word that her father had died in a car accident. By the time she and her husband finally arrived at their destination, a year had passed since the day they left Michigan, and they
were exhausted and ill. About this year she does not say, "I never felt
the pain because I had so much joy in God's service." Instead she
admits: "It was a nightmare."

Even Mother Teresa, the modern saint renowned for her love for
Christ, did not always feel joy in her work at the Nirmal Hriday house
for the dying in Calcutta. Some of her recently published letters to
her spiritual directors reveal that she suffered not so much from the
sights and smells of her daily work but from a sense of God's absence.
After the extraordinary mystical experiences of communion with
Christ that prompted Mother Teresa to begin her work with the destitute and dying, she experienced a "dark night of the soul" that seems
to have lasted the rest of her life. Smith College professor of religion
Carol Zaleski, in reflecting on the published letters, writes:

> We may prefer to think that she spent her days in a state
> of ecstatic mystical union with God, because that would
> get us ordinary worldlings off the hook. How else could this
> unremarkable woman, no different from the rest of us, bear to
> throw her lot in with the poorest of the poor, sharing their
> meager diet and rough clothing, wiping leprous sores and
> enduring the agonies of the dying, for so many years without
> respite, unless she were somehow lifted above it all, shielded
> by spiritual endorphins? Yet we have her own testimony that
> what made her self-negating work possible was not a subjective
> experience of ecstasy but an objective relationship to God shorn
> of the sensible awareness of God's presence.

God gave Mother Teresa a passionate faith but not the "spiritual consolation" we might expect she depended on to keep going. It seems
she shared not only in the physical suffering of Calcutta's destitute but
in the philosophical suffering of all those who experience doubt.[5]

Everyone who sets out to serve in the name of Jesus will end up
carrying a parcel containing a little bit of the world's suffering. Mother

Teresa carried a very large parcel because she had very great love. Compared to her it's easy to feel small, fearful, empty of love, and quite useless. I know I have the feeling that I could never be like her or other great servants that I admire, no matter how hard I tried. I try to remember that service is only partly a matter of trying. Mostly service is a matter of accepting the passions we have been given by God—and that in itself is difficult enough. When, through prayer and small daily choices, we can accept the passions we already have, then God can water them, prune them, and let them flourish for the sake of the world God loves.

EPILOGUE: MYSTERY

To reach the tiny island of Iona, Scotland, you must travel, it seems, to the end of the world. First, you make your way by train or car to Oban, a fishing village turned resort town on the western coast of Scotland. Then you take a ferry across to the Isle of Mull, where a bus will wind you across the island for an hour on one-lane, curvy roads, away from the mainland and toward the open sea. At last you arrive at Fionnphort, on the westernmost shore of Mull, where you catch your first glimpse, most likely through heavy mist, of Iona. Another short ferry ride and you arrive on the isle itself, a mile wide and about three miles long, hanging off the edge of Scotland like a jeweled earring. Iona is beautiful in a rough, windy sort of way, with its jagged highland hills rising from boggy pastures; its lonely beaches heavily exposed to the North Sea; its working sheep crofts, one-lane village, and restored stone abbey. But people don't flock there all summer for the views; they can find better ones with far less trouble. People come to Iona on pilgrimage because they have heard that there the veil is thin between the physical world and the spiritual world. There at the end of the earth, people say, you are closer to heaven.

A young monk named Columba founded a tiny Christian community on Iona in 562 A.D., making his own harrowing journey from Ireland in a small boat. He had gotten himself into some trouble back home, so he chose this little grass-covered piece of rock as his new home mostly because even from its highest hill he could no longer see Ireland. Iona became the base for Columba's missionary efforts into the land of the Picts (ancient Scots), and it has been a place of Christian community and a pilgrimage site almost ever since.

Is the veil really thinner there? I've been there twice for short stays, and I sometimes felt that the more people told me how thin the veil was, the more opaque it became. Mostly I struggled to stay warm against a chilly, rain-spattered wind that even in summer blows almost ceaselessly across the island. Perhaps the wind makes one appreciate more keenly the calm shelter of the abbey church. Worshiping in the abbey, walking through the ruins where monks and nuns used to pray and work, I did apprehend as never before how ancient is this Christian faith and how ancient is this Jesus whom we worship. We do not possess him, we moderns. We are only the latest latecomers to the worship of Christ. Christ, the Ancient of Days, a mystery before all time and in all time, imprinted in the wind and the sea as much as in the worn Celtic crosses near a little abbey at the end of the world.

THE QUEST TO KNOW

I want so much to know everything, to understand everything. When I consider the vast diversity of life on this planet, the unimaginable distances of space, the puzzling uniqueness of each person, the terrible sorrows that crush our spirits, the enormity of love, the beauties of every ordinary day—I am overwhelmed. Where do I fit into all this? How can I begin to understand it all? It seems the more I think and experience and master small areas of knowledge, the more the wonders expand, broader and deeper beyond all telling.

To make sense and meaning out of our lives, to find some way to sort out our days and our place in the world, we need to simplify and organize it all while still giving full scope to the wonder, full weight to that something more. As a framework of understanding, the Christian faith rests on great pillars of certainty; yet those certainties are mysteries. When Christians believe in God as Creator, Redeemer, and Sustainer; when we pray and worship; when we build community with one another; when we suffer and ease the suffering of others; when we seek to conform ourselves daily, body and soul, to Christ's dying and rising to unending life, in all these things we are basing our lives on certainties we can believe with confidence but not fully comprehend. We cannot master these mysteries; we can only place ourselves continually in their presence.

When we acknowledge that the Trinity is a mystery, that suffering is a mystery, that the resurrection is a mystery, does that mean we have given up trying to understand or that about some things we should not try to understand? Perhaps, like me, you don't like to accept things without question. Perhaps you share the impatience of people who, when they hear the word *mystery* used in the context of religious faith, suspect that behind the veil of that word, there may be nothing at all—or something altogether silly, like the puffing, frantic little man behind the curtain in *The Wizard of Oz*.

I have found that the mysteries of the faith do not require that we shut down questions but that we open ourselves to greater answers and perhaps to questions we have never asked. We perceive the energy of the atom and its infinitesimal particles only through a combination of higher mathematics, powerful electron microscopes, and theorizing minds. Similarly the mysteries of God call from us a combination of all our capacities and then some—intellect, imagination, will, feeling, and the gift of the Spirit—before we can touch their truth.

Developing these capacities takes time and daily practice. When it comes to apprehending mystery, we cannot expect, as we do in so many areas of life in the postmodern world, to follow a programmed pattern of behavior and receive instant and repeatable results. We tend to expect these days that we can purchase experiences in convenient packages—the thrilling movie, the perfect restaurant meal, the fabulous vacation. The capacity to apprehend mystery is not like that. It cannot be packaged or purchased. Instead it requires, as writer and pastor Eugene Peterson puts it, a "long obedience in the same direction."[1]

So the Christian faith invites us into daily practices in the same direction, into what soon begins to look like a pilgrimage: we study the Bible, worship together, serve in Jesus' name. We pray and hope and seek God's guidance and wait. We face discouragements and setbacks. As we do these things, it's not so much that we understand the mysteries more clearly but that the mysteries have their effect on us, slowly molding us over time. Our behaviors change; our thoughts change; our desires and hopes slowly transform. We start becoming the people God has designed us to be, people in communion with God—friends of God who take on the reflected light of God's presence. As the psalmist observes, "Those who look to him are radiant" (Psalm 34:3).

ALWAYS BEGINNERS

As we seek to hold on to the mysterious certainties of the Christian faith, it's only human nature to grip too tightly and compress these certainties into too-limited, too-simple formulations. Part of us wants truth to come in portable sizes. In trying to explain who Jesus is, for example, Christians can manage to reduce him to the good moral teacher in sandals, the wise founder of a social justice movement, a model CEO, their personal life consultant, the knight who defends their version of the truth, or even—if the worst contemporary worship songs are an indication—the perfect boyfriend.

If I were viewing Christianity from the outside, what would I think of the small, fold-up, portable truths that are sometimes presented as the sum of the faith? Would I find them compelling? Would they invite me to find true answers for my deepest questions and longings?

The simple formulations have their limits, but we do need them. We must have ways to talk about God and salvation, death and life, suffering, time, and eternity—we must try to explain things in words. Sometimes we let these formulations flatten the mysteries, and sometimes we use flattened mysteries to hurt one another. That's when the Spirit needs to remind us, through each other or the Bible or some other way, that we have not owned the mystery, not yet. There is always so much more beyond the words, beyond what we see, beyond what we now understand. So much more is waiting to be revealed to us as we travel further along on this pilgrimage.

Thomas Merton remarked that, when it comes to prayer, "we will never be anything else but beginners."[2] He could have said the same of the Christian life as a whole. Those who have spent a lifetime journeying faithfully with others, who have earnestly sought the presence of God, who have suffered and held to hope—such people do gain in wisdom, trust, joy, radiance. But they know, having glimpsed God's glory, how much more there is, how far they still have to go. All of us on this journey—saints and stumblers—perceive the mysteries more or less dimly in this life, yet we live in hope that our longings for wholeness will be satisfied, that one day God will reconcile all things to himself. Then we will fully comprehend the deep connections, the purpose and pattern of it all. Paul wrote: "Now we see but a poor reflection; then we shall see face to face. Now I know in part; then I shall know fully, even as I am fully known" (1 Corinthians 13:12).

Here and now we put our trust in the certainties of the faith not because they completely contain truth but because they teach us how to trace its breadth and depth. They lead us to the center of all truth, the ordering principle of the universe, which is not an impersonal force but a loving person. In Jesus Christ we see this loving person most clearly—Jesus the Wisdom of God, ordering the household of all things from before time and into eternity with strength and sweetness.

May you find many places where the veil is thin. May you receive the full riches of complete understanding. May you know the way to the mystery of God, which is Christ, for in him are hidden all the treasures of wisdom and knowledge, all provision for the journey, and the journey's end.

NOTES

Preface

1. C. S. Lewis, *Mere Christianity* (New York: Macmillan, 1960), 6.

Chapter One

1. Huston Smith's book *Forgotten Truth: The Common Vision of the World's Religions* (San Francisco: HarperSanFrancisco, 1992) is a lovely, concise introduction to the consonance of the great wisdom traditions.

2. A brief summary of Alvin Plantinga's main works appears in Andrew Chignell, "Epistemology for Saints: Alvin Plantinga's Magnum Opus," *Books and Culture*, 2002, 8(2), 20–21. In "Mind over Skepticism," John G. Stackhouse argues that Plantinga has successfully "defeated two of the greatest challenges to the Christian faith," the problem of evil and the problem of knowledge as logical defeaters to the rationality of faith; *Christianity Today*, 2001, 45(8), 74–76. See also the Suggestions for Further Reading.

3. Of course, Pascal scribbled in French. A transcription of his scribblings appears in many places. I found an account of Pascal's epiphanic experience, including the notes he wrote about it, in J. H. Broome, *Pascal* (London: Edward Arnold, 1965), 224.

4. For an account of Wesley's conversion in his own words, see *John Wesley*, ed. Albert Outler (New York: Oxford University Press, 1964), 66.

5. Paul Willis, "Bright Shoots of Everlastingness," *River Teeth,* 2002, 3(2), 56–65.

6. Augustine of Hippo, *The Confessions of Saint Augustine,* books I–X, trans. F. J. Sheed (Kansas City, Mo.: Sheed and Ward, 1970), bk. 8, chap. 12, 146.

7. Anne Lamott, *Traveling Mercies: Some Thoughts on Faith* (New York: Anchor Books/Random House, 2000), 49–50.

8. Barbara Brown Taylor, *When God Is Silent* (Cambridge, Mass.: Cowley, 1998), 90.

9. Dante Alighieri, *The Divine Comedy: Paradiso,* trans. John Ciardi, *Western Literature in a World Context,* ed. Paul Davies and others, vol. 1 (New York: St. Martin's Press, 1995), canto 33, ll.121–123.

10. "Spirit of God, Dwell Thou Within My Heart" appears in *Psalter Hymnal,* Centennial Edition (Grand Rapids: Publication Committee of the Christian Reformed Church, 1959), as hymn no. 394.

Chapter Two

1. For many of the insights into first-century Judaism in this section, I am indebted to N. T. Wright, *The Challenge of Jesus: Rediscovering Who Jesus Was and Is* (Downers Grove, Ill.: InterVarsity, 1999); see Wright, 106–108, for the first-century understanding of the terms mentioned here.

2. Wright, *The Challenge of Jesus,* 126–149, especially 138.

3. Wright, *The Challenge of Jesus,* 134–137.

4. Wright, *The Challenge of Jesus,* 106–111.

5. The Jews have recited this formula, called the Shema after its first word in Hebrew, since the beginning of their formation as a people. Moses uses it in his speech to the Israelites after the Exodus (Deuteronomy 6:4): "Hear, O Israel: The Lord our God, the Lord is one."

6. "O Come, All Ye Faithful" appears in *Psalter Hymnal,* Centennial Edition (Grand Rapids, Mich.: Publication Committee of the Christian Reformed Church, 1959), as hymn no. 341.

7. See Jeff Guinn's delightful retelling of the history of Christmas observations, *The Autobiography of Santa Claus as Told to Jeff Guinn* (New York: Tarcher/Penguin, 2003), 134.

8. G. K. Chesterton, *Orthodoxy* (New York: Dodd, Mead, 1959), 245.

9. The term *perichoresis,* "to dance around," had been in use since the fourth century to describe the coinherence of the two natures of Christ (divine and human). Since the eighth century, the Greek term and its Latin equivalent, *circumincessio,* are associated both with the dual nature of Christ and with the Trinity. See the *New Catholic Encyclopedia,* 2nd ed. (Detroit, Mich.: Thomson Gale, 2002), s.v. "Circumincession."

Chapter Three

1. John Milton, *Paradise Lost,* ed. Merritt Y. Hughes (New York: Macmillan, 1962), quotations from bk. 9, l. 999; bk. 3, l. 99.
2. Milton, *Paradise Lost,* bk. 9, ll. 781–782.
3. Garry Wills, *Saint Augustine* (New York: Lipper/Viking, 1999), 22.
4. G. K. Chesterton, *Orthodoxy* (New York: Dodd, Mead, 1959), 24.
5. For an excellent exploration of the relationship between addiction and sin, including references to other writers who explore this relationship, see Cornelius Plantinga Jr., *Not the Way It's Supposed to Be: A Breviary of Sin* (Grand Rapids, Mich.: Eerdmans, 1995), 129–149.
6. Introduction to *Othello, the Moor of Venice, The Complete Works of Shakespeare,* ed. David Bevington (4th ed.; New York: Longman, 1997), 1119.
7. Numerous versions of the Anglican Book of Common Prayer are available online at http://justus.anglican.org/resources/bcp/. The prayer of confession quoted dates back to the order of service for morning prayers in the 1552 Book of Common Prayer. It continues to appear in the service for morning prayer in the most recent edition (1979), although without the last phrase "and there is no health in us."
8. C. S. Lewis, *Till We Have Faces* (San Diego, Calif.: Harvest/Harcourt, 1984), 289.
9. Lewis, *Till We Have Faces,* 307.
10. In *Not the Way It's Supposed to Be,* p. 141, Cornelius Plantinga Jr. references a book called *AA: The Story* (New York: HarperCollins, 1988), 48–52, for a description of how Alcoholics Anonymous was derived from a Lutheran college chaplain's stages toward a changed life.
11. Quoted in Kathleen Norris, *Dakota: A Spiritual Geography* (Boston: Mariner/Houghton Mifflin, 2001), 174.

12. Ronald Ferguson, *Chasing the Wild Goose: The Story of the Iona Community* (Glasgow, Scotland: Wild Goose Publications, 1998), 157.

13. The phrase appears more than once in Forster. It is a key phrase in the novel *Howard's End*—for example, in chap. 33. E. M. Forster, *Howard's End* (New York: Penguin, 2000).

Chapter Four

1. I am indebted to S. Mark Heim, *The Depth of the Riches* (Grand Rapids, Mich.: Eerdmans, 2001), especially chap. 2, for pointing out this emphasis on relationality as a distinctive dimension of Christian salvation.

2. G. Fackre, *The Christian Story: A Narrative Interpretation of Basic Christian Doctrine* (Grand Rapids, Mich.: Eerdmans, 1978), 196, quoted in Heim, *Depth of the Riches,* 55.

3. I am indebted to Leanne Van Dyk's fine book *Believing in Jesus Christ* (Louisville, Ky.: Geneva, 2002) for an explanation of Anselmian atonement theory and for a helpful summary of other atonement theories.

4. *Hamlet,* 3.3.36–38. *The Complete Works of Shakespeare,* ed. David Bevington (4th ed.; New York: Longman, 1997). The radio program was episode 218, "Act V," of *This American Life,* originally broadcast on August 9, 2002 (http://www.thislife.org).

5. "Nothing But the Blood," *Celebrate the Blood: A Collection of Contemporary Songs from the Celebration Hymnal* (compact disc; Portland, Oreg.: MIDI Marvels, Inc., 2001).

6. C. S. Lewis, *Mere Christianity* (San Francisco: HarperSanFrancisco, 2001), 56–61.

7. Van Dyk, *Believing in Jesus Christ,* 65.

8. Technically the seed doesn't die. But as a seed, it does not show the standard biological requirements to be considered alive: metabolizing, growth, and reproduction. It requires planting, water, and sun to do that. I like the quirky thought of Jesus as the seed planted in the tomb who then sprouted in three days.

9. My Greek New Testament notes that the subjunctive mood is used here to "express purpose"; see *Novum Testamentum Graece,* ed. Eberhard Nestle, Erwin Nestle, and Kurt Aland (27th ed., rev.; Stuttgart: Deutsche Bibelstiftung, 1993).

10. The song quoted is a traditional spiritual usually called "Do, Lord." It appears in *Songs* (San Anselmo, Calif.: Songs and Creations Inc., 1992), 64.

11. Lewis, *Mere Christianity,* 147.

Chapter Five

1. See the cathedral's Web site, http://www.coventrycathedral.org.uk/, for information about the cathedral's history and current programs.

2. "Miracle Debris Cross?" from The *Valley Skeptic* (http://www.valleyskeptic.com/wtc_cross.html), Feb. 26, 2004. I do not recommend this site.

3. *King Lear,* 4.1.36. *The Complete Works of Shakespeare,* ed. David Bevington (4th ed.; New York: Longman, 1997).

4. For a short summary of Plantinga's argument, see John G. Stackhouse, "Mind over Skepticism," *Christianity Today,* 2001, *45*(8), 74–76.

5. *Hamlet,* 3.1.57. *The Complete Works of Shakespeare.*

6. Craig's way of describing his suffering is derived from a novel by Peter DeVries called *The Blood of the Lamb* (Boston: Little, Brown, 1961), 238. The protagonist at one point finds himself in the position that "was said to be the only alternative to the muzzle of a pistol: the foot of the Cross."

7. Nicholas Wolterstorff, *Lament for a Son* (Grand Rapids, Mich.: Eerdmans, 1987).

8. *Macbeth,* 5.5.27–28. *The Complete Works of Shakespeare.*

9. *The Cloud of Unknowing,* ed. William Johnston (New York: Image/Doubleday, 1996).

10. According to *Newsweek,* a recent National Institute of Health study indicates that "People who regularly attend church have a 25 percent reduction in mortality—that is, they live longer—than people who are not churchgoers. This is true even after controlling for variables intrinsically linked to Sundays in the pew, like social support and healthy lifestyle." See Claudia Kalb, "Faith and Healing," *Newsweek,* Nov. 10, 2003, 44 and following.

11. I am indebted to N. T. Wright for the insight that connects this passage with the call to bear the suffering of others as Jesus did; see *The Challenge of Jesus: Rediscovering Who Jesus Was and Is* (Downers Grove, Ill.: InterVarsity, 1999), 174–197.

12. Julian of Norwich, *The Revelation of Divine Love in Sixteen Showings Made to Dame Julian of Norwich,* trans. M. L. del Mastro (Liguori, Mo.: Triumph, 1994), 108.

13. Madeleine L'Engle, *A Wind in the Door* (New York: Bantam Doubleday Dell, 1973).

14. A summary of Terry's story appears on the Calvin College Web site: "Mourning Terry Etter," http://www.calvin.edu/news/releases/2003_04/etter.htm.

Chapter Six

1. John Chapman, "The Spiritual Letters of Dom Chapman," in Lorraine Kisly (ed.), *Watch and Pray: Christian Teachings on the Practice of Prayer* (New York: Bell Tower, 2002), 90.

2. Richard J. Foster, *Celebration of Discipline: The Path to Spiritual Growth* (rev. ed.; San Francisco: HarperSanFrancisco, 1988), 33.

3. Mechthild of Magdeburg, "The Flowing Light of the Godhead," in Karen J. Campbell (ed.), *German Mystical Writings* (New York: Continuum, 1991), 46–47.

4. Two recent articles summarizing study results and the controversies surrounding them are Cullen Murphy, "Innocent Bystander: Physician Herbert Benson's Research on Benefits of Intercessory Prayer," *Atlantic Monthly,* 2001, *287*(4), 18 and following; and Claudia Kalb, "Faith and Healing," *Newsweek,* Nov. 10, 2003, 44 and following.

5. C. S. Lewis, *Letters to Malcolm, Chiefly on Prayer* (New York: Harvest/Harcourt Brace Jovanovich, 1964), 21.

6. Thomas Merton, *Contemplative Prayer* (Garden City, N.Y.: Image/Doubleday, 1971), 37.

7. Don Postema, *Space for God: Study and Practice of Spirituality and Prayer* (Grand Rapids, Mich.: CRC Publications, 1997).

8. Gerard Manley Hopkins, "God's Grandeur," *The Poetical Works of Gerard Manley Hopkins,* ed. Norman H. Mackenzie (Oxford: Clarendon, 1990), 139.

9. "Why and How Do I Pray?" Alpha Course (videotape series; New York: Alpha North America, 2002), talk 6.

10. *Psalter Hymnal,* Centennial Edition (Grand Rapids, Mich.: Publication Committee of the Christian Reformed Church, 1959).

11. I am indebted to my mother-in-law, Marchiene Vroon Rienstra, for pointing out in her book *Swallow's Nest: A Feminine Reading*

of the Psalms (Grand Rapids, Mich.: Eerdmans, 1992) this wonderful idea of praying the Psalms from others' points of view. The book is now available through Xlibris (http://www2.xlibris.com/).

12. Anne Lamott, *Traveling Mercies: Some Thoughts on Faith* (New York: Anchor Books/Random House, 2000), 82.

13. John Milton, Sonnet XIX: "When I Consider," in *Complete Poems and Major Prose,* ed. Merritt Y. Hughes (New York: Prentice Hall, 1957), 168.

14. "What a Friend We Have in Jesus" appears in *Psalter Hymnal* as hymn no. 436.

15. Elie Wiesel, "What Ancient Masters Could Teach Our Generation," Festival of Faith and Writing lecture at Calvin College, Grand Rapids, Mich., April 2, 1998.

16. Augustine of Hippo, "A Discourse on the Psalms," in Kisly, *Watch and Pray,* 108–109.

Chapter Seven

1. Because I used the Revised Standard Version (RSV) of the Bible as a teenager, the passages quoted in the early sections of this chapter are from that version.

2. Quoted in Lance Morrow, "Evil," *Time,* June 10, 1991, 48–53.

3. From Robert G. Ingersoll's essay "The Gods," printed in *"The Gods" and Other Lectures* (Peoria, Ill.: C. P. Farrell, 1874). The essay is usually dated 1872 and appears at http://www.infidels.org/library/historical/robert_ingersoll/gods.html.

4. Saint Augustine, *Confessions,* trans. Henry Chadwick (Oxford: Oxford University Press, 1991), bk. 3, section 5, xx.

5. Karlfried Froehlich, *Biblical Interpretation in the Early Church* (Minneapolis: Augsburg Fortress, 1984).

6. Saint Augustine, *On Christian Doctrine,* bk. II, chap. 6, sec. 8. Available at *Christian Classics Ethereal Library,* http://www.ccel.org.

7. Group discussion with N. T. Wright on June 3, 2003, in the Jerusalem Chamber at Westminster Abbey, London.

Chapter Eight

1. Colleen Carroll argues that a revival is taking place among young Americans; see *The New Faithful: Why Young Adults Are Embracing Christian Orthodoxy* (Chicago: Loyola, 2002).

2. C. S. Lewis, *Mere Christianity* (San Francisco: HarperSanFrancisco, 2001), 175–183.

3. I would like to thank Ron Rienstra for permission to reproduce this chart, which he has developed for use in his teaching about worship.
4. Group discussions with Matt Redman on June 3, 2003, and with Alison Adam on June 4, 2003, both in London.
5. Group discussion with N.T. Wright, June 3, 2003, in the Jerusalem Chamber at Westminster Abbey, London.
6. The phrases "then and there" and "here and now" in the context of biblical study come from Gordon D. Fee and Douglas Stuart, *How to Read the Bible for All Its Worth* (2nd ed.; Grand Rapids, Mich.: Zondervan, 1993).

Chapter Nine

1. I obtained information from the Web site of the United Reformed Churches in North America, http://www.covenant-urc.org/urchrchs.html.
2. C. S. Lewis, *Mere Christianity* (San Francisco: HarperSanFrancisco, 2001), 12.
3. The church is Willow Creek Community Church in South Barrington, Illinois (http://www.willowcreek.org/).

Chapter Ten

1. Neil Howe and William Strauss, *Millennials Go to College: Strategies for a New Generation on Campus: Recruiting and Admissions, Campus Life, and the Classroom* (Great Falls, Va.: LifeCourse Associates/American Association of Collegiate Registrars and Admissions Officers, 2003), 9.
2. Sietze Buning, "An Open Letter," in *Style and Class* (Orange City, Iowa: Middleburg Press, 1982), 55–59. The poem notes that the idea of "Holiness to the Lord" being inscribed on every farm implement comes from Zechariah 14:20–21, a vision of the restoration of Jerusalem in which "HOLY TO THE LORD will be inscribed on the bells of the horses."
3. The novel is *Flabbergasted* by Ray Blackston (Grand Rapids, Mich.: Fleming Revell, 2003).
4. Frederick Buechner, *Wishful Thinking: A Seeker's ABC* (San Francisco: HarperSanFrancisco, 1993), 118.
5. Carol Zaleski, "The Dark Night of Mother Teresa," *First Things,* May 2003, *133,* 24–27.

Epilogue

1. Eugene Peterson, *A Long Obedience in the Same Direction: Discipleship in an Instant Society* (Downers Grove, Ill.: InterVarsity, 2000).

2. Thomas Merton, *Contemplative Prayer* (Garden City, N.Y.: Image/Doubleday, 1971), 37.

SUGGESTIONS FOR
FURTHER READING

℘ **C**hoosing a few good books out of the thousands available is daunting, but I would like to offer a list of books that have been especially formative for me or that others have warmly recommended to me as among the most helpful and formative for them. (Special thanks to Dawn and Andrew Burnett, Sheryl Fullerton, Mary Hulst, Ron Rienstra, and Jana Riess for their suggestions.) The following list includes some classics as well as brand-new books, covers a range of broad topic areas, and focuses on titles that are both accessible and challenging. Books cited in my notes in older editions are here listed in recent editions for the convenience of book buyers.

The list is, naturally, rather idiosyncratic. I hope you'll forgive its limitations and feel free to find your own way. A great place to find contemporary authors and books that combine Christian faith with literary excellence in all genres (but especially novels and poetry) is at the Calvin College Festival of Faith and Writing Web site: http://www.calvin.edu/academic/engl/festival.htm. Scores of Christian classics in the public domain are available online at http://www.ccel.org. For intelligent reviews of new books both Christian and non-Christian, try *Books & Culture: A Christian Review* (see http://www.christianitytoday.com/books/).

M. Craig Barnes, *When God Interrupts: Finding New Life Through Unwanted Change,* InterVarsity, 1996.

Barnes chronicles his own experiences of tragedy and grief, transforming these into an account of how God's interruptions can lead us
on the path to grace.

Dorothy Bass, ed., *Practicing Our Faith: A Way of Life for a Searching People,*
Jossey-Bass, 1998.
In each of the essays in this collection, a different author thoughtfully
considers how Christian faith shapes daily practices, including hospitality, simplicity, honoring the body, resting, community gathering, and so on. This book inaugurated the Practices of Faith series,
a collection of excellent book-length meditations on Christian
practices, also published by Jossey-Bass.

Frederick Buechner, *Beyond Words: Daily Readings in the ABCs of Faith,*
HarperSanFrancisco, 2004.
Buechner is a favorite of those who struggle with doubt but want to
stay alive in the faith. His earthy, poetic style helps present his unique
angle on a huge range of matters related to faith. This book is a
combination of three previously published favorites dealing with
biblical characters, theological terms, and spiritual dimensions of
ordinary words.

Robert Ferrar Capon, *Kingdom, Grace, Judgment: Paradox, Outrage, and
Vindication in the Parables of Jesus,* Eerdmans, 2002.
Capon's readings of the parables present the radical grace of God and
the radical challenge of the gospel in equally pungent doses.

G. K. Chesterton, *Orthodoxy,* Ignatius, 1995.
About one hundred years old now, Chesterton's spiritual autobiography
contains some of the most eloquent and funniest Christian writing ever. Some of the contemporary debates to which Chesterton
refers seem puzzling now; but his basic approach to Christianity
as the worldview that satisfies the mind, heart, and imagination
still convinces.

Fyodor Dostoevsky, *The Brothers Karamazov,* Penguin Classics, 2003.
This enormous tome will keep you busy for a long time, but it's worth
the effort because no other novelist matches the depth and
breadth of Dostoevsky's vision. This story of Russian brothers
and their father is a murder mystery, an exploration of basic

human types, and a profound meditation on Christian faith all
rolled into one.

Richard Foster, *Prayer: Finding the Heart's True Home,* HarperSanFrancisco,
1992.
Quaker writer and teacher Foster offers a comprehensive and challenging but accessible and encouraging guide to prayer. A contemporary classic.

Mark S. Heim, *The Depth of the Riches: A Trinitarian Theology of Religious
Ends,* Eerdmans, 2001.
For those plagued by questions about salvation for people of other
faiths, Heim presents a subtle, intriguing argument about various
possibilities for what happens after death.

James C. Howell, *Servants, Misfits, and Martyrs: Saints and Their Stories,*
Upper Room Books, 2000.
In this concise book, Howell gathers stories of admirable Christians
from different branches of the faith, ancient and modern, famous
and obscure, and organizes them according to the very different
spiritual characters and calling they each exemplify.

Melanie Jansen, *From the Darkest Night: Meditations for Abuse Survivors,*
Faith Alive Christian Resources, 2001.
Nothing simplistic or cheesy here; Jansen gives only the genuine com-
fort of truth and God's healing power.

Anne Lamott, *Traveling Mercies: Some Thoughts on Faith,* Anchor Books/
Random House, 2000.
Lamott's spiritual autobiography is couched in wickedly funny, totally
engaging vignettes of her life. Her self-deprecating honesty makes
her struggle to believe and keep believing all the more convincing and recognizable as one's own struggle too.

C. S. Lewis, *Chronicles of Narnia,* HarperCollins, 2004.
It's never too late to read these beloved fantasy tales of the Pevensie
children and their surprising adventures in Narnia. Lewis's seven
novels, meant for children but enjoyable at any age, offer unfor-
gettable pictures of forgiveness, repentance, sacrifice, deception,
trust, hope, and all manner of fundamental spiritual matters.

Nothing beats these for "baptizing the imagination" (as Lewis himself said George MacDonald's books did for him) into a Christian worldview.

C. S. Lewis, *The Great Divorce,* HarperSanFrancisco, 2001.
Lewis's narrator takes a bus ride to hell that invites the reader to consider the consequences of everyday good and evil. In contrast to the burgeoning genre of apocalyptic fiction, this book offers a useful corrective to popular commonplaces when imagining eternal destinations.

C. S. Lewis, *Mere Christianity,* HarperSanFrancisco, 2001.
First published in the 1940s, this reasoned account of central Christian beliefs is still a best-seller for good reason.

C. S. Lewis, *The Screwtape Letters,* HarperSanFrancisco, 2001.
In this slyly hilarious examination of sin, Lewis creates fictional correspondence between a senior devil and his protégé, who is busily engaged in tempting an average Joe into every possible pitfall. Another book to awaken the reader to the way pride, vanity, and other sin creep into the smallest actions and thoughts, as well as to the beauty and relief of God's love and grace.

C. S. Lewis, *Till We Have Faces: A Myth Retold,* Harvest, 1980.
This absorbing retelling of the myth of Psyche seems at first just a good story, then a meditation on the problems of faith. But then you realize it's about divine love.

Frederica Mathewes-Green, *At the Corner of East and Now: A Modern Life in Ancient Christian Orthodoxy,* Tarcher/Putnam, 2000.
As an American convert to Eastern Orthodoxy, Mathewes-Green gives an enthusiastic explanation of Orthodox Christian ways of thinking and practicing, particularly of the influence of liturgical worship on daily life.

Richard Mouw, *When the Kings Come Marching In: Isaiah and the New Jerusalem,* Eerdmans, 2002.
Mouw considers possible ways to understand the complex relationship between the Christian church and culture through a careful study of Isaiah 60 and related passages.

Andrew Murray, *With Christ in the School of Prayer,* Whitaker House, 1981.
Murray examines the gospels to discover what Jesus teaches about prayer
    through word and example.

Leslie Newbigin, *Foolishness to the Greeks: The Gospel and Western
    Culture,* Eerdmans, 1986.
Newbigin brings his decades of experience as a missionary in Africa
    to this book, in which he considers the Western world as an
    outsider. He examines how the gospel of Jesus invites a radical
    reconsideration of Western notions and ideas that we typically
    take for granted.

J. Philip Newell, *Celtic Benediction: Morning and Night Prayer,* Eerdmans,
    2000.
There's a reason for the current popular recovery of Celtic spirituality:
    it seems to speak with special eloquence for our times. This book
    of prayers guides the reader in prayer and meditation for morn-
    ing and evening.

Kathleen Norris, *The Cloister Walk,* Riverhead, 1997.
Norris compresses her years of experiencing Benedictine monastic
    life as a layperson. Her meditations range wide but offer an
    unusual and insightful consideration of how spiritual practices,
    worship, and prayer infuse everyday life.

Henri Nouwen, *Reaching Out: The Three Movements of the Spiritual Life,*
    Image, 1986.
This slim, beautiful classic describes basic movements of the spiritual
    life: from loneliness to solitude, from hostility to hospitality, and
    from illusion to prayer. I read this book in college, and it has
    shaped my understanding of the spiritual life ever since.

Michele Novotni and Randy Petersen, *Angry with God,* Pinon, 2001.
Rooted in a story of terrible suffering, this book analyzes the different
    means through which people become angry with God and offers
    biblically based steps for moving through that anger to a deeper
    relationship with God.

John Ortberg, *The Life You've Always Wanted,* Zondervan, 2002.
A basic introduction to the spiritual disciplines without the guilt.

Alan Paton, *Cry, the Beloved Country,* Scribner, 2003.
This story of a Zulu Christian pastor and his son is set in the 1940s in South Africa. It's a classic novel about suffering from a Christian point of view.

Eugene Peterson, *A Long Obedience in the Same Direction: Discipleship in an Instant Society,* InterVarsity, 2000.
By meditating on the Psalms of Ascent (Psalms 120–134), Peterson considers various themes in a life of discipleship such as worship, work, blessing, and repentance.

Alvin Plantinga, *Warranted Christian Belief,* Oxford, 2000.
A serious work of epistemology for those who take their philosophical doubt seriously. This is the third volume in Plantinga's trilogy on warrant; this one sets out a defense of Christian belief against philosophical objections to it.

Cornelius Plantinga Jr., *Not the Way It's Supposed to Be: A Breviary of Sin,* Eerdmans, 1995.
An anatomy of sorts that awakens the reader to all the dimensions of sin, from the grand and dramatic to the subtle and almost imperceptible. This would be a terribly depressing book except for the gorgeous writing and the epilogue on grace.

Marchiene Vroon Rienstra, *Swallow's Nest: A Feminine Reading of the Psalms,* Xlibris, 2003.
For women who need to heal their relationship to God, this devotional guide is like living water. The Psalms are carefully paraphrased and arranged into a monthlong series of devotions, including prayers and songs as well as readings. I used this book for several years to guide my prayer times and found that it taught me to pray the Psalms and expanded my too-limited view of God's nature and action.

Ronald Rolheiser, *The Holy Longing: The Search for a Christian Spirituality,* Doubleday, 1999.
Rolheiser, a Roman Catholic priest, invites readers to take the unrest and passions within and let that energy be directed and shaped by basic Christian beliefs and practices.

Huston Smith, *Forgotten Truth: The Common Vision of the World's Religions,* HarperSanFrancisco, 1992.

In this deeply philosophical but lucid book, Smith seeks the places where the world's wisdom traditions converge. It was originally published as *Forgotten Truth: The Primordial Tradition* (HarperCollins, 1976).

Huston Smith, *The World's Religions: Our Great Wisdom Traditions,* HarperSanFrancisco, 1991.
Smith's wise and articulate voice has provided the best introduction to the world's religions since the first edition of this book appeared in 1958. Without judging among the religions, Smith presents each in its best spirit, getting to the heart of each faith and explaining it clearly and insightfully.

Dallas Willard, *Renovation of the Heart: Putting on the Character of Christ,* NavPress, 2002.
An in-depth book about inner transformation, by the power of God and not ourselves, that produces outward results.

Lauren Winner, *Girl Meets God: A Memoir,* Random House, 2003.
Winner recounts her journey from nominal faith through Orthodox Judaism to Christianity in this fascinating, humorous, and beautifully written memoir.

N. T. Wright, *The Challenge of Jesus: Rediscovering Who Jesus Was and Is,* InterVarsity, 1999.
In this examination of Jesus' actions and words, Wright's feisty orthodoxy reveals Jesus' deep relevance to his own time in order to clarify how we should respond to him in ours.

N. T. Wright, *The New Testament for Everyone* series, Society for the Promotion of Christian Knowledge and Westminster John Knox, 2002–present.
Wright is a New Testament scholar and historian and an Anglican bishop who translates serious biblical scholarship into very readable, compelling explanations.

Philip Yancey, *What's So Amazing About Grace,* Zondervan, 2002.
Many readers can relate to Yancey's story of being raised in a judgmental, legalistic Christian world, rebelling against religion and God, and then at last discovering the grace of Jesus all over again. Because of this life story, Yancey's presentation of God's radical grace has proven especially compelling.

ACKNOWLEDGMENTS

M y husband, Ron, contributed theological insight, book recommendations, half his theological library, advice about "the X factor," and enormous patience and strength. I lean on him so heavily for so much. Only he knows what this book cost.

My children—Miriam, Jacob, and Philip—good-naturedly accept the oddity of having a mom who's a writer, even though that means, among other things, that they never know when something they do or say might turn up in a book.

Sheryl Fullerton is the sort of editor any writer would wish for—the kind who, with care and persistence, makes your writing far better than you can make it on your own. This book came into being at her invitation and took shape with her wise guidance all the way. She kept believing despite some awfully bad first drafts.

My agent, Lorraine Kisly, offered her gifts of tenacity and of knowing the right thing to say at the right time.

Lugene Schemper of the Calvin College Hekman Library lent his consummate professionalism to a number of tedious research tasks, cheerfully assisting me from across the ocean while I was living in London.

Leanne Van Dyk, dean of the faculty and professor of theology at Western Theological Seminary in Holland, Michigan, read through the entire manuscript to make sure I avoided major heresies. For any errors or other foolishness that remains, I take full responsibility.

Tony Jones and Geneviève Duboscq, by serving as skeptical readers, usefully spurred me to refine and polish beyond what I thought I could do.

Marchiene Vroon Rienstra has for many years inspired my spiritual growth with her clarity, creativity, wide perspective, and adventurousness. As I worked on this book, she also, as always, rescued me from several crises with encouragement and the expert child care only a grandma can give. Dorothy Shreve has taught me much about faithfulness, not least through her faithful prayers for me.

During the process of writing this book, I reached a new appreciation for the many people who have inspired me with their wisdom about God and practical examples of living faithfully as Christians. God works through the power of Christian community in marvelous and surprising ways. I'm especially grateful for my family, my students and colleagues at Calvin College, and the staff and congregation of Church of the Servant Christian Reformed Church.

Many friends contributed ideas and personal stories to this book: Alison Adam, Chip Andrus, Dawn and Andrew Burnett, Amy Byerley, Jeff Chandler, Steve Chase, Janell Colley, Dale Cooper, Kristy Dykhouse, Mary Hulst, Craig Knot, Neal Plantinga, John and Marchiene Rienstra, Rachel Rienstra, Sue Rozeboom, Trevor and Linda Rubingh, Linda Schaefer, Dorothy and Ed Shreve, Sean Starke, Susan Van Winkle, Elizabeth Vander Lei, Karen Ward, Paul Willis, Charlotte Witvliet, and many others whom I have mentioned in the book either by their real name, by a name I changed to protect their privacy, or by a description. Some of these people, besides inspiring me in other ways, read pieces of the book in rough early stages and offered helpful suggestions.

Finally, thanks to the production and marketing staff at Jossey-Bass, especially Andrea Flint and Sandy Siegle, for their expertise and good cheer.

THE AUTHOR

Debra Rienstra was raised in West Michigan and educated at Calvin College and the University of Michigan, graduating with highest honors in English literature. She received her doctorate in literature from Rutgers University in New Jersey in 1995. Since 1996 she has taught literature and writing at Calvin College in Grand Rapids, Michigan. Besides publishing academic articles, poetry, and articles for general readers, she is also the author of *Great with Child: On Becoming a Mother* (Tarcher/Putnam, 2002).

Debra is married to Rev. Ron Rienstra, an ordained pastor in the Reformed Church in America. They and their three children make their home in Grand Rapids but are currently residing in Sun Valley, California, while Ron is teaching and studying at Fuller Theological Seminary.

INDEX